Working Together in Vanuatu

Research Histories, Collaborations, Projects and Reflections

Edited by John Taylor and Nick Thieberger

ANU
THE AUSTRALIAN NATIONAL UNIVERSITY

E PRESS

ANU E PRESS

Published by ANU E Press
The Australian National University
Canberra ACT 0200, Australia
Email: anuepress@anu.edu.au
This title is also available online at: http://epress.anu.edu.au/

National Library of Australia
Cataloguing-in-Publication entry

Title: Working together in Vanuatu : research histories,
                 collaborations, projects and
                 reflections / edited by John Taylor and
                 Nick Thieberger.

ISBN: 9781921862342 (pbk.) 9781921862359 (pdf)

Subjects: Cross-cultural studies--Vanuatu--Congresses.
                 Social sciences--Methodology--Congresses.
                 Social sciences--Network analysis--Congresses.
                 Vanuatu--Social conditions--Congresses.

Other Authors/Contributors: Taylor, John.
                             Thieberger, Nicholas.

Dewey Number: 303.4833

Cover design and layout by ANU E Press

Cover image: Cover photograph by John Taylor, taken at the Vanuatu Cultural Centre, November 17, 2006, during the ceremony to award Ralph Regenvanu (former Director of VNCC and VKS) with the customary title of Libehkamel Tah Tomat. The title was bestowed by the late Chief Matthias Batick, former fieldworker from Lorlow, South West Bay, Malakula.

Printed by Griffin Press

Contents

Introductions

Histories

Collaborations

Projects

Reflections

Illustrations

Acknowledgements

The diverse combination of shared work that has gone into producing this volume, as with the conference from which it derives, is aptly summarised in the title. We would first like to acknowledge the blessing and support of the National Government of Vanuatu and of the Vanuatu National Council of Chiefs, and our appreciation of the Vanuatu National Cultural Council in allowing this project to take place. We are especially grateful for the ongoing efforts of the Vanuatu Cultural Centre and National Museum in sharing a growing wealth of human, archival and other resources with all researchers, in continually driving forward new, exciting and socially-relevant research projects, and in providing the facilities required for hosting events such as the conference Afta 26 Yia, from which this book originates. The conference was funded by the Australian Research Council's (ARC) Asia-Pacific Futures Research Network. During the course of this project and the subsequent editing of the manuscript, John Taylor has been first a postdoctoral fellow and then visiting fellow at the Gender Relations Centre (ANU), and then Simon Research Fellow at the University of Manchester, and received funding from the Wenner-Gren Foundation. Nick Thieberger was an ARC Postdoctoral Fellow at the University of Melbourne, Assistant Professor at the University of Hawai'i and an ARC QE2 Fellow at the University of Melbourne.

In the production of this volume we are especially grateful to Margaret Jolly and Stewart Firth. For her careful and sensitive copyediting, we thank Carolyn Brewer. We thank all of the Vanuatu Cultural Centre staff members who assisted the conference conveners, Nick Thieberger, John Taylor and Stephen Zagala; especially former director Ralph Regenvanu, current director Marcelin Abong, and Heneline Halele and colleagues for recording and transcribing the conference proceedings. Likewise we thank Mary Patterson and Stephen Zagala for their work in producing this manuscript. We applaud all of those conference participants—ni-Vanuatu and foreign researchers, fieldworkers, dignitaries, and all others who took part—who worked together so enthusiastically in producing what turned out to be a most memorable event, and who in the majority of cases travelled great distances to do so. While acknowledging and celebrating what for some might appear an over-optimistic idealism, as expressed in the title to this volume, we sincerely hope that the unique spirit of collaboration that characterises Vanuatu's research environment continues into the future.

N

Torres
Islands

Banks Islands

Vanua
Lava

P A C I F I C

Olpoi

Espiritu
Santo

Ambae
Nduindui
Navuti

Maewo

Wusi

Tutuba
Malo

Pentecost

Fanafo
Luganville

Vao Island

Ranon

Ambrym

Malakula

Utas

O C E A N

Epi

Nguna
Lelepa
Mangaliliu
Mele-Maat

Pele Island
Emao

Efate

Teouma
PORT VILA

Erromango

Aniwa

Tanna

Futuna

0   100 km

Aneityum

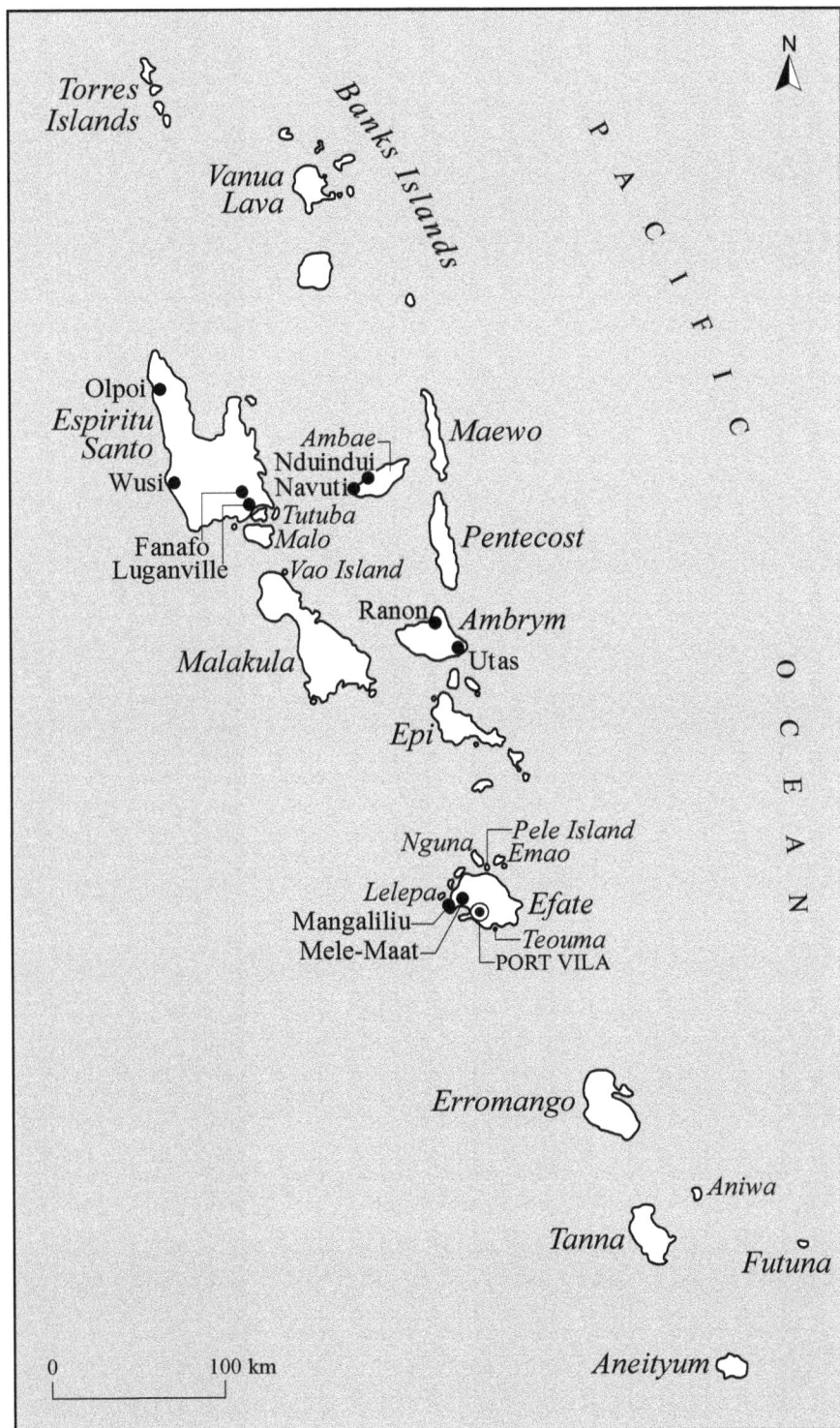

Map of Vanuatu

Introductions

Welkam Toktok

Jif Kalkot Murmur

Daerekta blong miusiem, ol jeaman mo presiden blong ol man filwoka, woman filwoka, riseja from defren kantri long yumi long Pasifik mo long Europe, olgeta we oli save stap long ples ia, ol obsevas, ol midias, ol jifs, fren we hemi stap long ples ia. Mi mi tekem tis taem, mi tekem hona ia, blong save welkamem yufala evriwan bak long aelan blong yumi long Efate, ples we sam long yufala i bin stap bifo mo kontiniu blong stap kam, mo yufala i laekem tumas!

Mi wantem mekem wan smol toktok olsem se, olsem mi neva save se bae mi kam wan jif. Mi bin bon olsem pikinini mi wan twin, twin pikinini wetem brata blong mi. Mi skul afta save blong mi long skul i karem mi go go mi kam wan skul tija we mi tij blong plante plante yia. Mi kam wan Presbyterian elda we mi prijim tabu tok blong God long jos fo plante ples truaot ol aelan long Vanuatu go go long 1993 olsem bifo 1983 i kam 1993 i kam toktok i stap kam long mi nao se: 'Yu mas kam wan jif'. Be mi harem se jif hemi no wan samting blong mi nating. Mi neva bin tren blong kam wan jif. Mi no gat save long wan samting abaot jif. Mi save nomo blong mi, mi tij long klasrum, stanap long blakbod toktok long Inglis long pikinini nomo evridei. Hemia nao hemi wok blong mi. Taem mi mi stap long skul mi stap talem long ol pikinini, mi panisim olgeta se, 'Don't speak in language speak in English', sam taem mi panisim olgeta, yu raetem handred taems long pepa blong yu se: 'I must talk in English, I must speak in English.' Hemia nao wok blong mi bifo.

Be i hapen se taem we long 1990 hem i kam go go i kam naoia hat blong mi, i stap filim o mi stap harem save se yes ating i mo gud mi mi go jif mekem se 1993 mi kam wan jif nao. Taem mi kam jif nao mi harem se mi mekem wan bigfala trabol i stap finis, bigfala trabol blong mi i stap we mi mi tijim narafala kalja long ol pikinini blong mi stret. Oli nomo save toktok long lanwis blong mi, i nomo save sing long lanwis blong mi, i nomo save tanis long kastom tanis blong mi we mi mi sapos blong mekem fastaem be mi mekem nara samting i stap fastaem blong mi winim hemia no gat nao vilej blong mi long Mangaliliu taem we mi mi stap toktok, pikinini i toktok i kam: 'He yu no toktok spos yu toktok long Bislama yu no stap long yad blong mi yu aot long yad blong mi, yu go long yad blong yu.' Rao rao blong mi naoia i stap olsem nao.

Be mi mi praod ia mi wan praod jif naoia mi flas gud ia naoia mi mi stanap ia, mi stap talem from se taem we Jean Guiart long 1950 we hemi kam blong mekem risej long ol smol smol storian blong yumi, Jean Guiart hemi wan prapa stamba man nao i mekem ol samting ia se oli stap in ples taem we José Garanger i kam papa blong mi nao i talem yes long José Garanger olsem se bambae risej i tekem ples. Fasin blong digim kraon i go go kasem 1996 i kam ia mi mo boe blong mi Douglas mitufala i pat blong hem tu mi praod se mi tu mi stat blong talem yes taem we Matthew Spriggs wetem ol narafala oli kam blong mekem kastom long mi wetem Ralph, Daerekta, taem oli kam mekem kastom long mi blong mifala i statem dedikesen. Olsem mi bin talem mi tijim fastaem mi mi praod mi flas tumas ia from se mi save karem bak mo naoia taem we mi mi toktok mi no toktok nating nomo be toktok blong mi hemi paoa from se mi stap filim se mi stap go bak long stret rod. Witaot ol risej blong yufala we yufala i bin mekem mi ting se mifala olsem bebe long wan pat blong wol.

Be fastaem mebi ol bubu blong mifala oli kam, taem samfala oli kam, 'E man ia i kam blong mekem wanem bakegen ia', be naoia we mi mi stap stanap long ples ia tudei mi mi luk se kaming blong yu, yufala long taem ia we yufala stap wokbaot hemi wan gudwan, mo wan impoten wan, mo hemi wan gudfala samting blong mifala. We mi glad tu we i stap long ediukesen buk naoia we wan gel i stap naoia wetem yumi Sara we hem tu i bin mekem i stap long buk naoia ol pikinini oli ridim. Naoia mi tu samtaem mi toktok mi ron i go bak long buk blong Sara blong mi mi ridim bakegen be olsem mi no save talem plante toktok mo be yufala i bin save finis mo kontiniu blong mekem, mi samtaem mi kros, mi krae, mi kros se hu i talem long ol misinari se oli kam long Vanuatu mo mi mas ones long yufala mi resaen long elda finis long last yia. Naoia mi stap klisim jos bakegen nao, mi stap wantem se bae mi nomo go prea long Sande nao from se taem mifala i mekem wan smol donesen i kam long olgeta long New Zealand High Com se bae Sande mi mi tanis kastom nao from taem turis blong mi o i kam wan Wol Heritij blong yumi we hemi no yet, spos hemi kam in ples bae Sande i kam, bae mi mi go tanis nao bae mi mi nomo go prea. So mi jes ritaea mi jes karem eli ritaeamen blong mi long saed blong jos long last Oktoba and naoia mi karem wan hat nomo wan mat blong jif, wan mat blong kastom. Ating hemia nomo tangkiu tumas an welkam long miting ia.

Welcome Speech

Chief Kalkot Murmur

Museum Director, Chairman and President of the man fieldworkers, woman fieldworkers, researchers from around the Pacific and from Europe, everyone who is able to attend here, observers, media, Chiefs, and friends who are here today. I would like to take this time, and take this honour, to welcome you all to our island, Efate, where some of you have been before and still visit, and seem to like rather a lot!

I want to tell you briefly that, before, I never thought I would become a chief. I was born with a twin brother. I went to school and with that learning I went on to become a teacher, and I was a teacher for many years. I became a Presbyterian elder and preached the word of God in churches all over Vanuatu from 1983 to 1993, but then a voice told me, 'You have to become a chief.' But I thought that being a chief was not for me at all. I had never trained to become a chief. I didn't have any knowledge of anything to do with chiefs. I knew about my own things, classroom teaching, standing up in front of a blackboard and talking in English to the kids everyday. That was my work. When I was running a classroom I would punish the kids, saying, 'Don't speak in language speak in English.' Sometimes I'd punish them by making them write a hundred times on paper, 'I must talk in English, I must speak in English.' That used to be my job.

So, when 1990 came around, my heart told me and I understood it would be better if I became a chief, so in 1993 I became a chief. But becoming a chief caused me some problems because I was teaching another culture to the children, they couldn't speak in my language, they couldn't sing in my language, they couldn't do the custom dances which I was supposed to be able to do for them, but I was busy doing other things. So in my village Mangaliliu when children come around I say, 'Hey don't you talk in Bislama in my yard, you get out of my yard, go to your yard.' I told them like that.

But I was proud, I was a proud chief, I was too flash, now I am here telling you that Jean Guiart recorded our stories in 1950, he did some research. Then José Garanger came, my father said yes to him and so his research went ahead. So they dug the ground until in 1996 me and my son Douglas were also able to approve the team with Matthew Spriggs and the others who made custom to me with Ralph Regenvanu, the Director of Vanuatu Kaljoral Senta, and we started the dedication. As I have said, I am very glad now because we can take back that knowledge, and my talk now is powerful because I have gone back on the right path. Without all the research which all of you have done we would be like babies in one part of the world.

But back then when the researchers came, maybe all our grandparents said, 'Hey, what have they come here to do?' But today, as I am here with you all I see that when you came to visit us it was good for us and it was important, and it was useful for us. I'm glad too that the research is in this textbook (Lightner and Naupa 2005) for children to read. Sometimes I also go back to this book and I read it and sometimes I'm angry. I cry. I'm angry because who told the missionaries to come to Vanuatu? I have to be honest with you. I resigned as elder last year. Now I avoid the church, I don't want to pray on Sundays, and we got a small grant from the New Zealand High Commission so that on Sundays we can do *kastom* dance for the tourists because my place is becoming a World Heritage area, well not yet, but if it does then we can do *kastom* dance. I won't be praying again. So I have retired, I took early retirement from the church last October and now I wear just one hat, the chief's mat, a *kastom* mat.

Reference

Lightner, Sara and Anna Naupa, 2005. *Histri Blong Yumi Long Vanuatu: An Educational Resource*, vols. 1–3. Port Vila: Vanuatu Cultural Centre.

Fes Toktok

Chief Paul Tahi (Presiden blong Malvatumauri)

Tangkiu tumas. Yumi stap long rum ia wetem yumi Second Political Advaesa blong Ministri blong Intenol Afea, Daerekta blong Nasonal Kaljoral Kaonsel mo Kaljoral Senta blong Vanuatu. Jif Murmur mo ol man riseja mo ol woman riseja mo ol filwokas, Dipiuti Daerekta blong Kaljoral Senta mo Jif Exekiutiv Ofisa blong Malvatumauri, mi glad tumas blong stanap long fored blong yufala from se fulap long yufala i bin apruv blong mekem risej long Vanuatu tru long kaonsel blong mi an mebi yufala ino save, mi tu mi no bin save long ol feses blong yufala be tede mi save lukim fulap long yufala. Hemi impoten tu blong yumi save sidaon tugeta insaed long rum ia, yumi save kam tugeta mo yumi wok tugeta. Hemi impoten blong yumi save wok tugeta from we long kalja blong Vanuatu yumi mas wok tugeta, long kalja blong Vanuatu yumi mas kam tugeta, yumi mas yunaet bifo yumi save mekem ol narafala wok. Hemia hemi fasin blong ol man Vanuatu.

Tangkiu tumas tu long evriwan we i save mekem se yumi gat konfrens se i save stap long Vanuatu from we yufala olsem, foma spika hemi bin talem oltaem mifala i stap diskasem Vanuatu long ol narafala ples we hemi no Vanuatu. Be tede yumi save sidaon tugeta long ples ia mo wok tugeta blong yumi save diskasem Vanuatu long graon blong Vanuatu. Hemia hemi tumas. Tede yumi kam tugeta long ples ia blong openem taem blong yumi blong yumi save wok tugeta, yumi save tok tugeta insaed long rum ia. Wae hemi kolem yumi bakegen blong yumi save sidaon tugeta long ples ia? Long twenti sikis yias blong indipendens blong Vanuatu, since we Foma Hed of Stet blong Vanuatu hemi bin talem, mebi from we bigfala nambangga we hemi stap long Vanuatu i gat tumas toti long rus blong hem. Ol riseja yufala i bin wok plante blong karem bak samfala samting we hemi nid blong yumi brum. Yumi klinim ol rus blong Vanuatu blong yumi save lukluk long defren daereksen we mi ting se hemi wan foma spika blong Malvatumauri hemi bin toktok long ples ia. Wantaem hemi talem long ol filwokas se, blong lukim olsem wanem wan nasiko hemi flae hemi go sidaon long branj hemi no save lukluk i go oltaem olsem, taem we hemi go sidaon hemi mas lukluk bak bifo hemi save tanem raon blong i lukluk rod blong hem, i tekem narafala daereksen blong hem i go. Tede Vanuatu, nesen blong Vanuatu ia, nesen ia Vanuatu hemi nid blong lukluk bak bifo hemi save tekem narafala daereksen i go. Hemia hemi bilif blong mifala plante we mifala i stap wok wetem Malvatumauri mo Kaljoral Senta blong yumi save gat taem naoia blong yumi lukluk bak and ten yumi save lukluk fowod blong save tekem narafala daereksen blong go.

Samtaem tu plante wok we yufala i mekem fulap taem hemi bin stap olsem ino propeti blong mifala long Vanuatu. Hemia blong mekem se mifala i save strengtenem mifala blong mifala i save stanap long hem ten blong lukluk bak blong tekem narafala daereksen blong yumi. Bambae yumi faenem se long manis ia bambae yu lukim gavman blong Vanuatu bambae hemi save kam blong mekem lonjing Yia blong Kastom Ekonomi we bambae hemi save sapotem laef long Vanuatu mo samtaem tu hemi save sapotem stret gavman ia blong hemi save lukluk long narafala rod, tekem niu daereksen ia blong olsem wanem nao hemi save lidim pipol blong Vanuatu mo nesen ia Vanuatu. So mi ting se ol wok we yufala i bin mekem o yufala i stap mekem oli mo oli veri veri impoten wok blong yumi save lukluk olsem wanem nao bae, bae yumi ridaerektem ol muvment blong yumi, ol lukluk blong yumi, ol tingting blong yumi mo ol, ol wei blong ol lisning. Samtaem tu yumi mekem ol aksens folem wanem nao yufala i stap blong faenem bak. Mebi i gat fulap tok wisdom oli stap insaed long ol samting ia, be nao mifala i stat blong lusum. Mifala i bin lisin long toktok blong jif Murmur we hemi bin talem se hemi bin stap long klasrum ten hemi fosem pikinini blong i tok long Inglis, i fosem pikinini blong i tok long Franis so yumi nid blong luk bak. Yumi luk bak an ten yumi luk fowod blong tekem narafala daereksen blong nasiko i save flae taem we hemi flae hemi save go sidaon long narafala daereksen hemi save tekem mo. So wetem sora blong yufala evriwan we yumi stap mebi toktok hemi no longfala i naf hemi sot be mi wantem se yumi stap traem blong yufala i helpem mifala long kalja. Mo tu long ol jifs long Vanuatu mo pipol blong Vanuatu yumi nid blong lukluk long wanem wei naoia blong yumi save lukim Vanuatu blong yumi tekem Vanuatu i go long narafala jeneresen i kam. So wetem sot toktok olsem, mi olsem jeaman blong Kaljoral Kaonsel blong Vanuatu mo semtaem Presiden blong Malvatumauri, Woking Tugeta konfrens blong yufala ol riseja blong Vanuatu hemi nao ofisoli open.

Opening Speech

Paul Tahi (President of the Malvatumauri)

Thank you very much. We share this room with the Second Political Advisor to the Ministry of Internal Affairs, the Director of the National Cultural Council and Cultural Centre of Vanuatu. Chief Murmur and all the male researchers and the female researchers and *filwoka*, Deputy Director of the Cultural Centre, and the Chief Executive Officer of the Malvatumauri, I am very glad to be standing here before you all, especially since so many of you have been approved to undertake research in Vanuatu through my council, and yet perhaps you don't know me. I, too, have not known all of your faces, but today I can see many of you. It is also important that we can sit together in this room; that we can come together, and we can work together. It is important that we can work together because in the culture of Vanuatu we must work together in the culture of Vanuatu we must come together, and we must unite before we can go ahead and make any other work. This is the way of all people from Vanuatu.

Thank you to everyone who has made it possible for this conference to take place in Vanuatu because, it is like the former speaker said, that we discuss Vanuatu in many other places, but not in Vanuatu itself. But today we can sit in this place, and we can work together to discuss Vanuatu on the soil of Vanuatu. This is a big thing. Today we have come together in this place to open the time during which we can work together, and we can talk together in this room. But why have we been called to sit together in this room? In the twenty-six years of Vanuatu's independence, since the former Head of State of Vanuatu declared, maybe because the big banyan tree of Vanuatu has too much dirt in its roots. All you researchers have worked hard to return some things that need to be swept. We clean the roots of Vanuatu so that we can look for a different direction, just as a former speaker of the Malvatumauri once told us at this place. Once he told the fieldworkers that, to see how a *nasiko* flies, he goes and sits on a branch, but he can't look forward all of the time. When he sits he must look behind him before he can once again turn his head around to see his road, or to choose another direction. Today Vanuatu, this nation of Vanuatu, this nation must look back before it can take another direction and move on. This is the belief of many of us who work in the Malvatumauri and Cultural Centre, that we can have this time to look back, and then we can look forward and move on in a different direction.

It is sometimes also the case that much of the work that you have done has not remained the property of us in Vanuatu. But this is how we can strengthen ourselves so that we can stand up with it, and then look back to take another direction. This month we will see the government of Vanuatu launch the Year of Kastom Economy, this can support life in Vanuatu, and at the same time it can support the proper government so that it can find another road, and take a new direction in how it leads the people of Vanuatu and nation of Vanuatu. So I think that all the work that you have made, or are making, is very, very important work for us to see how we can redirect all of our movements, all of our visions, all of our thoughts, and all of what we hear. Sometimes we act according to what you recover. Maybe there is a lot of wise talk contained in all of these things, but now we are starting to loose them. We've listened to Chief Murmur's speech, who told us how he was taught in a classroom in which they forced all the children to speak English, or forced the children to speak in French, and so now we need to look back. We can look back, and then we can look forward to take another direction so that the *nasiko* can fly, and can then sit down and take yet another direction still. Perhaps to your ears this speech is not long enough, but I want to say that we continue to try to help you to help us in our culture. And the Chiefs of Vanuatu, and the people of Vanuatu, we need to find a way to see Vanuatu, and take Vanuatu through to the coming generation. And so with this short speech, I as the Chairman of the Cultural Council of Vanuatu and also the President of the Malvatumauri, the Working Together conference of the researchers of Vanuatu is now officially open.

Editors' Introduction

John Taylor and Nick Thieberger

This collection is derived from a conference held at the Vanuatu National Museum and Cultural Centre (VCC), during November of 2006. This forum brought together a large gathering of foreign and indigenous researchers to discuss diverse perspectives relating to the unique program of social, political and historical research and management that has been fostered in that island nation. *Afta 26 Yia* (After 26 Years), as the conference was called in the national lingua franca Bislama, marked the silver anniversary of the publication of a landmark edited volume, *Vanuatu: Politics, Economics and Ritual in Island Melanesia* (Allen 1981), one year after Vanuatu gained independence in 1980. The combination of that volume, the beautifully produced *Arts of Vanuatu* (Bonnemaison *et al.* 1996) and a special issue of the journal *Oceania* (Bolton 1999), demonstrates the growth of a vibrant and diverse community of social, linguistic and archaeological researchers of Vanuatu. The ongoing spirit of collaboration and quest to produce productive relationships based on mutual respect that defines this community is primarily focused around the operations of the innovative VCC—first established as the New Hebrides Cultural Centre in 1957 (Tryon 1999: 9)—but has much deeper historical roots. At *Afta 26 Yia* we sought to celebrate that research history, while at the same time showcase the diversity and relevance of past and current research.

Of primary importance was the proviso that the conference be held in Vanuatu itself. Numerous exciting and valuable Vanuatu-specific colloquia had already been held outside of Vanuatu, most recently at two annual conferences of the Association of Social Anthropologists of Oceania (Lihue 2005, San Diego 2006), and before that at an innovative multi-disciplinary workshop called Walking About: Travel, Trade, and Movement in Vanuatu (Canberra 2000), and at a research seminar also held at the Australian National University in 1998 (see Bolton 1999). At the same time, ni-Vanuatu fieldworkers (Bislama, *filwoka*: ni-Vanuatu cultural researchers, advocates and advisors) had been meeting annually at the Vanuatu Cultural Center (VCC) in Port Vila for over two decades (Tryon 1999: 10). *Afta 26 Yia* was to provide a timely opportunity to bring the discussion of this research together for the first time within Vanuatu, and maximise the involvement of ni-Vanuatu researchers and a ni-Vanuatu audience.

The conference was timed to fall between the annual Cultural Centre's women's and men's fieldworkers' workshops, and papers were given primarily in Bislama to provide the opportunity for foreign researchers to make joint presentations with their ni-Vanuatu collaborators as well as allowing for fieldworkers and other ni-Vanuatu researchers to report on their own research projects. The conference was held at the National Museum in Port Vila and received support from the Australia Research Council-funded Asia Pacific Futures Research Network, the Vanuatu Cultural Centre and the Friends of the Vanuatu Museum. As stated in the conference announcement, *Afta 26 Yia* sought to engage the following questions: What is the significance of collaboration between international and indigenous researchers in Vanuatu? How does social, linguistic, archaeological and historical research on Vanuatu impact upon or benefit local communities, and how might the benefits be enhanced? How might research on Vanuatu be more effectively communicated to local audiences (in publications, film, exhibitions, school curricula or otherwise)? What new initiatives, strategies and institutional linkages might be developed to further enhance research that is both effective and socially relevant? The papers presented here are representative rather than exhaustive, and reflect the wide range of subject matter, presentation styles, and stages of progress that were apparent across the many projects and initiatives discussed at the actual conference. It is also to be noted that the majority of papers presented by ni-Vanuatu Vanuatu Kaljoral Senta (VKS) fieldworkers and staff, and the opening speeches, appear in both Bislama and English. These are translations of the actual oral presentations. For a full description of the actual conference, please refer to the epilogue of this volume (by Margaret Jolly).

It might be said that the history of social, linguistic and political research in Vanuatu stretches as far back as those most early voyages of re-discovery, made on the vessels of Quirós (1606), Bougainville (1768) and Cook (1774). While often avowedly violent in nature, the dialogues that took place in those early encounters produced innumerable written and oral 'texts' that did much to shape broader cross-cultural impressions and motivations for both sides (for Quirós, see Mondragon 2006; Jolly 2009). Looking further back in time, given the likelihood of multiple waves of primordial migration to the archipelago, such formative projects in cultural knowledge production no doubt predate even this. We also have the later arrival of Roi Mata, to central Vanuatu, probably some time during the 1600s (Bedford 2006: 19). One can only speculate the degree to which such Pacific pioneers engaged with locally established populations in mutual acts of social, linguistic and political research as they figured out how they might live successfully together.

Clearly, however, the specific methodological, pedagogic and institutional roots of the research projects discussed here are more historically proximate. These emerged as a part of the colonial activities of European powers to the Pacific region, and continue as a part of what might be described as neo-Colonial interests today; including especially the joint British and French 'condominium' administration of the New Hebrides, and more recently Australia and New Zealand. However misguided their methods and agendas may have been, both the evangelical and ethnological work of missionaries, such as the Anglican Reverend Robert Henry Codrington (1891) or Marist Father Elie Tattevin (1929–31), necessarily proceeded on the basis of dialogue, and on the desire to foster some degree of mutual religious, linguistic, social, cultural and political-economic understanding. Indeed, missionaries sought to educate the European public 'back home' about the ways of 'native island life', just as they sought to educate and convert those populations to their own ways. Like them, the work of early social scientists such as W. H. R. Rivers (1914), Felix Speiser (1923), John Layard (1942), Bernard Deacon (1934), or the mercurial Tom Harrisson (1937), was undertaken with at least the partial aim in mind of safeguarding aspects of local social or cultural life, if not the physical health and very survival of local populations as a whole.

As noted by Bob Tonkinson (Ch. 2), a significant hiatus separates those nineteenth- and twentieth-century pioneers from the research that followed World War Two. It is through the substantial combined efforts of specific individuals during this pre-Independence period that the current collaborative ethos most clearly emerged (see Bolton 1999; Tryon 1999). That many of these passionate and untiring pre-Independence researchers of Vanuatu language, history and culture are now household names in Vanuatu—whether across Vanuatu as a whole or in the immediate regions in which they worked—is testament to the high esteem in which their efforts are held. In this volume, and providing a most interesting counterpoint to Bresnihan and Woodward's account of *Tufala Gavman* (2002), the remarkably candid and evocative testimonies of three anthropologists who undertook research in the post-war/pre-Independence New Hebrides show something of the influence that both the joint British and French condominium government and local ni-Vanuatu community leaders had in directing research during this period. Both of the colonial authorities evidently encouraged social scientific research, and in both Michael Allen's and Bob Tonkinson's cases, played an important hand in defining their research projects and sites, if not the direction of research itself. By contrast, in Ellen Facey's case (Ch. 3), as in Michael Allen's (Ch. 1), we witness the growing power of ni-Vanuatu to curtail or otherwise control projects within the context of a fast approaching political independence.

Following Independence in 1980, the new Vanuatu government sought to promote *kastom* alongside Christianity as a part of a specifically 'Melanesian socialist' vision. However, given that the governing party had been formed, in the words of its leader Father Walter Lini, on the basis of the struggle against 'any form of colonialism, and any tendency towards neo- colonialism' (1980: 27), a moratorium to block foreign research was established in 1985. While this no doubt came as a disappointing impediment to most foreign researchers of Vanuatu at the time, in hindsight it can be seen to have had the positive effect of spurring on the current collaborative turn. While some foreign researchers simply undertook shorter research trips on tourist visas, others came to Vanuatu to undertake projects that were approved on the basis of their national importance, collaborative methodologies, and for their inclusion of provisions for local training or knowledge production. Linguists working in Vanuatu at the time, including Terry Crowley, John Lynch and Darrell Tryon established long-term research projects in a number of parts of the country (see Phillip Tepahae this volume on his project in Aneityum with John Lynch) and fostered a new generation of linguistic research students. The further development of the national fieldworkers program during this time through the inclusion of women's *filwokas*, developing out of the collaboration between Lissant Bolton and Jean Tarisesei on the Women's Culture Project (1991–92), represents a case in point (see Bolton 1999; Tryon 1999; also Chs 8 and 9 in this volume). So, too, does the World War Two Ethnohistory Project, coordinated by James Gwero and Lamont Lindstom (1987–89) (see Lindstrom and Gwero 1998, and Ch. 4 and Ch. 5 in this volume). The recent publication of a path-breaking collaborative ethnography, derived from the Vanuatu Housegirls Project (Rodman *et al.* 2007, and this volume), leads the way in demonstrating the profound value of Vanuatu's unique collaborative turn to readers and researchers internationally (compare, for example, Lassiter 2005).

The moratorium lasted for just under a decade, from 1985 to 1994, and was ultimately lifted to help fulfil the Vanuatu Cultural Centre's mandate 'to preserve, protect and develop *kastom*' through the encouragement of collaborative projects between foreign researchers and local communities (Regenvanu 1999: 98). While not diminishing the importance of individual or sole-authored methodologies, project-centred collaborative approaches have today become a defining characteristic of Vanuatu's unique research environment. This emphasis on collaboration has emerged from an ongoing awareness across Vanuatu's research community of the need for trained researchers—both ni-Vanuatu and foreign—to engage directly with pressing social and ethical concerns, and out of the proven fact that it is not just from the outcomes of research that communities or individuals may be empowered, but also through their modes and processes of implementation, as through the ongoing strength and value of the relationships they produce. With this in mind, it is hoped that the papers presented here, in their collectivity, go beyond the mere celebration of collaboration by confronting Vanuatu's specific environment of cross-cultural research as a diffuse set of historically-emergent methodological approaches, and by demonstrating how these work in actual practice.

References

Allen, Michael (ed.), 1981. *Vanuatu: Politics, Economics and Ritual in Island Melanesia*. Sydney: Academic Press Australia.

Bedford, Stuart, 2006. *Pieces of the Vanuatu Puzzle: Archaeology of the North, South and Centre*. Canberra: Pandanus Press.

Bonnemaison, Joël, Christian Kaufmann, Kirk Huffman and Darrell Tryon (eds), 1996. *Arts of Vanuatu*. Bathurst, NSW: Crawford House.

Bolton, Lissant (ed.), 1999. *Fieldwork, Fieldworkers, Developments in Vanuatu Research*. Special issue of *Oceania* 70(1).

Bresnihan, Brian and Keith Woodward, 2002. Tufala Gavman: Reminiscences from the Anglo-French Condominium of the New Hebrides. Suva, Fiji: USP Press.

Codrington, R.H. 1891. *The Melanesians: Studies in their Anthropology and Folklore*. Oxford: Clarendon Press.

Deacon, A. [Arthur] Bernard, 1934. *Malekula: A Vanishing People in the New Hebrides*, ed. Camilla H. Wedgewood, with a preface by A.C. Haddon. London: George Routledge & Sons.

Harrisson, Tom, 1937. *Savage Civilisation*. London: Gollancz.

Jolly, Margaret, 2009. The Sediment of Voyages: Re-membering Quirós, Bougainville and Cook in Vanuatu. (Ms)

Lassiter, Luke E., 2005. *The Chicago Guide to Collaborative Ethnography*. Chicago: University of Chicago Press.

Layard, John, 1942. *Stone Men of Malekula: Vao*. London: Chatto and Windus.

Lindstrom, Lamont and James Gwero (eds), 1998. *Big Wok: Storian blong Wol Wo Tu long Vanuatu*. Suva: Institute of Pacific Studies, University of the South Pacific; Christchurch: Macmillan Brown Centre for Pacific Studies, University of Canterbury.

Lini, Walter, 1980. *Beyond Pandemonium: From the New Hebrides to Vanuatu*. Wellington, NZ: Asia Pacific Books.

Mondragon, Carlos, 2006. 2007. Ethnological Origins of the ni-Vanuatu 'Other': Quirós and the early Spanish historiography of Asia and the Pacific. In *Pedro Fernández de Quirós et le Vanuatu: Découverte mutuelle et historiographie d'un acte fondateur 1606*, ed. Frédéric Angleviel, 145–67. Port Vila: Groupe de Recherche sur l'Histoire Océanienne Contemporaine / Délégation de la Commission Européenne au Vanuatu / Sun Productions.

Regenvanu, Ralph, 1999. Afterword: Vanuatu perspectives on research. *Oceania*. 70: 98–101.

Rivers, W.H.R., 1914. *The History of Melanesian Society*. Two volumes. Cambridge, UK: University of Cambridge Press.

Rodman, Margaret, Daniel Kraemer, Lissant Bolton, and Jean Tarisesei, 2007. *House-Girls Remember: Domestic Workers in Vanuatu*. Honolulu: University of Hawai'i Press.

Speiser, Felix, 1991 [1923], *Ethnology of Vanuatu: An Early Twentieth-Century Study*. Bathurst, NSW: Crawford House Press.

Tattevin, E., 1929–31. Mythes et Légendes du Sud de L'Ille Pentecóte'. *Anthropos* 24: 983–1004 and 26: 863–6.

Tryon, Darrell, 1999. Ni-Vanuatu research and researchers. *Oceania* 70(1): 9–15.

❧ Histories ☙

1. Some Reflections on Anthropological Research in a Colonial Regime

Michael Allen

When I first began research in Nduindui district in west Aoba (subsequently renamed Ambae) in November 1958, not only was it well and truly prior to independence, but very few had even begun to seriously contemplate that they might live to see such a day. In other words, there was a feeling that though independence would most probably occur one day, it was still a long way off, maybe half-a-century or more away. If we had known that it would be a reality in a mere 22 years we would without doubt have been astonished.

It might help if I begin my story with a brief outline of just what set of circumstances led to my arrival in Port Vila on that, for me, highly auspicious day, 30 October 1958. And I still well remember when I stepped ashore from the Messageries Maritime mini-liner the *Polynesie* the truly astonishing sight of Keith Woodward (Assistant Secretary for District Affairs, British Residency) clad in resplendent and glittering white colonial gear, waiting to formally greet me with that intense yet slightly lost look that his already failing eyesight conveyed.

Just one year earlier I had completed an MA Honours Qualifying course in anthropology at Sydney University (SU) and for my fourth year's honours thesis I had carried out a library-based comparative study of male cults and initiations throughout Melanesia (Allen 1967). Of all the early ethnographic material that I had then saturated myself in none fascinated me more than the work of Robert Henry Codrington (1891), William Halse Rivers Rivers (1914), Arthur Bernard Deacon (1934) and John Willoughby Layard (1942), most particularly on both the public-graded societies and the secret societies of the northern New Hebrides. Hence, when I was offered a four-year postgraduate scholarship by the Australian National University (ANU) I expressed a strong preference to locate my PhD research in one of the less-studied communities in the northern district. But, by mere coincidence, at much the same time that I was offered my scholarship, the ANU had received a letter from the Colonial Social Science Research Council (CSSRC) in London, at that time the principal source of social science research funding in the UK, asking whether the ANU knew of a suitable anthropologist who might be interested in making a study of the social structure of Aoba Island (Comfort to Freeman). As I subsequently discovered, the applicant for the funding of such a project was John Rennie, the then British Resident Commissioner in the New Hebrides. Rennie had seemingly been motivated by two factors—first, he had studied anthropology at Oxford University and as a result strongly believed that colonial administrations would benefit greatly should its officers acquaint themselves with the results of good fieldwork-based anthropological research. Second, he chose Aoba for a number of reasons that I think are worth recording. Let me quote directly from Rennie's application to the CSSRC for funding:

> I should like to see a social anthropologist undertake a study of social structure on the island of Aoba. I tentatively suggest that the study should have particular reference to the bases of social cooperation in this society, which has evolved in a climate of laisser-faire [sic] under the influence of uncontrolled pressures from missions, traders and war and ineffective administration by the Government.

> In making my recommendation I have not lost sight of the survey made by Professor Elkin in Social Anthropology in Melanesia [Elkin 1953]. The project falls into one of his priority categories, a study of a disorganised community, but I prefer Aoba to the areas he lists and am fortified in this opinion by the knowledge that Monsieur Jean Guiart, the anthropologist who has the closest recent acquaintance with the New Hebrides, independently assigned the highest priority to a study of Aoba. (Rennie to Comfort).

John Barnes, who had supervised my fourth-year thesis at Sydney University (SU) and had subsequently been appointed to the chair of anthropology at the ANU, immediately suggested to me that in view of my preference to work in the northern New Hebrides he would be prepared to recommend me to the CSSRC. So, when I stepped ashore in Port Vila, I knew that I had, as it were, two sponsors with perhaps not entirely identical expectations as to the final outcome of my research. As regards the financial arrangements, my understanding was that the CSSRC would fully fund two years of fieldwork on Aoba with the ANU funding the time spent in Canberra analysing my material and the writing-up of my thesis. I do not, however, remember experiencing any undue anxiety regarding this arrangement, mainly because first Woodward and then Rennie soon assured me that they had no specific expectations other than the hope that I would eventually come up with a thesis that would satisfy my intellectual mentors and examiners. Rennie, however, seemed pleased enough when I promised him that I would make carbon copies of all of my reports to my academic supervisors and send them to him. For my part, the arrangement worked very well, indeed quite often I found Rennie's comments and observations at least as insightful and helpful as those that came from Canberra, and certainly a good deal more prompt.

Figure 1.1. Port Vila, October 1958

(Michael Allen, photographer)

Before I finally managed to disentangle myself from the pleasures of Port Vila, Rennie elaborated a little more on what especially intrigued him about Aoba, most especially the Church of Christ-dominated Nduindui area of the western end of the island. What little he knew of this area, mainly from the occasional brief report from the northern district British Agent based in Luganville, was that the Nduindui people, far from being disorganised, took much pride in the fact that they could look after their own affairs, including the settlement of internal disputes and conflict, with the minimum of either interference or help from the colonial authorities. Indeed, the evidence was clear that they were inclined to resent any kind of outside interference within the district. In like manner, they regarded their resident white missionaries primarily as temporary professional helpers skilled in such matters as education and health. The actual running of the local church was firmly in the hands of the indigenous church elders.

Rennie was clearly of the opinion that if my research findings could document and analyse the means whereby the Nduindui successfully ran their own affairs then the British administration might indeed learn something that would enable them to facilitate similar developments elsewhere in the New Hebrides. As I subsequently discovered, the British Administration was at this time particularly keen to establish government-sponsored local councils on as many islands as possible. Prior to leaving Canberra, Barnes strongly recommended that on my arrival in Port Vila I should endeavour to meet Jean Guiart and hopefully get some useful advice as to how to successfully carry out fieldwork in the New

Hebrides. Since I had previously received no fieldwork training or even casual advice at either SU or at the ANU, other than some hasty instruction in John Barnes's useful method for recording genealogies, this seemed like a good idea. When I asked Woodward if this were possible he informed me that Guiart was most probably somewhere in North Efate carrying out research on chiefly titles and that he, Woodward, would straightaway drive me up there and seek him out. But when we arrived at Paonangisu village we were told that the good professor had left on the previous day for the nearby island of Pele. An hour later I set out with a guide on a small outrigger canoe but on arrival at a coastal village we were told that Guiart had left that morning for a village on the other side of the island. This went on for two more days until I eventually caught up with him in Mangorango Village on Emau Island. He was sitting under a tree in the middle of the village surrounded by some of the older men.

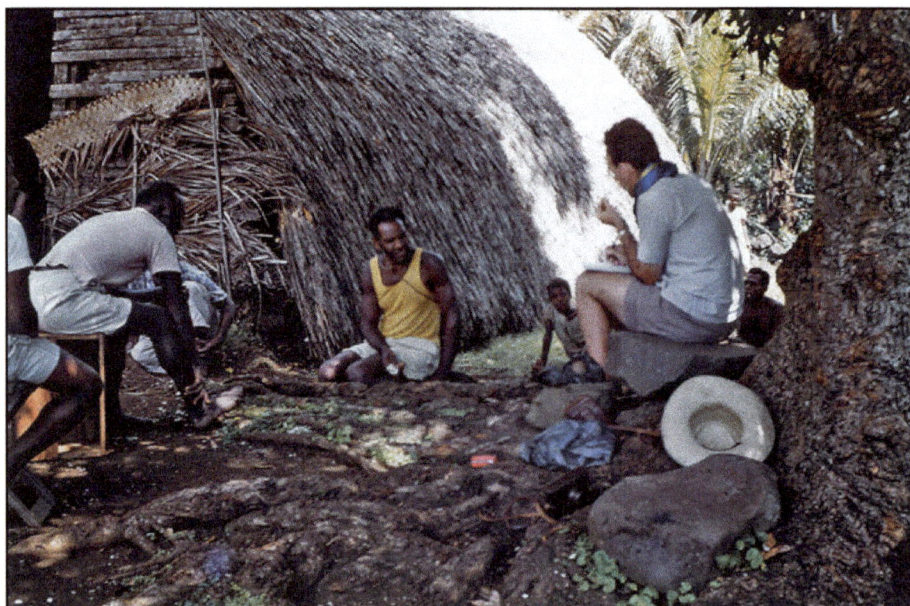

Figure 1.2. Jean Guiart at work in Mangarongo village, Emau, November 1958

(Michael Allen, photographer)

He immediately welcomed me, and when I told him that I hoped to get some fieldwork tips from him he generously invited me to sit and observe; which I duly did. For the next few hours he recorded the names of various titles and kinship terms, then closed his notebook and announced that it was time for us to proceed to the next village where he would record similar information. He added that in his opinion one or two days was the maximum time that one could expect a small Melanesian village to put up with the presence of a foreign anthropologist. Furthermore, it was, he asserted, good for one's health to spend most afternoons walking from one village to the next. Needless to say, this information seriously alarmed me, for if there was one thing I had learnt from my professors it was that good fieldwork depended on long residence, preferably from one to two years, in one's chosen community! Jean also strongly recommended that I should endeavour to record my information in my notebooks in such a manner that it could be prepared for publication with the minimum of additional work. This also astonished me!

But let me turn now to the other and more important side of the collaboration equation; that between myself as anthropologist and the Nduindui people. When I first arrived in the district, collaboration of any kind seemed, for the best part of the first two months, a remote and impossible dream. I soon found that the Church of Christ district council was indeed a powerful organisation dominated by a formidable elder by the name of Abel Bani. After my first meeting with Abel and my no doubt quite feeble attempt to explain that I would like to live in a village for a year or more in order to study and record as much as I could of their way of life, their stories, their knowledge of traditional custom as well their contemporary life style, Abel promptly informed me that they knew nothing whatsoever of *kastom* and hence I would be well advised to instead carry out my investigations in east Aoba, where *kastom* was still strong. Here, he said, with a somewhat severe expression on his dauntingly strong face, we follow the Christian way and regard *kastom* as the way of darkness. Nevertheless, he did agree to inform the Council of my desire and would in due course let me know their decision. At that point I began to fear that indeed Guiart's advice regarding the impossibility of prolonged residence in a small community was all too true.

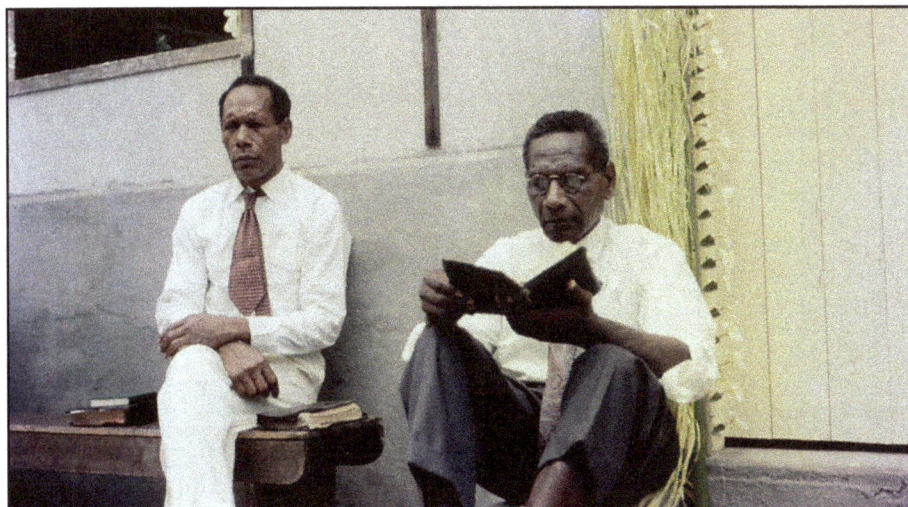

Figure 1.3. Isaac Vira (Navuti Elder) and Abel Bani outside Nduindui Church, November 1960

(Michael Allen, photographer)

For the next month, while living with the piratical-looking yet kindly French trader Paul Leroux and his Tahitian wife, I paraded myself daily throughout Nduindui, stopping to talk with anyone prepared to listen and endlessly trying to explain what anthropology was and especially my desire to live in a village, and whilst there to attempt to learn the Nduindui language and to record as much as I could of both past and contemporary culture. Though many seemed friendly enough and even expressed some interest in my proposed work, they all confirmed Abel's opinion that everything depended on the Council's decision.

Three weeks later I was told by Abel that the Council had decided that they would prefer me to leave, but should any individual village invite me to live with them then they would have no objection. And sure enough, the following day Isaac Vira and Solomon Gamali, two good friends that I had recently made in Navuti village, informed me that the village council had decided to invite me to stay and that they would provide me with a small one-roomed hut to live in. They also told me that the principal reason for Abel's reluctance to welcome me was his fear that I might bring trouble to the district, as had frequently been the case in the past both on Aoba and on neighbouring islands, when whites were allowed to come and live in their midst, mostly as either traders or missionaries. My friends felt that Abel, and many other senior members of the district council, because they could not really understand what anthropology was about or what possible benefit it might bring to them, feared that I must really have other motives, above all that I might seek to acquire land or introduce yet another Christian sect. I even heard it said that some feared that if I fell ill or some other misadventure befell me then might not the Irish government send a gunboat to wreak vengeance, as had often enough occurred in the past when mishaps befell whitemen!

Needless to say I was transported into seventh heaven when a few days later I moved from Leroux's fortress-like trading post to my hut in the centre of Navuti and before long had begun language lessons and had recorded my first few genealogies. Though I did not use the word then, on looking back I can now say that I had begun to enjoy true collaboration. As the months went by a small number of men in Navuti and in surrounding villages became not just informants and friends but enthusiastic collaborators in the task of collecting whatever kind of information I was then interested in. To begin with it was mostly genealogies but it soon extended to using tape recorders to record songs, stories and myths. Foremost amongst those early collaborators in the anthropological enterprise were two who subsequently became amongst the first fieldworkers to work for the Cultural Centre, one of whom is still active today and has already made his valuable contribution to this conference—I refer of course to James Ngwero (also Gwero in this volume, see Ch. 5) of Nambangahage Village. I still remember very vividly when James came to me one day during that first spell of fieldwork and told me that he had written down a number of stories about the culture heroes Takaro and Mwerambuto that he had obtained from a knowledgeable old man in east Aoba called Harry Mala. I still hold those twenty or so beautifully handwritten pages of some five or six such stories that James very generously gave to me. Another early recruit as a Cultural Centre fieldworker was Emmanuel Vira Lalau. I have recorded many hours of Emmanuel singing traditional songs in that beautiful voice of his.

Figure 1.4. Emmanuel Vira Lalau with a bag of kava roots, Lovanualigoutu, May 1980

(Michael Allen, photographer)

There were, however, incidents that, though not of a lasting kind, nevertheless momentarily threatened this on-going happy collaboration. Perhaps the most notable occurred during my second period of fieldwork. By then I had begun to envy the two local missionaries, Ron Maclean of the Church of Christ and Paul Grant of the Apostolic Church in nearby Walaha, both of whom owned light though powerful motorbikes that whisked them with ease over rough tracks to the most remote villages whilst I spent many hours lugging notebook, camera and sometimes tape recorder over the same routes. One day I wrote to Woodward and asked if by any chance the British Administration in Vila happened to have an unused motor bike. To my surprise they evidently had and a week or two later it arrived via the Burns Philp trading vessel at Nduindui anchorage. So down I eagerly rushed to receive it. But my heart sank when I saw that in place of the usual uninformative number plate it had a large plate clearly labelling it as 'BR 3' (British Residency 3). After almost 18 months of carefully distancing myself from the British Administration as much as I reasonably could, here I was driving up to Navuti on a British Residency bike! But by then it seemed that my credentials were well enough established to laugh this one off and soon every young man in Ŋavuti was begging to have a go on the bike.

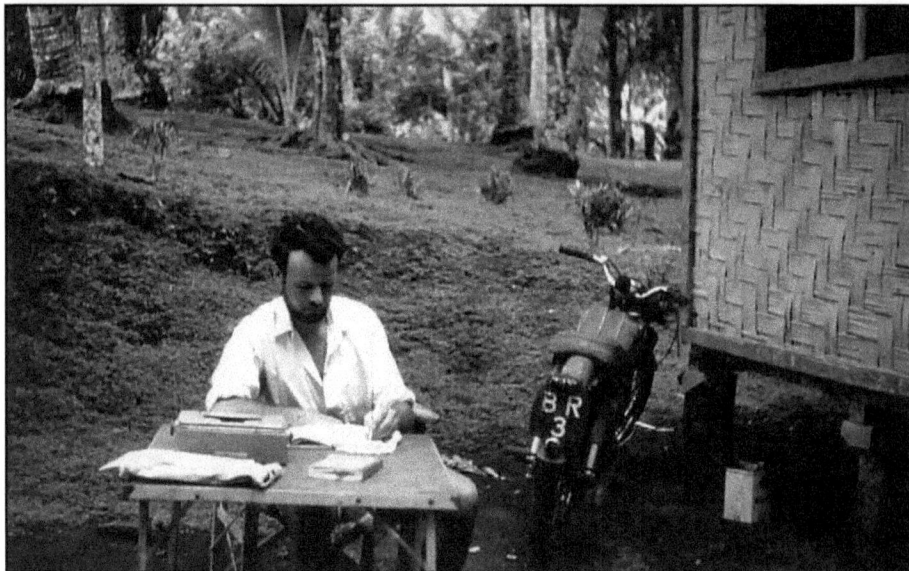

Figure 1.5. Michael outside his hut in Navuti Village with the BR 3 bike, September 1960

(photograph taken by Joel Tari of Navuti Village)

But, perhaps most important of all, what in retrospect I most value as a product of my collaboration both with the British Administration and with the Nduindui people was that as part of my promise to Rennie, though by then he had left to become the Governor of Mauritius, I had indeed submitted to his successor Colin Allan copies not only of all my reports to the ANU but also of various seminar papers that I had read to my anthropological colleagues. These remained for some years in the offices of the British Administration in Vila until one day Caroline Leaney, by then the ex-wife of a British District Agent, came across them, edited them and put them put together in 1969 as a kind of soft-back publication (Allen 1969). Very kindly, she not only sent me some 20 copies, of which I now possess only one, but arranged for about a dozen more to be sent to individuals whom I nominated in various villages throughout West Aoba. As I know from subsequent visits to Nduindui, the last being in 2003, most if not all of these are still held by families in the same villages. Needless to say this gives me considerable pleasure to contemplate—indeed far more so than the copies of my much more arid PhD thesis that can be found languishing in a number of university libraries.

References

Allen, M.R., 1967. *Male Cults and Secret Initiations in Melanesia*. Melbourne, VIC: Melbourne University Press.

Allen, M.R., 1969. *Report of Aoba: Incidental Papers on Nduindui District, Aoba Island*, ed. C. Leaney. Vila: British Residency (Mineographed).

Codrington, R.H., 1964. *The Melanesians: Studies in their Anthropology and Folklore*. Oxford: Clarendon Press.

Comfort to Freeman, 1957. File RES.88/47/01, Colonial Office, October.

Deacon, A. Bernard, 1934. *Malekula: A Vanishing People in the New Hebrides*. London: George Routledge and Sons.

Elkin, A.P., 1953. *Social Anthropology in Melanesia: A Review of Research*. London: Oxford University Press

Layard, J., 1942. *Stone Men of Malekula*. London: Chatto and Windus.

Rennie to Comfort, 1957. File RES.88/47/01, Colonial Office, October.

Rivers, W.H.R., 1968 [1914]. *The History of Melanesian Society*. 2 volumes. The Netherlands: Anthropological Publications, Oosterhout N.B.

2. The Research Context in New Hebrides-Vanuatu

Robert Tonkinson

When I began fieldwork in the New Hebrides in 1966–67, late in the colonial period, conditions for research were benign. As is well known, an incompatibility between British and French foreign policies with respect to just about every facet of colonial administration had inevitably given rise to a distinctly *laissez-faire* approach to joint governance, which came to characterise the archipelago beyond the main towns and large centres of plantation activity. The hands that guided research in the Group, at least back then and in the run-up to Independence, were similarly light in their touch—perhaps because the influx of researchers was so small. There was a long hiatus separating the early twentieth-century anthropological pioneers (Speiser, Deacon, Harrisson, Layard, and others) from the post-WW2 era, which began with the commissioned research of Jean Guiart, then Americans Robert and Barbara Lane, who were followed by Michael Allen.

My paper is necessarily some what personal and anecdotal, since it is based heavily on memory, supplemented by what my correspondence and notebooks suggest about the political context of research back in the colonial era. Almost half of my 30-something visits since then have entailed some fieldwork, but in relation to the post-independence era, many other researchers are better placed to comment on research administration in Vanuatu. From personal experience they can attest to the signal importance of the Cultural Centre in transforming the research context. Formerly characterised by individualism and virtual autonomy, it is now one of fruitful collaboration and cooperation between overseas researchers and ni-Vanuatu, directed towards the achievement of a more satisfactory balance of the 'purely academic' with national interests and priorities.

In 1980, having attended the independence celebrations in Vila as one of two Australian National University (ANU) representatives, I came away greatly impressed by the manner in which the symbology of this great occasion demonstrated and affirmed for all ni-Vanuatu (and the world at large) a crucial message: that although *kastom* had been elevated to be an integral element of national unity, only those components of it deemed ethically and morally congenial to mainstream Christianity would be supported; in other words, sorcery, revenge killing, spouse-beating and so on were excluded (Tonkinson 1982a, 1982b, 2004a). Creative tension and negotiation would inevitably persist as the new nation dealt with the ambiguities and blurred edges of 'good' and 'bad' *kastom*, and so the need for a home-based anthropological presence struck me as compelling. With this imperative in mind, I wrote informally to an old friend, Donald Kalpokas, making a case for the training of some ni-Vanuatu anthropologists and requesting that his government consider sending students to ANU. He agreed with the sentiment, but couched his reply in terms of more pressing priorities facing a newly independent nation, understandably favouring the training of lawyers, accountants and doctors.

This was, of course, before the moratorium on overseas academic researchers was decreed, not long after independence. I suspect that we researchers had all anticipated some flexing of the muscles of autonomy and anti-imperialism on the part of youthful, newly independent nations such as Vanuatu, but the severity and the longevity of the ban came both as a surprise and a great disappointment. Thanks to tourist visas, however, it was still possible for researchers to come back to the islands and keep abreast of developments among those local peoples with whom they had worked. As practitioners of the 'extended case method', those fieldworkers who made frequent returns to Vanuatu possessed language skills and a strong knowledge base that had been forged pre-independence. We enjoyed close ties to 'our' people, so we were able to gain much from these brief visits, over and above reaffirmations of mutual attachment and on-going commitment to our friends-become-kin. Years later, having moved to Perth, I was delighted to hear that Ralph Regenvanu was studying anthropology at ANU, and we all know the rest of that story, notably the subsequent renaissance of anthropological research in Vanuatu.

In 1966, I was recruited from the University of Western Australia to join a large research project involving ten studies of displaced communities in the Pacific, aimed ultimately at enhancing our understanding of social change processes.[1] The project director was a famous US anthropologist, Homer Barnett.[2] He wrote to the British administration here asking permission for me to do research on Epi among recently relocated villagers from Lopevi Island after its volcano erupted and forced them out.

---

1 Research Assistants were given two year appointments, with a generous salary, airfares and expenses. After a year or so of field research, the appointee would be expected to spend the second year in residence at the University of Oregon, writing up the results as a monograph. This meant not only a guaranteed book-length publication but also the freedom to use one's data for a higher degree. Ron Crocombe told me that he urged Professor Barnett to advertise for researchers in Australasia because, at that time, Barnett was having difficulty recruiting suitable fieldworkers in North America! Those were indeed the heady days of the prosperous sixties.

2 In 1953, Barnett, a distinguished scholar, published *Innovation*; adopting an 'ideational' or 'mentalistic' approach, he made a major contribution to theories to culture change. See Lieber, ed. 1977 for an assessment of the Barnett project's objectives and outcomes.

The quote that follows is from a handwritten P.S. on a letter dated 22 February 1966 from Keith Woodward, the Assistant Secretary for District Affairs, British Residency, Vila, to Barnett.

> I am sorry about the delay [in getting permission for me to undertake fieldwork in 1966–67] but your omission to write to both Resident Commissioners has caused some difficulty with the French Residency which is very sensitive about these matters and has in effect declined to take cognisance of your proposal since it was not addressed at the same time as we were. You were not to know this but it is one of the facts of life in the Condominium.

Not knowing, for example, that a major diplomatic flap had once supposedly transpired in Vila from allegations that one nation's flag was flying centimetres higher than the other's outside a Condominium building, my American boss could perhaps be forgiven for the mistake he made in not writing simultaneously to both colonial authorities. Eventually, after Professor Barnett had done as directed, a response, co-signed by both Resident Commissioners (31 March 1966) declared that they 'had no objection' to my project. While leaving the choice of field site to Professor Barnett, they put a strong case for an alternative research location: the village of Maat, on Efate, which had been established by south-east Ambrymese people some 15 years previously. They noted also that the villagers' subsequent purchase of adjoining land suggested an intention to remain there. Not only would the Maat study yield valuable data on rural to peri-urban adaptation, the authorities suggested, but it would also be a useful complement to a socio-geographical study of Vila and its hinterland undertaken the previous year by two Australian National University researchers, Harold Brookfield and Paula Brown (Brookfield and Brown Glick, 1969).

Such talk of benefit was a clear indication that the colonial authorities saw potential value in anthropological research. Since both the Maat people and their village's whereabouts were secondary to the fact of relocation, Barnett was happy to go along with the Maat, Efate, suggestion—and so was I. I had already endured, over a three-year period in Australian's forbidding Western Desert, the trials of remoteness, fundamentalist Christian missionaries, extremes of climate and luxury-free conditions. I was really ready for peri-urban propinquity and all that it promised, including early morning baguette deliveries to Maat village by an excellent Vietnamese baker.

This being the colonial era, permission to undertake research never hinged on a prior approach to the people among whom one intended to study, either back in Western Australia, where I had commenced Honours fieldwork in 1962, or in the New Hebrides. I do not recall receiving any instruction regarding rules or protocols governing the proper conduct of research, or any listing of obligations and responsibilities, especially towards the people among whom I would be living and working. As far as I know, neither British nor French officials had even informed the villagers at Maat that a European would soon arrive in their midst with a request to invade their domain. This was not surprising, since the French never (and the British rarely) ever visited the place, and professed to know next to nothing about it.[3]

In July, 1966, I sailed from Sydney on the Messageries Maritimes copra-cum-passenger ship, the *Tahitien*, to Vila via Santo. Once anchored in the harbour, we were put ashore by lighter, but because it was a Saturday and the British Residency offices were closed I was unable to locate any officials to let them know that I had decided to continue to Noumea to do some research in the South Pacific Commission's library and archives, and would return to Vila from there in about a week. This no-show vexed the British, as I subsequently learned when I was dressed down about it. Happily, Professor Barnett's gaffe with the letter of application did not put me offside with the French officials, who were amenable and offered me access to files on Maat. This generosity proved fruitless, however, as they failed to locate any, and there probably were none, since the Maat people, as Anglophones, were not their concern. The British made the same offer, but the crucial files on the relocation to Maat and its aftermath were by then in the Pacific Archives in Suva, so I spent a week working on relevant New Hebrides materials while en route to the U.S. in 1967.

It was clear that, since I was a British subject, the British side would be in charge of me, and they kindly installed me in the transit house in the British Paddock (now Independence Park).[4] Once I was settled at Maat, and the villagers had grasped what I needed to learn from them, they were enormously helpful, and data on the variables affecting their relocation poured in. The following year, when it came time for the Ambrym segment of my research, Elders Maxi Solomon and Yonah Taso Vovaen, two of the most respected and knowledgeable southeast Ambrymese leaders, escorted me and rendered invaluable assistance with my enquiries into remaining elements of *kastom* there. The British gave us a lift north in one of their vessels, and I was able to reciprocate by letting them persuade me to take charge of the census exercise in Southeast Ambrym, so I ended up doing my bit for Empire.

---

3   While going through old papers recently, I discovered that my 'Permit to Enter and Reside in the New Hebrides' required the University of Oregon to lodge a 'security bond' (amount not specified) on my behalf. I have no idea whose security was being thus guaranteed.

4   The legendary Keith Woodward, an invaluable friend to all researchers, was a great help and a fount of local knowledge, as was Tessa Franklin (later Fowler), who had assisted with an economic survey carried out in the early 1960s.

Figure 2.1. Elder Maxi Solomon with some of his family at Maat Efate; he was a major force for change in both Southeast Ambrym and the relocated village of Maat

(Robert Tonkinson, photographer)

Someone back in Australia had told me that, once I'd signed the visitors' book at the British Residency, I would eventually receive an invitation to a Residency occasion, so I should take some formal wear to New Hebrides, which I did. Then it was my turn to be vexed when no such invitation was forthcoming, especially since the then British Resident Commissioner, New Zealander Colin Allan, had a research-based Master's in anthropology, on Solomon Islands land tenure, and would surely be genuinely interested in the relocation research and would therefore wish to be apprised of my progress. Alas, there was just the initial interview-welcome in his office, and then a year later I was summoned for an equally brief and formal exit-interview, with no cocktail party invitations to the Residency that would have given me the chance to don formal wear.

Ironically, it was the French Residency, initially offended by Professor Barnett's oversight, which came to the rescue. Perhaps the fact that one of my dancing partners at local balls was a daughter of the French Resident Commissioner may have had something to do with my invitations to dine at the Residency; from this remove, I cannot recall. However, I clearly remember the day the Mouradians made a visit to Maat, turning up unannounced to say hello and to ask if I would show them around the village. This was probably the first and only time any senior colonial official had set foot there, so the locals were shocked, and more than a little perturbed at first. Our esteemed visitors spent an hour or so (happily, as far as I could discern) negotiating the muddy paths and chatting with the villagers, while I bent their ears about both administrations' neglect of Maat, and answered questions about how the research was going. M. Mouradian, reputedly a noted historian and scholar, was certainly a gentleman and a great host, even if, as we've since learned, he was heeding President de Gaulle's instruction to oppose any moves towards independence (Van Trease 1995: 15–18).

Figure 2.2. Colonial Vila: awaiting the arrival of General De Gaulle at the French War Memorial, 1966

(Robert Tonkinson, photographer)

Two years later, the Ambrymese relocation monograph had been published and copies were sent to both administrations and to the Maat people and other interested parties. I was a visiting lecturer for a year at the University of Oregon, and by then had made the decision to enrol for my doctorate at the University of British Columbia. Since my intention was to base my thesis on Aboriginal material, I was planning a return to Australia for further fieldwork, but with a stopover in New Hebrides en route, for more research there as well. Much to my surprise, a handwritten congratulatory letter arrived from the British Resident Commissioner, concerning the Maat monograph, which he had just read. I responded, thanking him for the kind remarks and announcing my imminent return to Vila.[5] He replied, saying that his Administration was embarrassed by

---

5   There were many issues deserving of further research, especially the ambiguities inherent in being identified with both homeland and relocated village (Tonkinson 1977, 1979), and the issues of identity that would be central as long as the Maat people remained in Efate (Tonkinson 1985).

what I'd written about the gross neglect of Maat by the colonial authorities, and would welcome my advice as to how best to assist the village. The long-awaited invitation to the British Residency did ensue after I returned that year (1969); but this time as an author, a Ph.D candidate and a critic of the regime who had been judged worthy.

Out in Maat, my return triggered a minor upsurge of bureaucratic interventional activity. The British District Agent and sundry other British officials, in full do-gooder project mode, dashed back and forth from town, and the poor bemused villagers, wondering what had hit them, were dragooned into community labour every Saturday. They must have been so relieved when I left, because in subsequent letters they reported that the status quo was soon restored and the officials had reverted to their old invisible man routine. Maat once again became 'that scruffy little village behind Mele'.

Figure 2.3. Maat and Mele children re-enacting at a school concert the arrival on Efate of the first Christian missionaries

(Robert Tonkinson, photographer)

Having jumped ahead, I now return to the beginnings of the New Hebrides fieldwork and the colonial context. What of my desire and intention to live at Maat? After several meetings and lots of explanation about why a European would want to live in a malaria-infested village some seven miles from town, the villagers acceded to my request. I paid them to build me a two-roomed hut in their midst, and this was quickly done. The reason for their hesitation, I was told at the time, says much about their perceptions of their colonial masters. It went as follows: the older women, particularly, were convinced that, as whites have thin skin, I would be ravaged by Anopheles mosquitoes and die of malaria, whereupon the colonial authorities would blame them for failing to look after me properly, and, as punishment, the villagers would all be sent back to Ambrym.[6] These strong fears spoke volumes about the deep concerns of some older Maat people regarding their security of tenure at Maat and their conviction that they could be sent packing at the whim of their colonial overlords, despite the villagers' purchase of enough extra land to make their village economically viable.

It was some years later when, over a few drinks, a southeast Ambrymese friend who taught school suddenly asked me if I knew the 'real' reason for the strong opposition of the older women to my request to live at Maat. He said it wasn't the weak skin story, but one that arose from my unsettling ability, as a total stranger—and a paleface to boot—to know the names not only of spouses and children but long dead forebears as well. What had happened was that, while still living in town, I had obtained from the British District Agent some census details about Maat so that I could know its approximate population and begin to familiarise myself with the villagers by learning some names. On my first ever visit to Maat, with two Ifiran friends, one of whom had taught there and was happy to introduce me, I repeatedly referred to the census material to identify people, and in a few cases also identified their deceased parents. I am sure that I had told my listeners where the information was obtained from, but probably did so in English, and as rumours later spread this fact would have been obliterated. Since only a returning spirit of the dead would possess such knowledge, and since these beings can be highly dangerous (earning them the label *temat*), the last thing these women wanted was a potential murderer loose in the village. So the 'real' reason entailed some strong continuities in 'traditional' beliefs despite decades of Presbyterianism, and was anthropologically more compelling, though less relevant to the present discussion than the first explanation.

I had no difficulties with the British administration, and enjoyed fairly frequent informal contacts with Keith Woodward; after all, for most of the 13 months I was living close to town, had an old car, played and danced at the tennis club and divided my leisure time between village and Vila, so there was ample contact for the British to feel that they had their eye on me, and the French too for that matter, since many of my fellow tennis players were Francophone. My only brush with the French, if it can be called that, arose immediately after a visit I had made to Santo, during which I went to a French-owned copra plantation one Sunday afternoon to say hello to a large group of Southeast Ambrymese who lived and worked there. No one was at the homestead when I arrived there

---

6   A few widows were even reported to have begged their sons to remove corrugated iron from their roofs and store it, ready for transportation to Ambrym—much to the amusement of the men who related this to me, though their laughter sounded a little forced.

to announce myself, so my friends took me through to the workers' quarters. There, over two or three hours and in the course of asking scores of questions on all sorts of topics so as to gain some idea of what their lives as migrants in Santo were like, and what their residence intentions were for the future, I must have included a question about their wages.

Back in Maat, Efate, a day or so afterwards, a French Residency vehicle pulled up in the village and Hubert, a friend of mine who worked as a radio broadcaster, sought me out: had I just been in Santo, he asked. Yes. Had I been on such-and-such plantation asking questions? Yes. He then informed me that the Residency had received a complaint from plantation owners on Santo that an English-speaking *agitateur* trespassed on their property and, they alleged, was stirring up the natives by asking provocative questions. The complaint was discussed that morning at the Residency, and he guessed that, from the description of the villain and the fact that he was talking to people from Southeast Ambrym, it could well have been me, so he was sent out to check on it. My reactions were mixed; this news was ominous but also amusing. I assured my friend that the wages question was one of a great many, and had been asked for comparative purposes, not to foment a revolution! Thus reassured, Hubert returned to the Residency to inform the officials that all was well, and nothing further came of it. The incident, however, was a powerful reminder of how very small the colonial world was in New Hebrides at that time, and how, breaching basic tenets of colonialism by living among the colonised, anthropologists were often under suspicion of inciting them to resistance.

Figure 2.4. Maat village, Efate: the village choir in an open-air performance of hymns

(Robert Tonkinson, photographer)

The ways in which that world had moulded attitudes were brought home in other ways, illustrative of the fact that colonialism's worst single feature is its imbuing of subject peoples with a consciousness of their own inferiority. Being called 'masta' in the Vila market, though, was initially both troubling and funny, because after firmly scolding the vendor: '*Mi mi no masta blong yu; nem blong mi Bob,*' he would invariably follow up with '*I gud Bob, mi glad blong mitim yu…nao masta, prais blong bananas ia i gud tumas!*' During my first visit to Ambrym, when I visited other villages, there was mild panic whenever I sat on the ground, as people raced around in search of a chair, then insisted I must sit on it, because only black people sit on the ground, and whites must be positioned above the locals.[7]

I still remember one young man in Utas village, where I normally reside in Southeast Ambrym, telling me knowingly that, although I pretended to be ordinary in Ambrym, I was a big man back in Australia, being driven around in a large car and protected by my own bodyguards. One thing I need to tell you at this point is that no Europeans live in Southeast Ambrym, owing largely to its exposed windward aspect and lack of good anchorages. Official visitors were also rare; in one eight-year period (1946–54), no District Agent or other colonial officer is said to have visited the region. No wonder small children either fled in panic or froze, transfixed with fright at the sight of me; here at last is that white man their parents were constantly warning would come to kill and eat, or abduct, them for bad behaviour.

Back in Maat Efate, it took a while to dawn on me that I was not only the first European to live among them but, for most I was the first European they could get close to and freely touch (at that time, very few worked as 'house-girls' in town and minded their employers' children). After all, colonialism, as we well know, relies for its reproduction on the maintenance of strict social and spatial boundaries—the very things that we as anthropologists are intent on abolishing in our quest for rapport and empathy. While visiting Santo, I was hanging out with a group of southeast Ambrymese friends when they suggested we go to see a Western movie at the open-air picture theatre. On arrival, they confronted me with the question: did I want to sit in the rear section with the Whites, and pay 100 francs, or sit in the front with them, and pay only 50? On social rather than financial grounds (of course), I opted for the latter, but then, to my horror, I realised that all the locals were cheering for the cowboys. I remember shouting to my friends above the din, 'No, no, don't you realise, *you're* the Indians?!' To which my good friend, policeman David Persi, replied, with a big grin, 'We *know* that, but the Indians always lose!'

---

7   This makes one wonder what the British were doing when they decided to put their Residency down on Iririki Island; the French, perched way above, on the hill overlooking the harbour, certainly got that one right!

Figure 2.5. Southeast Ambrym: loading copra, the area's major cash crop

(Robert Tonkinson, photographer)

One advantage of working in a colonial situation is that it quickly confronts you with the defining power of the colour of your skin: you are rich and influential by definition, and both respect and fear are implicated in the views of you held by the colonised, regardless of your personality. As anthropologists, we can be made extremely uncomfortable by such perceptions. The other issue is our inability to define ourselves adequately to the world. To this day, the vast majority of Southeast Ambrymese do not understand what I've been up to these past forty years, despite my earnest attempts to explain my discipline and my mission to them. 'Ongelxiax?' they say, 'So you're on holiday.' Their understanding of *polien* 'work' does not include asking countless questions, scribbling in a notebook, chatting to a tape recorder and wandering from village to village. In the early years they were certain I would not come back, but my riposte about investing so much time and effort in language learning gradually eroded their certainty on that score. It all came down to trust rather than any understanding of my motives, and never once have I been asked to explain why I asked a particular question, or what I planned to do with the answer. Whatever I do or have done, they have not seemed perturbed or threatened by it. By the same token, however, as a woefully neglected people living in one of the least developed areas of the nation, most could well ask what my periodic presence among them has done for their material welfare, outside the few villages where I sleep and a circle of decades-old exchange-relationship beneficiaries. I did not undertake collaborative or directed applied research aimed at bringing about some much-needed developmental change in Southeast Ambrym, though I certainly offered plenty of advice and suggestions.[8]

Figure 2.6. Southeast Ambrym: Bonne Annee celebrants, early New Year's morning, 1978

(Robert Tonkinson, photographer)

Also, in the Maat Efate case, despite my criticism of the authorities' neglect of the village, one conclusion I drew from a comparison with the other nine communities studied in the same project was that this relocation was among the most successful, to a great extent *because* the government played no part in it (see Lieber, ed. 1977; Tonkinson 1977). The absence of bureaucratic interference maximised villager initiatives aimed both at addressing the many challenges consequent upon relocation and taking advantage of the opportunities for innovation that it enabled. In the Maat case it was the Presbyterian Church, and its officers and parishioners on Efate, whose support, particularly in the

---

8   Excuses: My appointment to the Chair in Anthropology at the University of Western Australia (UWA) in 1984 meant a large expenditure of time and energy in rebuilding, restructuring and running the Department and its programs. Also, the Vanuatu research moratorium, combined with my relocation to the west coast, directed my attention strongly back to the Western Desert. For a decade from 1992, I was senior consultant anthropologist on the Mardu land claim (later Native Title claim) by the people among whom I'd worked since 1963. This culminated in my writing the bulk of the Connection Report, the documented bases for claim, on which the 2002 decision to grant them native title over the bulk of their traditional homelands largely rested.

campaign that saw the villagers pay off their land purchase loan, was crucial to the economic viability and prospects for permanency of the relocated community at Maat.

Figure 2.7. Southeast Ambrym: preparing Sunday *laplap* puddings, Endu Village

(Robert Tonkinson, photographer)

Had Dr. Barbara Lane been able to attend this conference, she would have focused her talk on a theme that I have not been able to address via the Ambrymese, either in their homeland or in the Efate village, since in both locations officials were scarce;[9] namely, the manner in which the people in south Pentecost used the two-government rule effectively to free themselves from any disruptive interference in their affairs by either administration. The astute political strategies via which the traditional villages, in the region where Barbara and her late husband Bob did their research, managed to preserve their culture is a fascinating story that we hope Barbara will in time publish.

In a brief but excellent discussion on the responsibilities entailed in long-term research, written shortly before his untimely death, Roger Keesing (1994: 189–91) posed a set of questions, most of which would be quite familiar to us. One that perhaps is not so common, though, concerns the effects of an anthropological penchant for studying atypical and unrepresentative 'traditionalist' communities

---

9   The sole and very important exception was British District Agent Darvall Wilkins, who persuaded the British to use Australian aid money for the building of a water supply, airfield and road –apart from clinics and schools, until today the only visible evidence of any official interest in Southeast Ambrym. Despite this dismal history of neglect, the southeast Ambrym region has never been a locus of millenarian thinking or activity (cf. Tonkinson 2004b).

that plays into Western cravings for 'romanticised primitivity and exoticism', and more recently for 'ecological and spiritual wisdom', when the realities of life reveal the vast majority of Melanesians as committed both to modernism and to Christian life. Roger fessed up as a culprit, given his work on the pagan Kwaio in the Solomon Islands, and so do I for reconstructing 'traditional life' among the Mardu Aborigines of Australia's Western Desert (Tonkinson 1978–91).[10]

I conclude with some observations that I hope will be relevant to Vanuatu's present circumstances, based on my hidden part-time role as an expedition ship lecturer since 1981. What the mostly aged, predominantly American travellers crave more than anything is a reassurance about the 'authenticity' of their brief experiences ashore. Many are disquieted about the status of *kastom*, and will ask, for example: 'Is the Rom performed other than for tourists, and is the secret society still functioning as it would have done in the past?' 'Would the village be this clean if they hadn't known we were coming?' 'Do women bare their breasts in public when there are no tourists around?' 'Does the shipping company pay the community for the trouble they go to for our visit?' As much as they enjoy the dance spectacles put on for them, seventh heaven for a surprising number is when we are forced to move to Plan B, perhaps because the landing site at Plan A is too hazardous on the day, and they are put ashore in a village that has virtually no prior warning (past the scout boat that takes the Expedition Leader and me ashore to ask permission for a visit). Once in the village, most tourists are both pleased and eager: this, then, they are certain, is village life as it is normally lived, so they are in absolutely no doubt that 'what we see is what we get'. Of course, if *all* the 'cultural' landings were like this, without colourful artistic performances or artefacts for sale, many would soon be grumbling about boredom, but I can say with absolute conviction that nothing brightens the expeditioner's day like making new friends among the locals, thanks to that universal Melanesian ability to draw strangers rapidly and warmly into 'family' relationships. The afterglow of this, when people come back on board, is palpable.

For me, the shipboard work has added an interesting and different dimension to my experience as an anthropologist. Having observed a colonial situation in which I at times found myself interpreting the one to the other, I now deal with a highly privileged minority bent not on ignoring or changing a subject people but determined, however briefly, to engage in what they hope will be an authentically exotic and interesting encounter with fellow humans. I began in the days of colonialism, saw the transition to independence and now, in my

---

10 Defence: that was *after* writing a monograph on the clash between Mardu and Christian fundamentalists at a remote mission (Tonkinson 1974), and many articles about social change processes since 1963. Also, my work in this country has been with long-time Christians who, by the 1960s, had grown very comfortable with a view of their pre-European past as all darkness and evil, and remembered very little of their old religion.

'retirement', am still somewhere in the middle, but find value and satisfaction in being able to facilitate, albeit fleetingly, some communication and understanding between two sets of people, for each of whom the other holds some fascination.

References

Barnett, Homer G., 1953. *Innovation: The Basis of Cultural Change*. New York, NY: McGraw-Hill.

Brookfield, Harold C. and Paula Brown Glick, 1969. *The People of Vila*. Department of Human Geography, Research School of Pacific Studies, Publication HG/1 (1969). Canberra: ANU.

Keesing, Roger M., 1994. Responsibilities of long-term research. In *Culture-Kastom-Tradition: Developing Cultural Policy in Melanesia*, ed. Lamont Lindstrom and Geoffrey M. White, 187–97. Suva: University of the South Pacific.

Lieber, Michael D. (ed.), 1977. *Exiles and Migrants in Oceania*. Honolulu: University Press of Hawai'i.

Tonkinson, Robert, 1968. *Maat Village, Efate: A Relocated Community in the New Hebrides*. Eugene: University of Oregon Press.

Tonkinson, Robert, 1974. *The Jigalong Mob: Aboriginal Victors of the Desert Crusade*. Menlo Park, CA: Cummings.

Tonkinson, Robert, 1977. The exploitation of ambiguity. In *Exiles and Migrants in Oceania*, ed. M.D. Lieber, 269–95. Honolulu: University Press of Hawai'i.

Tonkinson, Robert, 1978. *The Mardudjara Aborigines: Living the Dream in Australia's Desert*. New York: Holt, Rinehart and Winston. [1991 *The Mardu Aborigines*. (revised and enlarged) Fort Worth, TX: Holt, Rinehart and Winston.]

Tonkinson, Robert, 1979. Divination, replication and reversal in two New Hebridean societies. *Canberra Anthropology* 2(2): 57–74.

Tonkinson, Robert, 1982a. National identity and the problem of *kastom* in Vanuatu. *Mankind* 13(4): 306–15. (*Special Issue: Reinventing Traditional Culture: The Politics of Custom in Island Melanesia*, ed. Roger M. Keesing and Robert Tonkinson).

Tonkinson, Robert, 1982b. Vanuatu values: A changing symbiosis. In *Melanesia: Beyond Diversity*, ed. R. May and H. Nelson, 73–90. Canberra: Research School of Pacific Studies, Australian National University. Republished in *Pacific Studies* 1982, 5(2): 44–63.

Tonkinson, Robert, 1985. Forever Ambrymese? Identity in a relocated community, Vanuatu. *Pacific Viewpoint* 26(1): 139–59.

Tonkinson, Robert, 2004a. Spiritual prescription, social reality: reflections on religious dynamism. *Anthropological Forum* 14(2): 183–201.

Tonkinson, R., 2004b. Encountering the other: Millenarianism and the permeability of indigenous domains in Melanesia and Australia. In *Cargo, Cult and Culture Critique*, ed. Holger Jebens, 137–56. Honolulu: University of Hawai'i Press.

Van Trease, Howard, (ed.) 1995. *Melanesian Politics: Stael Blong Vanuatu*. Christchurch: University of Canterbury.

Woodward, Keith, the Assistant Secretary for District Affairs, British Residence, Vila, to Barnett, 22 February 1966.

3. Threading Many Needles: Ins and Outs of Anthropological Research in Pre-Independence Vanuatu

Ellen E. Facey

In this paper I explain the circumstances surrounding research I conducted in the Pacific nation of Vanuatu in the late 1970s, or the New Hebrides/Les Nouvelles Hébrides as it was known at the time.[1] On applying for an extension of my permit to remain in the New Hebridean community in which I had been living for much of 1978, I was asked to adhere to the limit agreed on prior to my arrival, and to leave within a few days. My reasons for writing about this now are several. For one, it has become more acceptable in the anthropology of recent years to write explicitly with and about the 'I' of the writer/researcher/ fieldworker, no longer veiling ourselves in the no-one that is 'One' (as in 'One thinks/can conclude', etc.), in passive verb constructions that create an air of distance and impartiality (such as, 'it appeared to the observer'), and in the various other means used in past decades to mask our own personal features as well as the often personal nature of fieldwork.

That is, however, perhaps only a sufficient cause. The necessary cause has to do with my own personal and professional self. Whether it is a good thing or not, anthropologists still place much emphasis on one another's performance as fieldworkers. In this business it is a precious and also very vulnerable aspect of one's professional persona. I have had the unfortunate experience of finding out what this means at first hand, having been stung by gossip generated by 'colleagues' who came to know one fact about my fieldwork but were blissfully ignorant of any of the details or context behind it. Gossips are remarkably uninterested in details or context, much as tabloids are uninterested in thorough or balanced reporting, so this is not surprising. Nonetheless, in the first stage of my career as a professional, I felt unable to write about these events.

What follows is, first, my tale of arrival in my field site, on the island of Nguna, central Vanuatu, as faithful a representation as I am able to provide of my 'first contact', based on memory and my field diary. I then compare it with similar ones found in the Pacific ethnographic literature. The differences among them lead to consideration of anthropological fieldwork in decolonising and post-colonial situations, and to the specific variables that influenced my experiences

---

1   I have chosen to use the old name, the New Hebrides, throughout, except where reference is made to post-Independence Vanuatu.

in the New Hebrides—the experience of arrival and, later, that of departure and also of return or re-entry. Finally, I offer some ideas with the intention of stimulating a discussion of the value of field research within anthropology today and in the future.

Threading many needles

I flew into the New Hebrides' capital, Port Vila, in March 1978, a 23-year-old post-graduate student eager to prove herself. I then spent what seemed an inordinate amount of time and money languishing in its hotels and restaurants, waiting for local permission to go to my chosen research site, Nguna, an island just off the northwest coast of Efate. I could not calculate the expenditure of mental energy spent in daily visits to the British Residency, and then to the Vanua'aku Pati office, which I had been told by my contact in the Residency, was 'unofficially' but most definitely in charge of visitors to this part of the archipelago. What my graduate advisor, Dr. Michael Allen of the University of Sydney Anthropology Department, had thought would be a straightforward entrée once my visa was approved by the Residency, had turned into a hot, dusty run-around, one that lasted a full month rather than the three or four days Michael had projected. But it was 1978, and the New Hebrides was no longer in the secure, if highly duplicated and confusing, grasp of its two colonial powers, Britain and France. Michael had had a number of successful advisees who had seemingly experienced a smooth passage in various parts of the New Hebrides. But it was not to be the case for me on my journey to Nguna.

I had originally booked to depart Sydney in December 1977, but a scant few weeks before my departure date I received a terse cable from the British Residency's Research Office in Port Vila, saying that my permission to travel to the New Hebrides to conduct research in the Central District had been revoked, indefinitely. Recent 'incidents' and an air of hostility toward Europeans in general had led the Residency to feel that its officers 'could not take responsibility for [my] security'. Not sure what to make of this setback, I contacted Michael who made a number of attempts by phone, eventually successfully, to reach a contact of his in Port Vila for some inside information on what might have caused this reversal. It turned out that there had been an incident in downtown Vila which was being described in some media as a 'riot' and all research permits had been put into limbo, not only mine. We also learned that leaders of the Vanua'aku Pati, an indigenous political independence movement, had declared itself to be the 'People's Provisional Government' of the country on 29 November 1977, a few days before the cable had been sent. Michael's contact claimed that the so-called 'riot' was really nothing more than a few scuffles in the streets of Vila and in some of the small towns on other islands that took place when Pati members ran up their new flag. This clarified the situation, but left us hanging as to whether my research would ever be carried out. We would just have to wait and see.

Subsequent news reports confirmed Michael's contact's opinion that the events of late November/early December 1977 were relatively minor. After a few weeks, there were no signs of spreading or increasing violence, so I appealed for reinstatement of my research permit. This was granted and I was able to fly to Vila in late January 1978.

Nonetheless, on my arrival in the capital, officials were at pains to impress upon me two facts: first, that my position was to be a neutral one. Under no circumstance was I to begin making anthropological inquiries, nor to travel outside Vila for such a purpose, until I had been granted permission by the Research Office to do my study in a specific location. Second, the area in which I had proposed working (Nguna Island, in the central District) was considered by all and sundry to be a stronghold of the pro-Independence Vanua'aku Pati. I would have to stay clear of any perception of involvement with their or any other pro-Independence movements. I wondered how much pressure I might be subjected to locally in order to get me to do just the opposite. If Nguna were such a pillar of Vanua'aku Pati strength, what were the chances that I could maintain the neutral stance demanded by the official government?

And then it got worse. My final interview in the Residency was with the government agent most closely involved with Nguna. In respect of his memory, I will leave him nameless. In a quiet, but sombre kind of way, he repeated the warnings I had already been given. Then he added this bombshell, 'Now I'm going to tell you something and, if you should ever repeat it, I shall deny having said it.' My heart sinking, I listened as he explained that Independence was not far off now, and that he and some of his fellows had been for some time providing intellectual, strategic encouragement to the leaders of the independence movement, believing that the colonial hold on the archipelago should and would soon be removed. In light of the fact that the Vanua'aku Pati was the only viable indigenous political party, it was likely to become the first governing party. Therefore, I would have to seek permission from the Pati itself, albeit quietly and unofficially. This was not a suggestion, but a clear instruction. A successful entry and stay in Nguna would depend on obtaining this permission.

So I took myself off to the Vanua'aku Pati's office, and attempted to speak to someone there. For a month I trod a path to their door, to make and then re-make missed appointments to be seen by Fr. Walter Lini. Barred from initiating any inquiries in or out of town while my application was reviewed by the Vanua'aku Pati leaders in consultation with their Nguna branch ('Nguna-Pwele

Cultural Association') representatives, I waited restlessly, spending my slim research funds on a series of increasingly cheap hotels/motels/rest-houses and restaurants.

Eventually I was told that the Pati leaders were awaiting the decision of the Nguna-Pwele Cultural Association representatives. Once that—a positive recommendation—had been received, I was then able to try to make an appointment with Fr. Lini. More time elapsed as the annual Vanua'aku Pati's all-member Congress intervened, but I finally met with the Vanua'aku Pati leader. He was an intimidating presence. Like the Residency officials he, too, gave me a severe lecture and warning regarding what would be acceptable behaviour on my part. But, I was indeed given permission which, in hindsight, I think was extremely generous given the far weightier matters he and the rest of the Pati leaders were dealing with at the time and what may have been to some of the Pati leaders a tempting opportunity to assert their authority by refusing my request in the face of the Residency's approval.

My (officially illegal) Vanua'aku Pati Passport was typed while I waited, a slip of blue paper about 3 inches long, containing my name, occupation, purpose of visit, and permitted length of stay. The last had been shaved down to nine months from the year I had requested, but there was clearly nothing to be gained by querying that, even though my (official and legal) research permit from the British Residency gave me the full year. The irony is that I was never asked at any subsequent time to show my Vanua'aku Pati-issued 'passport', nor even to declare my political sympathies. When on a few occasions the issue did arise in conversation, especially during the national elections of 1979 (during my second field stint), I protested that as a foreigner I was a disinterested spectator and it was inappropriate for me to voice an opinion, and that was always accepted graciously. I suspect that the fact that I attended whatever political rallies or meetings took place on Nguna was taken as silent assent, although I attended them simply as part of my fieldwork, just as I went to church and attended weddings and funerals or trips to market. There were times, though, when I perceived hostility and suspicion as to my motives or that of my 'boss' (advisor) who 'had sent me'. As a young, single woman I was perceived more as someone else's pawn or agent, rather than being myself a person to be concerned about. These instances, however, appeared to have nothing to do with permissions, official or unofficial, but rather with particular individuals' feelings of having being manipulated and cheated in the past by outsiders, or suspicion that the information I was seeking might be used by others, insiders or outsiders, to their disadvantage, for example, in land rights disputes.

The final hurdle to be passed before I could leave town and head to Nguna, was to meet with the in-town representatives of the Nguna-Pwele Cultural Association. In the meeting between myself and two men from the Association, in which I explained my purposes once again, I was assured that they had spoken to the chiefs on Nguna, and had 'cleared the path' for me. When the time to leave came, I would send a radio message to a particular person who would meet me and help me arrange for housing.

On the beach

A few days later…I came out of my reverie with a nasty jolt as the bow ground to a halt against the pebbles of the shallows. The boatman, who had yet to speak at all, began tossing my bags and boxes to the young boys and girls who had come running. The bigger kids caught them and dumped them in a pile up beyond the wet strip on the blinding white sand. As I climbed clumsily over the side of the launch, the littlest of the children stopped short, their faces registering a sort of stunned amazement, as if they had seen a ghost. As I was to find out much later, a few of them were looking at a white person at close quarters for the first time. Judging by their expressions, it wasn't a pretty sight.

Following the children at a more leisurely pace was a man in perhaps his late thirties. He asked, 'Where is Matthew?'[2] Startled, I responded in kind, in English, 'Who's Matthew?' At that, he appeared taken aback as I had been at his question, and he turned to address a question in another language to the boatman, who was already back in the launch and trying to re-start its reluctant engine. Over his shoulder the boatman made his reply, succeeded in starting the motor and, without further ado, roared away.

> Turning to me, the remaining man said, 'Who are you?'
>
> 'My name is Ellen Facey. I sent a message yesterday on the radio saying that I was coming today. It was to Jonathan. Um, I was told that a man named Jonathan was expecting me.'
>
> 'Jonathan?'
>
> 'Yes! Jonathan. Do you know him?'
>
> 'I am Jonathan. Was it your message that was on the radio yesterday?'
>
> 'Yes! Yes, I sent the message for you to meet me here this afternoon.'
>
> 'Oh.' This was said with a heavy air of disappointment.
>
> 'Didn't you get my message?'
>
> 'Yes, I heard your message.'
>
> 'Oh. Well, is something wrong?'

---

2   Pseudonyms are used throughout.

'I thought it was my son, Matthew. I thought the message was from my son, Matthew. I thought he was coming home from school on the launch today.'

Oh, dear. That would be disappointing, to expect your son and find this stranger, a woman, white woman, looking like she meant to stay for some time. Strange indeed.

I glanced toward the bay; the boat was long gone. Clearly a bit of patience and persistence was called for here, to salvage some sense and a plan of action out of this confusion.

'So, you are Jonathan?' Finally, remembering a crucial piece of information that had slipped my mind, I asked, 'You're the school teacher, aren't you?'

He smiled, and seemed relieved to find this common ground, 'Yes, I am the school teacher. That is the school.' He gestured, 'There. Up there. And these are my students.' Still gathered round, but not too near, the children were watching this exchange with keen interest.

'I'm sorry you misunderstood my message and thought your son was coming. But I was told you were expecting to hear from me, waiting for my message.'

This was met with silence. Possibly a bad sign, I thought.

'Uh, I spoke to your sister in Vila.'

'You spoke to my sister? Who?'

'I spoke to your sister, Mercy. The one who works at the newspaper...?'

'Oh, Mercy! Yes, Mercy works at the newspaper.'

'Yes, that's right, that Mercy. She told me she'd spoken to you, that you had a house I could stay in, a house I could rent for a few months.'

A broad smile lit up Jonathan's face: 'You want to stay in my house?'

'Yes, that's right.'

'Well, I don't know. You wait. Wait here.'

And with that, he was gone, striding back across an open field towards the nearby group of cement-block buildings, now taking shape in my mind as the school, complete with flag-pole in the centre of the yard. Some minutes later—during which time I contemplated the fact that I had neglected to prepare a Plan B in advance—he returned, calling as he came, 'Alright, come! You come!' He said something else to the children, still milling about, eyeing me, and they began to sort themselves and my belongings out according to size and began bearing them away, each with a package or box proportionate to his or her ability. As Jonathan and the first of the children began to recede into the distance, I decided that I had better get going and follow them or be left behind.

Where exactly we were headed I had no idea, but we were definitely going somewhere, and I would find out soon enough. I brought up the rear of the train of giggling children. As we approached the village I glimpsed a picturesque clapboard building, with a long veranda facing the sea, its white paint little more than a memory.

Modernising images of 'arrival'

In one way the above vignette is startlingly akin to Bronislaw Malinowski's off-quoted line: 'Imagine yourself suddenly set down surrounded by all your gear, alone on a tropical beach close to a native village, while the launch or dinghy which has brought you sails away out of sight' (1922: 4). It was through this device that Malinowski began the process of establishing himself as the Ethnographer with a capital E, the quintessential empathetic Other, as well as the 'inventor' of anthropological fieldwork as we know it—or think we do—today (Stocking 1983), until Malinowski's *Diary* was published, at any rate.

According to Mary Louise Pratt (1986) both Malinowski and, later, his renowned student, Raymond Firth, employed much the same literary conceit, that of the castaway making First Contact with a group of islanders. Thereby they placed themselves as ethnographers in their field of research just as the preceding generations of explorers and military men, as writers, had placed themselves in their fields of exploration and discovery.

Moreover, Pratt, argues, both Firth and Malinowski sought to portray themselves as 'larger-than-life' and twice as 'versatile', a 'subject that…can absorb and transmit the richness of a whole culture' (Pratt 1986: 39). In all, she says, these ethnographers presented themselves as 'anything but the self-effaced, passive subject of scientific discourse' (*ibid*.). In her article Pratt goes on to discuss more recent ethnographic portraits, such as E.E. Evans-Pritchard's, David Maybury-Lewis' and, coming to more modern times, those of Marjorie Shostak and others who have encountered San peoples. For each of these and, as well, for all the rest of us who produce ethnographic texts, Pratt asserts that we unavoidably generate self-portraits in how we construct such scenes of arrival and first contact.

In my own case I am struck by the continuity of the beach-side arrival scene found in the writings of my Pacific ethnographic predecessors. The visual image it calls up and the emotional responses the castaway image engenders are ever so familiar. I can scarcely have done anything other than reproduce the trope, it seems. The similarity only holds, however, at the most obvious, most superficial level. The reader cannot read the second section of this paper as the 'traditional castaway' tale, as Pratt describes Malinowski's and Firth's first contact scenes;

and I cannot be said, like Firth, to have 'show[n] up as a benevolent eighteenth-century scientist-king' (Pratt 1986: 39). In the first place, this is by no means a first contact, except for the ethnographer as an individual and perhaps some of the children. There is nothing pristine about the situation encountered; the conversation is conducted in the ethnographer's own language. Most of all, there is nothing triumphal about the arrival. This ethnographer is tentative, unsure, definitely not some kind of cool, detached scientist, not a commanding presence or any kind of royalty. In sum, this is not the glorious arrival of some powerful personage; rather, it is a scene of common ground being negotiated. The potential for economic exchange, in the form of rent, is there; yet there is reason to believe that it might be an equal exchange. It is certainly a situation in which the white stranger does not have the upper hand and the outcome, if optimistic, is not at all clear or predetermined.

Mostly, importantly, framing these tales of arrival as we do is misleading. Mine didn't really start 'On the Beach', as I've described it above. It started in Sydney, with permissions, and a cable and conflicting versions of what was happening. The prologue did portend the events to follow.

What is the source of these differences in arrival scenes then and now? It has to do with many differences: different ethnographers; changing eras in the discipline, in gender relations, and in the prevailing international political relations that underlie research in countries other than one's own. It is this last that I wish to address in the balance of this paper. Other readers/writers will analyse my tropes as they will, but the arrival scene I have sketched above is at least a reflection of certain realities that existed in many places in which anthropologists were working in the 1970s and 80s. The differences between the colonial Pacific and the decolonising and newly independent nations of the Pacific are substantial. In part, as a result of this, modern arrival tales will necessarily be unlike previous ones. Our means of gaining access to such fields for study must necessarily be novel, too.

Decolonisation as a fieldwork condition

Time passed quickly. Unbeknownst to me, it turned out that the house I had rented was for the use of the school teacher, and who should be the appropriate recipient of the rent that I had been paying became an issue. So, after the first two months living on the school grounds, where I had only one neighbouring family, I moved into another house in the village proper, which allowed me to become more involved in everyday matters and events over the next six months.

As the nine-month limit of my 'passport' was approaching, I wrote to the Nguna-Pwele Cultural Association, asking whether I might extend it for another month, so that I could stay through the Christmas season, 1978. A few more weeks passed, and the reply came that they would leave the question in the hands of the villagers. It seemed to them that this decision was up to those with whom I had been living since March. That seemed fair and reasonable to me, so I put the matter to the village high chief's 'tongue' (*manamena*), his assistant who chaired the village council and was his speaker at village meetings. I was asked not to attend the meeting; instead, I submitted a short written description of my work and intentions, in the Ngunese language.

The evening following the meeting the Council Chairman relayed to me the outcome of their deliberations: in view of the nine-month limit permitted by my Vanua'aku Pati 'passport', the village council felt that my stay could not be extended. By that point it had in fact expired, therefore the council had stipulated that I ought to depart within five days from then. They had further decided that, should I wish to return, while the possibility was open for me to do so, I would have to pursue the same avenue of permissions as before. I was also told that I should choose to live in a different village, and that the question of which village would be decided by the chiefs.

It was at this point that I first questioned whether the initial clearance for my arrival (the pledge of having 'cleared the path') had probably not been obtained at all by the local Nguna-Pwele representatives, or perhaps it had not been done in what was perceived by someone as the proper way. Perhaps it had not received assent from all those who felt they ought to have had a say. The other possibility was that some jealousy or irritation may have emerged from perceived advantages or disadvantages of my presence in that particular village. Perhaps there was one or more villager who found my presence tiresome. It might take only one dissenting voice. It might as easily have been, given how politically charged the times were, that the council members simply felt themselves bound to the limitation set on my 'passport', as a reflection of their commitment to the Pati leadership. But I had no way of knowing which, if any, of these possible explanations might be the case. In the end, though, it didn't matter. It was clear that leaving within the requested time-frame was the only option, and this is what I did. I said my goodbyes feeling heavily laden, with both disappointment and gratitude elicited by the gifts that people brought: woven mats; watermelons and other sorts of produce; a garland of frangipani for my hair, and many kind words and hugs.

A return

My return after eight months away was a complete anti-climax after the rather sudden end to my first field trip. I wondered whether my request for another research permit would put me into the same kind of political permission-seeking cycle as I had encountered the first time, and whether I would be denied entry, given what had gone before. To my relief, there was no problem whatsoever. First, in the official view of the British Residency, there had been no trouble reported involving me over the course of my stay on Nguna during 1978, and I had left well within the one year for which they had given approval. At an unofficial level they seemed to be well aware that I had also passed the inspection of the Vanua'aku Pati and had observed their time limit, too. So I received immediate approval to return.

Second, when it came to the Vanua'aku Pati officials, their reaction was much the same. No complaints had come to them and, at that point, they felt that it had become a local decision, as they had stated at the end of my first period of research.

It may be, as I heard from other researchers, that the Pati had made some political capital from my having submitted to their self-declared authority the year before. Albeit in a small way, my case had bolstered their claim to being able to control their heartland of support, the central district. During the months that elapsed since my departure, though, the Pati had reached a higher plateau of political development; so Pati officials gave me to understand that they were unconcerned with my further comings or goings.

At the local village level, I had decided to take the previous decision of the village council at face value. They had raised no objection to my returning, only to my living in the same village, for whatever reason. So I decided to approach one of my primary informants, an elderly man and his wife, pillars of one of the smaller communities down the road from where I had originally lived. When I wrote to them they immediately wrote back, offering to house me. I was glad to have the opportunity to live with a family, which included their two young grandsons, rather than living on my own as I had before. Their village was also only a 30-minute walk from my former village, so I was able to visit and maintain relations with people there as well as in my new location. Also, the new village was only a quarter the size of the first village, and considerably less affluent, so it provided a contrast in a number of ways that were very informative. In particular, in terms of village politics, my new location had fewer formal decision-making structures because they had chosen not to institute a new style of village council such as the first village had. Therefore, while much of the everyday business of village life—decisions, disputes, interpersonal problems— went on in the first village in camera within committees, in the second, all village business was conducted in the public weekly meeting of the whole.

In fact, knowing that I had been asked not to reside again in the first village, those of the second appeared to take particular pleasure in making sure that I was party to all discussions in their village (in keeping with a strong inter-village rivalry). As a result, I saw and heard much more of the dynamics of the kinds of things that I had not had the opportunity to see or hear before, for example, the trial of an allegation of adultery and the resolution of land boundary disputes. This allowed me to shine the light of contrast on some features of the first village, as well as to fill gaps in my ethnography that had been created by the more closed atmosphere and political structure of the first village.

Ethics of access in changing circumstances

In the years of my fieldwork there, 1978 to 1980, the New Hebrides was in a state of transition, from colony and Condominium to nation, as Vanuatu. This transitional era might be said to date from the 29 November 1977 declaration of a People's Provisional Government by the Vanua'aku Pati. From that time on researchers were subject to a series of levels of government, official and unofficial, national and local. Up until then, access by foreign researchers had been virtually unlimited, with relatively perfunctory examination of credentials and intentions by one or other of the foreign governments. Thereafter, the prototypical field-research situation had prevailed, wherein the anthropologist had but to arrive on the island of her/his choice and proceed to work through a personal network grounded in the asymmetrical power relation between Native and Western 'Other' and developed by assiduous management of material goods: money, Western medicines and luxury items, use of a boat or truck, and so on. In other words, having passed a cursory inspection for a visa, once in situ, the anthropologist had been subject only to the vagaries of local opinion.

Such situations certainly could be a source of considerable difficulties, especially in densely populated and socially diverse areas, or equally, in remote, ultra-conservative areas. Yet this is a far cry from the kind of complex situation researchers walked into in the New Hebrides when I did. It was a sign of the times that I was required to pass muster at four different political levels, each with different degrees of authority and ability to enforce their decisions. The strategy I employed was to cooperate fully and straightforwardly with representatives at all these levels. While I was concerned at the time with the resultant delays and expenses involved, and the multiple examinations of my plans and personal politics, this was compelled by that acutely sensitive context, especially in the part of the country in which I was interested. To do otherwise would have been to deny and disrespect existing forces, be they official or otherwise.

Having had this experience it troubles me when I hear, on occasion, that researchers have turned to sneaking into countries where the research approval process may be a lengthy one with a stringent and perhaps costly review process. Entering 'through the back door', either without a visa or on a tourist rather than a research visa, while fully intending to conduct research, is a kind of subversion of the structures in place in other countries—whatever one might think of them—that is dangerous and foolish. The international image of the anthropologist is already poor among some groups without further tarnishing it through open displays of cultural arrogance.

Perhaps in such situations we should do more of what we claim to do best—comparative research, using existing materials. We should also certainly do more of what recent researchers in Vanuatu are doing: collaborative, applied research. When I finished my research and completed my dissertation, which of course was in answer to my own purposes of obtaining a post-graduate degree in anthropology, I made the decision to try to render my research results in such a way as would be of interest and value to the people of Nguna, most particularly to those who had helped and encouraged me the most. What would be of greatest value and benefit to them? In my case it was not hard to identify what to do. Many of the men who had put in the most hours to help me understand their traditions were very elderly. Even by 1982, as my dissertation was heading out for binding, several of Nguna's Elders best known for their knowledge of stories and other types of oral knowledge had already passed away. I knew beyond a shadow of a doubt what would honour their memory and what would be appreciated by those who remained, and hopefully also their families and younger generations, too; a compendium of their stories in their own language. Using techniques available from studies of oral literature, particularly the work of Dennis Tedlock and Peter Seitel, I tried to re-create/re-present the experience of those people's stories as lived performances—their voice, their tones, the feelings they elicited from moment to moment. This I believed would be a far more satisfying legacy and tribute than any other scholarly product that I might create.

It was not easy to 'sell' even academic publishers on the idea of a bilingual book, one of those languages being spoken by a maximum of 3,000 to 4,000 people in one 'remote' part of the world. The book was written primarily for the Ngunese audience, so ultimately I went with a small Canadian university press because they were the first to agree to publish the volume as written, in particular with all the texts in both English and Ngunese, the complete text in Ngunese coming before the English to avoid the distraction of inter-linear translations. Providing the texts in English fulfilled a secondary purpose of opening the reading of the texts to a world-wide audience, while at the same time making the book more useful for teaching/learning English, or Ngunese. Likewise, the introductory chapters aimed at the anthropological audience were kept to a minimum so as not to overshadow the texts themselves. I made a whole series of such decisions and, not surprisingly, I have had complaints from everyone: an Appendix of inter-linear translations and glossary are not enough for the linguists; there is not enough ethnographic detail for the ethnographers. One reviewer actually asked what could possibly make me want to spend so much time trying to faithfully re-present all the details of different speakers' style, stress, intonation, non-verbal gestures, etc. in every text rather than analysing their content. Everybody, except the Ngunese, has not been satisfied. But that's OK, because all I have had from Ngunese people—people I know and people I've never met, by mail, in two languages, and most recently by e-mail, also in two languages—are notes of appreciation and requests for additional complimentary copies. That has made it all worthwhile.

Nguna Voices was special and novel when it came out in the later eighties. But already it is the past. The future may be collaborative, community-driven research. As long as it produces results that have value for local people, while not at the same time creating inequalities—that seems like a good thing. It is now fair to say that the researcher who fails to return something to the people with whom she/he has worked is unlikely to receive approval for a return engagement. Indeed, following from recent and ongoing changes to Canadian research ethics guidelines with Aboriginal peoples, the researcher who does not engage potential subjects of research as partners, with outcomes and benefits to those communities agreed to in advance, will not be able to do research. And appropriately so, in my view.

References

Facey, Ellen E., 1988. *Nguna Voices: Text and Culture from Central Vanuatu.* Calgary, Alberta: University of Calgary Press.

Malinowski, Bronislaw, 1961 [1922]. *Argonauts of the Western Pacific: An Account of Native Enterprise and Adventure in the Archipelagoes of Melanesian New Guinea.* New York: E. P. Dutton & Co., Inc.

Pratt, Mary Louise, 1986. Fieldwork in common places. In *Writing Culture: The Poetics and Politics of Ethnography*, ed. James Clifford and George E. Marcus, 27–50. Berkeley, California: University of California Press.

Stocking, George W. Jr., 1983. The ethnographer's magic: fieldwork in British anthropology from Tylor to Malinowski. In *Observers Observed: Essays on Ethnographic Fieldwork*, ed. George W. Stocking, Jr., 70–120. Madison, Wisconsin: University of Wisconsin Press.

Collaborations

4. *Big Wok*: The Vanuatu Cultural Centre's World War Two Ethnohistory Project

Lamont Lindstrom

By the 1980s, it was clear that the generation of older ni-Vanuatu that had experienced the remarkable and sometimes traumatic events of the Pacific War was passing away. Sponsored by the Vanuatu Cultural Centre (VCC), with support from the U.S. National Science Foundation and the Wenner-Gren Foundation for Anthropological Research, VCC fieldworkers between 1987 and 1989 interviewed more than 125 men and women who had lived through the war years in Vanuatu (1942–1946). Coordinated by James Gwero and Lamont Lindstrom, the project attempted to locate and interview throughout Vanuatu men and women with stories to tell.[1] A selection of these recorded accounts subsequently appeared in a book *Big Wok: Storian blong Wol Wo Tu long Vanuatu,* published entirely in Bislama (Lindstrom and Gwero 1998; for a second collection of war history in Vanuatu, see Moon and Moon 1998). The project also produced a weekly program for Radio Vanuatu in late 1988 and early 1989. The project's upcoming twentieth anniversary invites us to recall some lessons learned. War stories, and their collection, can tell us something about research collaboration and about Vanuatu's stories, storytelling, and storytellers in general.

The World War Two Project, which involved chasing down older men and women with stories to tell from Aneityum up to the Torres Islands, was certainly Big Work. Actually, we chose the name *Big Wok* to reflect that of a similar project of Pacific War ethnohistory then ongoing in the Solomon Islands. This had produced a collection of war memories called *Bikfala Faet: Olgeta Solomon Aelanda Rimembarem Wol Wo Tu* (The Big Death) (White *et al.* 1988). The Solomon Islands suffered months of violent land and sea battles. Down in Vanuatu, which was spared much actual fighting, most people's lives were instead shaken by the establishment of extensive Allied military installations on Espiritu Santo and Efate and also smaller coast-watching and other northern outposts located up through the Torres Islands. Whereas Solomon Islanders witnessed and sometimes were caught up in fighting, most ni-Vanuatu instead

---

1 Although coordinated by Gwero and Lindstrom, various Cultural Centre fieldworkers also helped record war stories and focused on war history during one annual fieldworker workshop. Vianney Atpatoun, Dickinson Dick, Joel Iau, Richard Leona, George Loren, Michael Matoa, Hosea Meal, Mathias Batick, John Peter, Phillip Tepahae, Lengi Tepu, and James Teslo, among others, recorded war stories while Cultural Centre Directors Kirk Huffman and later Ralph Regenvanu helped with project logistics and the eventual publication of *Big Wok*.

found themselves working, officially and unofficially, for military strangers. Wartime work, thus, was the main focus of our story collecting protocol—or the list of questions that guided our interviews with those who remembered the war.

Storytellers

Outside military forces began to arrive in Vanuatu in early 1942. Anyone born in 1940 and before, therefore, might have interesting war stories to tell. This was a sizeable percentage of Vanuatu's population—in 1987, any man or woman who was older than 47 years or so. Even if they stayed at home, anyone then living in the country must have noticed at least some impact of the war given the size of military occupation forces (Figure 4.1). In July, 1944 when Allied base operations peaked, up to 100,000 Americans were stationed in Vanuatu or were there in transit to the north (Lindstrom 1996: 11). Since Vanuatu's population was then roughly only 40,000, military personnel, mostly American, outnumbered ni-Vanuatu by more than two to one.

Figure 4.1. Santo, March 1944

(US National Archives)

With so many potential storytellers, how could we choose who to interview? Local knowledge helped. The VCC fieldworker program—which had many previous successes investigating joint cultural and historical topics throughout Vanuatu—promised to be an effective mechanism for widespread story collection. James Gwero and I started with elder men known for their narrative repertoires of which war stories were often only a small part. Some of these, like Erakor's Dick Lautu, were recognised locally as raconteurs of war history. We recruited storytellers through 'snowballing': asking each storyteller if he or she knew of others from whom we might request an interview. To spread as wide a net as possible, we relied on interested fieldworkers to record who they thought might be most knowledgeable (and most talkative) about war events. Although James and I recorded stories only on Efate, Southeast Santo, West Ambae, and Tanna, we had the support of VCC fieldworkers who found and interviewed people from across much of the rest of Vanuatu. Focusing our efforts on Vanuatu's two towns, we were also able to interview people from a variety of communities who were then present either in Vila or Luganville. We all followed local roads and connections to identify potential storytellers. For example, I called on friends from Southeast Tanna, including Thomas Nouar and Rabi Timo whose war experiences I had already recorded in the early 1980s (Lindstrom 1989). James Gwero, similarly, was interested to document the memories of his kinsmen Timothy Tako and Alfred Coulon, among others. In the end, the particular assemblage of war stories certainly reflected the personal networks of us story collectors.

As an outsider to Vanuatu society, I suspect I was more concerned, compared with some VCC fieldworkers, to pursue story content rather than some specific storyteller. If I could get a good account of Black Americans who served in the New Hebrides, I did not care who might be telling this. But it may be that particular storyteller identity weighed more heavily with some fieldworkers who tapped the memories of elders in their own families and villages. Others, too, were concerned with who was telling stories. During an eight-day recording trip to Tanna, for example, I was accompanied by an assistant nominated by the ministry in charge of cultural affairs whose presence, I suspect, insured that I talked mostly with reliable (in those days, non-John Frum) elders. I was happy to do so, however, as the personal roads that we followed led me to new storytellers around Lenakel on West Tanna.

In addition, I suspect that I was more interested than some in seeking *women's* war stories. Although we strongly recommended that fieldworkers talk with as many women as possible, in the end the project recorded only eight women of which just one of these was not interviewed by James Gwero or myself. It was true that many women were reluctant to share their memories, deferring to men who might speak for them. Nana Ouchida, for example, was able to talk about the arrest of her Japanese common-law husband but she was much helped in this by her son Henri. Similarly, Tom Kalsirik recounted to us the painful rape of his wife who was either still unable to speak about this experience or was prepared to let her husband speak for her. Other women, however, such as Margaret Kastin of Port Vila, were excellent storytellers. One of the best storytelling sessions we recorded involved a group of four women from Mele—Leiboe Kalosike, Janet Mansale, Fepi Mara and Annie Kaltiua—all of whom had worked at the Navy hospital established on Bellevue plantation. Sitting together around a table, their stories and laughing memories built one upon the other. We should have tried to record women in similar sorts of groups who might have become more talkative, more reminiscent, in numbers.

Story collecting

The World War Two Project built on previous research into the war that the VCC and also Radio Vanuatu had begun in the 1980s.[2] We also benefitted from the work of interested local experts such as Reece Discombe and Ernie Reid. The project's aim was to be as catholic and comprehensive as possible—to collect any sort of war memory that still lingered in the mind of anyone who might be willing to share this. We wanted story topics to emerge from individual and shared memory. What, in particular, were people bothering to remember of their war years? Nonetheless, we had to guess what at least some stories might be about and we approached story collecting with a protocol of issues and questions already in hand. Partly, this had served to convince funders (such as NSF and the Wenner-Gren Foundation for Anthropological Research) to support the project. And partly, this provided our crew of story collectors a shared starting point. The challenge, of course, was not to let our protocol overrun or drown out the themes that local stories and storytellers themselves might reveal. We told the Wenner-Gren Foundation that the project would

> address the question of why war stories and songs continue to capture the imagination of local audiences in island Melanesia. In so doing, we seek to understand the socially meaningful statements war stories make about identity, about power, and about relations between islands and others.

We hoped to determine the continuing importance of war stories within individual life histories, local notions of time and history, and war stories' relationship with other genres of island narrative and song. Specifically, we argued that war stories would reveal details of people's military employment and other interaction with outside forces, give insight into the social importance of the presence of many African-American servicemen, and provide information about the emergence of nationalism and other postwar movements in Vanuatu and beyond.

---

2   Including a James Gwero interview with Aviu Koli of Lamen Bay, Epi.

We developed a handwritten protocol of story topics, large and small, that we taped to the wall of the World War Two 'office' that was located in the old Cultural Centre building. This rolling protocol, which we added to as needed, listed a set of topics we thought were good starting places when asking people to remember the war and eliciting good stories. These topics ran from various sorts of '*Wok long Amerika*' (*long dok, sip, efil, rod, hotel, haospital*), to '*Halpem Amerika*', the New Hebrides Defence Force, '*Niufala samting blong wo*', '*Amerika halpem olgeta*', '*Niufala bisnis*', '*Skul/Jaj*', '*Taem wo i finis*', and ending up in some miscellaneous '*Trabol long wo*'. We tried to use this protocol as a shared starting place for collecting stories. The protocol allowed us to prompt storytellers when memory had, at least temporarily, run its course and also insured that we asked a range of people about what we suspected might have been shared experience. This helped broaden the perspective on particular events insofar as we asked people from throughout Vanuatu, men and women when we could get them, many of the same questions.

It is clear, however, that some of this protocol reflected my outside, in this case American, agenda as much as it did local concern. For example, I had long been interested in the Black American military experience in Vanuatu and I hoped to learn more about this from the local perspective. I was also already interested in the impact of American cargo, supplies, and presence on Tanna's John Frum movement and in the place of 'America' in general within Vanuatu's postwar anti-colonialism. I wanted to be careful, though, not to typecast the influence of some obviously "good" America of the 1940s vis-à-vis the 'bad' colonial powers France and Great Britain.[3] But other items on our rolling protocol did surface from local memories and stories and not from our outside interests. Some locally well-known events found their way onto the protocol because of sharp, island memories of American doctors who excised one person's filariasis-infected scrotum, the assault, murder, and rape of Maevo and his family by U.S. soldiers that took place near Santo's Sarakata River, and the postwar retrieval of American bodies that had been temporarily buried at Freswota near Port Vila.

Other Vanuatu themes soon became clear as the archive of recorded war narratives grew and we added these, too, to the protocol. Such themes included the various sorts of trouble and suffering that people had endured during the war years and the fact that ni-Vanuatu assisted military personnel (contributing labour, serving as scouts and guides, and more) as much as soldiers and sailors helped ni-Vanuatu (with food, money, medicine, and so forth). As always in Vanuatu, the exchange of goods and services is properly balanced.

---

3   See Zeleneitz and Saito (1989) for an analysis of the impact of the story collector's nationality on Papua New Guinean appreciation of American versus Japanese forces.

We also had gathered a small collection of official and private photographs from the 1940s. We showed these around as widely as possible in order to identify, if we could, the people captured in the pictures, and to spark memories about the events portrayed or similar events that people had experienced. For example, Captain Stephen Slaughter, who had worked with Tannese Labor Corps recruits encamped at Tagabe, gave us his wartime scrapbook. Joe Natuman was able to identify the men in several of these photographs. One captures Labor Corp boss Major George Riser along with Tannese labor supervisors Loumhan Isaac, Johnson Kiel, and Simon Nuvo (Figure 4.2). One of my favourite photographs, this one an official U.S. Navy shot, depicts military dentists checking the teeth of a small boy in August, 1943 (Figure 4.3). Titus Molirani of Tutuba recognised himself and his teeth in this some 45-years later. Official U.S. military photographs typically identify the Americans depicted but refer to others only as 'natives' or 'islanders'. My aim to identify, by name, all the individuals depicted in these photographs reflected my own interests but these, I think, were often also shared by many ni-Vanuatu storytellers. Even when no one could put a name to some of the people depicted, photos nonetheless were very useful spurs to memory, evoking much interest and often good stories.

Figure 4.2. American labor corps supervisors including George Riser with Loumhan Isaac, Johnson Kiel, and Simon Nuvo

(S.D. Slaughter photographer; copyright Lamont Lindstrom)

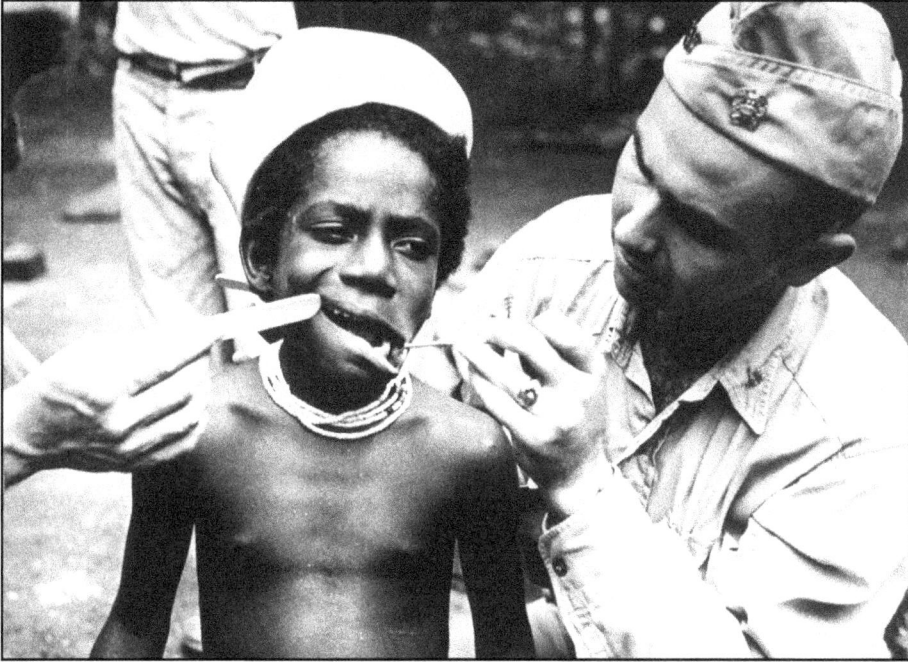

Figure 4.3. Titus Molirani

(US National Archives)

Storytelling

The other side of story collecting is storytelling. We recorded most stories in Bislama. Those few that came to us in vernacular languages required translation into Bislama (by me, for several stories told in Tanna's Kwamera (Nɨfe) language, James Gwero for a couple of West Ambae stories, or by Vanuatu Cultural Centre (VCC) fieldworkers). I argued then that Bislama was an appropriate language for telling war stories in that the wartime events that people endured were often novel, unknown in *kastom,* and that the war had brought together people from many communities who, in the 1940s, had to speak Bislama among themselves and also, occasionally, with interested Allied military personnel. I believe these arguments are still good ones and our Pidgin recordings, moreover, were easily transformed into a Bislama book that today is accessible to most ni-Vanuatu who can read the language.

One issue that is always topmost in Vanuatu storytelling is who owns the story? Who has rights to narrate this in public? And who has rights to hear the story? This is particularly so with *kastom* stories, whose copyright—the right publicly to tell—is frequently owned by individuals acting as representatives of family groups (see Lindstrom 1990: 76–82). We expected most war stories, however, still to be 'life stories', or narratives of personal experience (see Lacey 1984). As such, individual storytellers would have best rights to their own stories and they could decide whether or not they might want to share these with us. In some cases, many people had taken part in the same events and had their own perspectives on these. In others, a war story might already have been told and retold to become widely known. These narratives, through previous tellings, have become formalised—additions to Vanuatu's public domain which, of course, remains bounded and by local and kin claims. A number of men, for example, told similar stories about the attack on Maevo and his family near the Sarakata River (see also Moon 1998: 104–06). And many Tannese could tell of Kauas' wild escape from Labor Corps duties on Efate when he put on a *nambas* and disappeared into the bush. We figured, therefore, that most war stories—unlike many *kastom* stories—either still belong to the individual narrators who experienced or witnessed the events in question, or like many folktales and children's stories were 'free', belonging to ni-Vanuatu in common. We also supposed shared rights to listen to and record war stories. These are stories about the impact of a global war on ni-Vanuatu lives and land in which many others were also deeply involved including Americans, Australians, New Zealanders, Japanese, British, and French. The appropriate audience for Vanuatu war stories, thus, is far wider than that for many *kastom* stories that properly speak only to those with kin-based or other local rights to tell, listen, and learn.

Our arguments about 'free' stories, along with relatively meagre project funds, dictated that we did not pay people to tell their stories but only asked them to share them with us. We did promise storytellers an eventual larger audience. We were able to include a number of voices on a weekly Radio Vanuatu program that featured war narratives and song. We also explained that we expected to use stories in a book about the war in Vanuatu. We were careful therefore to ensure that *Big Wok*, when this finally appeared ten years after the project ended, does include at least a brief comment from almost every storyteller that we recorded between 1987 and 1989.

James Gwero was right to insist that storytellers were as important as the stories they told. Building on James' appreciation of the storyteller *and* the story, and ni-Vanuatu concern with establishing personal connections between storytellers and story collectors, where we could we photographed storytellers and subsequently shared around copies of these photographs.[4] These served as small gifts in return for a story. Some storytellers carefully posed in *kastom* finery (as did Timothy Tako and Matthias Vira of Ambae) or in wartime duds and equipment that they had saved since the 1940s (as did Samuel Tapahan of Tanna, Figure 4.4).

---

4 I believe that James, at one time, hoped to feature photographs of our storytellers along with their published texts. When we pulled together *Big Wok*, however, we only included war-era photographs of which only a few of which captured storytellers in their younger years.

Figure 4.4. Samuel Tapahan

(Lamont Lindstrom, photographer)

Stories

War stories differ from *kastom* stories in various ways including the fact that many of these still remain personal narratives that have not yet been formalised into oral texts, told and retold from one generation to the next. Some of the stories we collected were tightly structured and had clearly been shared before. Other storytellers provided looser, more rambling recollections as they paused to think back to what had happened to them during the war. Most had interesting, often gripping wartime memories whether or not their narratives were tightly or loosely structured. Occasionally, tape-recorder running, someone ran out of memory and James Gwero might then pepper them with questions from the Project's protocol.

Although less formulaic than many *kastom* stories, war and *kastom* narratives also have several things in common. Like many *kastom* stories, war narratives might possibly serve as charters or claims. Just as people tell *kastom* stories to assert their family's claim to land, to chiefly status, to rights to use certain weaving designs and motifs, and so forth, so might the telling of a war story stake claims. An obvious claim is that the storyteller either personally experienced or witnessed the events that he or she narrates. But stories can also stake more complex, more serious and expensive claims. When Vanuatu sought to assert its territorial rights to Matthew and Hunter Islands, located between Aneityum and New Caledonia, for example, it collected TAFEA *kastom* stories about these islands.

The counterpart World War Two ethnohistory project in the Solomon Islands, in fact, had sparked much local interest in possible compensation payments from the Americans, British, and/or the Japanese governments. People there sometimes told stories of suffering bombings, death, and destruction hoping that these stories could charter claims to rights to compensation. Perhaps someone at last would pay for bulldozing gardens and trees? Many people in Vanuatu also suffered during the war. A few lost their lives through accidents, illness, or overwork. Some women were raped or assaulted. Some surrendered their homes and gardens to the military, such as happened on Tutuba. Many worked hard for relatively little pay (Figure 4.5). However, we told storytellers that the project was not connected with any official interest in compensating wartime suffering but that we could help, at least, to publicise any stories and painful memories of loss that people might wish to share.

War stories possess other common features with *kastom* stories. These include the narrative importance of recollecting specific personal and place names. Memories of ancestral names and the places where one's family has lived are obviously important to stake claims to land and other rights. War storytellers, along these lines, similarly contextualised their narratives of wartime events within frames of places and people, as did Stephen Vusi of Longana, Ambae, who when interviewed by James Gwero anchored his story with the names of his supervisor Mr. White, military chaplain Mr. Brown, named places such as Bihu, Lolowai, Surunda, Chapuis, and Walaha along with other named people and places. These citations of personal and place names help establish the truth and the weight of what one has to say (see Lacey 1980: 84).[5]

Figure 4.5. Tannese labor corps members camped at Tagabe

(S.D. Slaughter, photographer; copyright Lamont Lindstrom)

Like many *kastom* stories that celebrate the accomplishments of ancestral or culture heroes, war stories too have champions; many with magical or special powers (see Lacey 1984: 13). One *kastom*-like hero, mentioned by several storytellers, was Santo resident Leon Giovanni. Giovanni served as ships' pilot and he also guided several US military patrols into the Malakulan bush and elsewhere. Local storytellers, however, were more interested to recall his special powers, especially those associated with *su* magic. Giovanni could make himself invisible and also discover hidden Japanese scouts and spies that no one else could see. Solomon Marakon of Ambrym recalled: *'Leon Giovanni, him i gat samting ya, him i gat su. Hem i faet long su. Taem we him i go, ol man oli no*

---

5   And James Gwero, seeking possible 'roads' of useful social connection as people in Vanuatu frequently do, probed further to discover whether or not Mr. Brown might, in particular, have been an Anglican chaplain.

save luk. Taem i sut, ol man oli no save luk' (Lindstrom and White 1998: 127). Similarly, Raqraq Charlie of Malakula, a second heroic figure who features in a number of war stories, reportedly drew on his courage and his military friends to challenge Condominium authority (see also Moon and Moon 1998: 97–9). In addition to heroes, war stories also celebrate trickster themes that recall traditional stories of wily ancestors such as Remeto on Tanna. Tanna's Nase Kapaho, for instance, boasted his ability to elude pursuit by Condominium police forces during the war by hiding behind the American servicemen that he had befriended (Lindstrom 1989: 411). Such tricks allowed him to taunt Condominium police without fear of punishment.

A final and notable similarity between *kastom* and war stories concerns the role of song as a historical medium. Song, throughout the Pacific, is a 'formulary device' that memorialises important historical events, people, and places (Lindstrom 1990: 107–13; see Ong 1982; Charlot 1988). Ni-Vanuatu preserve important historical information in song as well as in story. Songs, like stories, help fix historical events, and also certain perspectives on this, in collective memory. Some songs stand alone as independent texts; others are incorporated as components of *kastom* stories. The two genres are linked in that many *kastom* stories incorporate one or more songs as important constituents. When we asked people to tell us their war stories, many would sing to us as well. In the midst of a story, a narrator might burst into song to elaborate some significant point or to document an important observation. Such songs function like place and personal names to add weight and consequence to a story.

We thus made a point to ask people if they recalled any songs from the war— songs that they themselves had composed or had learned from others. Some of these latter included popular mid-century American songs (e.g., *You Are My Sunshine* or the *Marines Hymn*—Dick Lautu knew many of these). Other songs were local compositions some of which, since the war, have remained popular and widely known. A favorite example is a song about Shepherd Islands and North Efate men who British District Officer Geoffrey Seagoe recruited to do the initial clearing of what today is Bauerfield. This song is variously attributed to Willie Bertie of Nguna, among others (Moon and Moon 1998: 48). We recorded one version performed by Wallace Kalaunapapa in Paunangisu; fieldworker Michael Matoa provided (through Kirk Huffman) a translation of several verses of this. This along with other songs about Big Wok that people continue to sing today complement a rich heritage of stories that preserve Vanuatu's wartime memories:[6]

---

6   Moon and Moon (1998: 48–49) cite more complete lyrics along with an English translation provided by Kalsaf Graham of Tongoa in March 1994. They also recorded a second version of the song in January 1994, sung by Tom Tasong and family from Tikilasoa, Nguna.

Tai manga tu do dongo Vakalo

Endo pai taleva ni maramana

Ma tedo umai paki kuengida

E awi re te tunga vae esava

CHORUS:

Awi awi ri taimanga soldia teu rumai pak New Hebrides

Endape sara [Eu rumai pilaki] 'munition, eu pae United States of America

Rangi wain eurumai do town Vila

Epo masau tea suasua

En datango Hebrides thousand boy

Ngo Seagoe umai po musangi ngam

Tupei teaai sara nalauna

Efate, Nguna, Pele, Emau,

Mataso, Makura, Tongariki,

Tongoa, Malakula, Emae, Paama.

- - - - -

Brothers we used to hear about the war

On the other side of the world.

But it is coming to our country

Where are we going to go?

CHORUS:

Awi awi brothers, soldiers are coming to New Hebrides

They bring all sorts of ammunition; They come from United States of America.

When they came to Port Vila

They needed people to work

They asked for a thousand New Hebrides boys

And Seagoe came to pick us up

We are from many islands

Efate, Nguna, Pele, Emau,

Mataso, Makura, Tongariki,

Tongoa, Malakula, Emae, Paama.

Ol brata yumi harem faet

I stap nara saed long wol

Mo i stap kam long ples blong yumi

Mo i wantem ol man blong go wok

CHORUS:

Sori tumas ol brata ol soldia oli kam long Niu Hebrides

Oli tekem amiunisin oli kam long United States of Amerika

Mifala ol man aelan ya

Efate, Nguna, Pele, Emau

Mataso, Makura, Tongariki

Tongoa, Malakula, Emae, Paama.

It is now 51 years after the end of the Pacific War. Most of the men and women who lived through the war in Vanuatu have now passed on—although not all. There are still older people with excellent memories and with good stories to tell. And many war stories and songs now have been passed down to children and grandchildren, becoming part of family and village memory. As time goes by, war stories are gradually changing into *kastom* stories. We were only able to record stories from some 125 people back in the 1980s. But there are many more friends and family members still out there with important stories to tell. Although the project officially ended back in 1989, I hope that VCC fieldworkers will continue to seek out, interview, and record war stories and songs to add these to the growing and cherished archive of Vanuatu's history.

References

Charlot, John, 1988. Some uses of chant in Samoan prose. *Journal of American Folklore* 101: 302–11.

Lacey, Roderic, 1980. Coming to know Kepai: conversational narratives and the use of oral sources in Papua New Guinea. *Social Analysis* 4: 74–88.

Lacey, Roderic, 1984. '...No Other Voice Can Tell': Life histories in Melanesia. *International Journal of Oral History* 5: 5–35.

Lindstrom, Lamont, 1989. Working encounters: oral histories of World War II Labor Corps from Tanna, Vanuatu. In *The Pacific Theater: Island Representations of World War II*, ed. Geoffrey M. White and Lamont Lindstrom, 395–417. Honolulu: University of Hawai'i Press.

Lindstrom, Lamont, 1990. *Knowledge and Power in a South Pacific Society.* Washington, DC: Smithsonian Institution Press.

Lindstrom, Lamont, 1996. The American Occupation of the New Hebrides (Vanuatu). Macmillan Brown Working Paper Series No. 5. Christchurch: Macmillan Brown Centre for Pacific Studies, University of Canterbury.

Lindstrom, Lamont and James Gwero (eds), 1998. *Big Wok: Storian blong Wol Wo Tu long Vanuatu*. Suva: Institute of Pacific Studies, University of the South Pacific; Christchurch: Macmillan Brown Centre for Pacific Studies, University of Canterbury.

Moon, Margaret and Bruce Moon (eds), 1998. *Ni-Vanuatu Memories of World War II*. Diamond Harbour, NZ: Published by the authors.

Ong, Walter J., 1982. *Orality and Literacy: The Technologizing of the Word*. London: Methuen.

White, Geoffrey M., David Gegeo, Karen Ann Watson-Gego and David Akin (eds), 1988. *Bikfala Faet: Olketa Solomon Aelanda Rimembaren. Wol Wo To/ The Big Death: Solomon Islanders Remember World War II*. Suva: Institute of Pacific Studies, University of the South Pacific.

Zeleneitz, Marty and Hisafumi Saito, 1989. The Kilenge and the war: an observer effect on stories from the past. In *The Pacific Theater: Island Representations of World War II*, ed. Geoffrey M. White and Lamont Lindstrom, 167–84. Honolulu: University of Hawai'i Press.

5. Olgeta Stori blong Wol Wo Tu

James Gwero

Hemi [Lamont Lindstrom] talem se bae mi stori smol, mi wantem talem se mi wantem go hom be oli talem se bae mi stori smol insaed long Wol Wo Tu so nao mi stap. Stori blong Wol Wo Tu hemi olsem kastom stori nao, olsem wan ples long Ambae oli kolem big man ia *Tagaro* we naoia hemi stap mekem faea i wok be volcano, be hemi olsem nao. Wol Wo Tu stori naoia hemi siksti yias nao an yu save luk samting we Tagaro i mekem olsem long ples ia yu save luk ol man America oli mekem rod hemia raonem Efate o Santo, hemia ol America i wokem be spos ol man America ino kam Wol Wo Tu ino gat hemia bae rod ino gat. Wol Wo Tu ino gud mo i gud, yes taem mi wok insaed mi faenemaot olsem be hemi gud long hemia we mi talem ia spos hemi no gat olsem ia bae yumi indipenden, Vanuatu bae i indipenden be bae hemi had wok blong mekem rod blong raonem Efate o Santo.

Be hemi isi nao we ol man America i woKem so ol man oli save tingbaot se ol man America nao i mekem rod be wan samting mi wantem talem naoia se long risej ia i gud blong mekem wan buk bakegen, tu buks bakegen we long lanwis mo Inglis mo Franis. Mekem ol man oli save gud bikos samting ia stori ia hemi sud be *once and for all* ino save mekem bakegen olsem we mi go long America long ples we oli kolem man ia mi luk ol notis antap America hemi talem se bae hemi neva mekem *wo* bakegen olsem from hemi lusum plante man. So hemi min se ples ia o taem ia hemi impoten blong ol man oli save. Bambae mi singim wan singsing we ol man oli komposem be i tokbaot Wol Wo Tu ia. Mi glad blong talem se Wol Wo Tu ia ol man oli stap komposem plante song long lanwis samfala oli tanis long hem. Tanis kastom mifala i kolem 'Naboe' singsing blong faet ia long Wol Wo Tu.

Nao mi singim samtaem we mi finis be wan samting mo insaed long Noisy Boy string band taem hemi sing abaot wan taosen man Tanna hemi gud mo saon blong hem hemi gud. Miusik ia i gud wan be wan toktok we hemi talem insaed ia long namba tu veses 'America hemi girap long ful paoa blong hem', nao yu luk ol man ia i putum singsing ia tingting blong olgeta i gudwan bikos hemi girap long ful paoa blong hem hemi kam. Hemi kam blong blokem Japanis so mi sapraes long olgeta we oli komposem song ia, hemi kam wetem ol ting blong faet mo ol ting blong wokem taon long Santo mo Vila. Hemi kam wetem ful paoa blong hem bikos sam long olgeta man ia taem oli stori wan man Paama hemi se Japan hemi se bae hemi win long Santo afta hemi safa long Port Vila. Hao nao oli save? Hao nao hemi talem olsem ? Yes hemi tru taem ia hemi taem blong faet mifala man mifala i fraet ia from Japan bae i kam long bus o i kilim mifala. Nao bae mi stori, sori spos mi go longwe lelebet long woksop bae yufala, sori okei taem blong fraet taem blong fraet taem ia Japanese i mekem faet hemi mekem krul wan hemi kilim ol man olbaot kilim ol woman kilim olbaot long Solomon.

I gat wan man we ating yufala i save o no Addison spos yu stap long eapot blong Solomon bae yu luk wan memori ston i stap aotsaed oli talem se: *He gave his life for Guadalcanal*. Yu save storian blong man ia o no. Man ia Addison hemia hem nao hemi givim laef blong hem, hemi ded afta America i go tru insaed long Solomon blong faet bikos hemi no save go tru. America hemi no save go tru, tufala i faet long sanbis oli kolem 'a red fish' hemia blad blong tufala i ron long sanbis ia. Mi mi go long ples ia mi luk afta man ia Addison hem tingting blong hem se bae hemi ded ale ol merikel i kam tru, go tru insaed nao hemi go antap long plen i go antap antap olgeta wetem ol bom be yu save Japan hemi stap stap sat olsem ia oli no save kam insaed. So Japan hemi mekem eapot ia, hemia Addison fil ia hemi no komplitim so America hemi wantem ronem hem aot bikos spos hemi lan ia ten afta bae i kilim ol man Vanuatu nao bae hemi kam. Okei be taem hemi wantem kam, America i wantem kam be masket blong hem olsem hip blong hem, okei man ia hemi go antap long plen wetem ol bom evriwan hemi sat daon stret long ol masket ia hemi bosta hemi lus okei nao America i save kam insaed nao. Hemia stori blong *Addison* from hem nao oli talem se, *He gave his life for Guadalcanal*, hemi givim laef blong hem blong ol man Guadalcanal mo ol man America tu oli go insaed.

Okei hemia mi go longwe tumas mi go long Solomon stamba blong faet ia i kam long Solomon. Olsem man ia i talem se hemi kam be Japan hemi mekem stamba blong hem long Solomon aelan be hemi faet i go long America be hemi no go long America tufala i mekem nomo long Solomon. So faet ia hemi gud mo ino gud olsem man Solomon i talem se ino ples blong tufala blong tufala i faet long ples ia. Ples blong tufala longwe weswe tufala i no faet longwe from Japan i singaotem America i kam.

Yu save wae America hemi mekem wo from hemi bonem Arizona wan wo sip long Hawaii ten America hemi diklea wo. Ale yufala i save ating long 7 Disemba 1942 mi go luk ples ia so bae mi go go olbaot nao be hemia nao mi stap ting se ol man i mas save memori ia. Yufala evriwan ino save ia be hao nao bae mi mekem i klia long ol man blong save. Mi naoia mi talem long yufala, plante man oli stap singaotem mi nao tumoro bae mi go, mi go storian long Franis skul antap ia abaot samting ia Wol Wo Tu. So bae mi stori i long wan tumas fulap fulap long kaset blong mitufala we mitufala i rikodem ol man mitufala i wok sikis manis ia, rentem trak tri deis long ples ia, rentem trak long Santo 6 manis ten afta mitufala i go long Hawai'i. Yu save mi laki taem mi wok long hem mi go long Hawai be mi go tu taem, tu taem mitufala man ia be mi stil stori long stori blong Wol Wo Tu ating mi bambae mi man America from we mi stap storian long ol man America oltaem be las taem ia nomo sori bae mi talem nogud wan.

Long taon ia long Franis Embasi mi faenem olgeta man Japanese oli stap soem ol samting we America i sakem. He man mi lukluk mi seksek, he be wan woman ia hemi save Bislama mi se yes be mi mi wok long samting ia be mi mi no save stori blong samting ia. Okei hemi se long woksop ia oli mekem long namba 16 to namba 21 oktoba long taon ia, be woman ia i pulum mi i go insaed mi lukim TV blong samting ia atomik bom ia. Yu save 1945 America hemi sakem atomik bom ia long *Hiroshima,* seventi taosen man i ded, long *Nagasaki* long namba 9 hemi tu handred an fifti taosen so mi talem ia rabis wan ia mi jes save ia be mi talem long man ia se: be i rong blong hu? I rong blong bos blong man Japan be America i putumaot wo ia long ples blong yufala ia nao spos hemi no sakem eni bom be mifala i no gat nao.

So sori mi jes faenem an mi staon wetem hem smol an mi luk video blong hem be hemi no gud blong ol pikinini oli luk tis kaen so sori mi talem ia mi jes luk. Mi sapraes long America mi save se man we i wokem bom ia ating oli stopem hem blong ino mekem bakegen nao bikos hemi rabis wan. Spos i sakem long Vanuatu hemia evriwan i go so mi storian i long wan tumas plante plante storian be bae mi singim wan singsing. Singsing ia mi singim long TV finis be mi fogetem wan laen an ten be i gud blong oli mekem i gud bakegen be singsing blong ol man America be hemi sud America Nasonal Anthem be ol boe long taem ia America hemi no kolem olgeta boe. Long taem ia America hemi no kolem olgeta boe taem ol man oli wok wetem hem, hemi jes fren blong olgeta. Wan samting we hemi jensem ol man Vanuatu we Franis wetem Inglis tufala i neva mekem ol man Vanuatu i go wan ples o i go kakae long wan tebel be America nao i mekem from taem hemi tekemaot wan paket sigaret hemi openem hemi givim long evriman afta i laetem olsem wan pija yu luk hemi laetem nao ol man Vanuatu oli tekem tis kaen. Mi mi haos boe oltaem taem mi skul mi haos boe long wan Inglis man, be haf kakae i stap bae hemi talem long mi kakae spos no bae mi sakem long ol dog, be neva i singaot man i kakae wetem be ol man America nao oli mekem. Oli mekem tis kaen laef ia hemi jens long Vanuatu.

Be sori i gat longfala stori bae mi singim singsing ia blong ol man America. Ol boe ol man neva oli kolem olgeta boe be i gud olsem fren bikos bifo yumi kolem *Master* ol samting olsem ia. No America taem yu kolem boe hemi no wantem be hemia singsing ia taem oli ronron long trak oli wok oli singim.

Okei hemia las wan i gat plante be mi singim hemia be mi talem se i gat plante singsing an mi laekem. Mi laekem ol song ia hemia wan man i komposem abaot Vila taem oli kam so, be man ia i komposem long tri lanwis Paama lanwis, Ambae lanwis, and tis wan long Inglis. Yu save long taem ia ol woman oli fraet long ol man America so stori ia long en bae i talem be nogud pat blong hem nogud mi talem. Mi talem olsem se ol woman oli fraet long ol man America be oli stap werem traoses blong ol man blong olgeta mi mekem blong i sot olsem be afta hemi jens. Be naoia mi luk ol woman oli werem traoses we oli defren nao be hemi no kastom nating nao.

Okei man ia i komposem taem we oli kam so hemi tokbaot laef ia afta hemi tokbaot ol man America, be taem oli kam so long taem ia long PP wof be naoia oli berem wof ia oli mekem go go i longwe be solwota, wof basis hemia saed long gavman building taon ia. Samfala woman oli singsing raon long olgeta faea oli kam wom long faea be afta oli luk ol man America oli kam so afta oli silip oli jenis oli werem sus.

Okei Tangkiu.

The Stories of World War Two

James Gwero

He [Lamont Lindstrom] told me I should speak a little. I wanted to tell him that I wanted to go home, but since they told me I had to talk a little about World War Two, here I am. The stories of World War Two are just like *kastom* stories, just like the place on Ambae that has the big-man *Tagaro*, who is right now setting the volcano on fire. That's what they are. The stories of World War Two are now 60 years old, and in just the same way that you can see all the things that *Tagaro* made on Ambae, you can also see how the Americas made roads around Efate or Santo. But if man America had not come, and if there was no World War Two, these roads would not be here either. World War Two was both not good, and good. This is what I found through my research. It was good in that, if it had not have happened, we still would have achieved independence—Vanuatu would be independent now—but it would have been very hard to make roads around Efate or Santo.

I would like to say now that it would be good to make two more books out of this research [Big Wok], one in vernacular language, and in English and French, to make everyone understand the history well. This story should be 'once and for all', and it can't happen again. Just like when I went to America, the place of these people, and I saw notices that said that they will never make war like that again, because they lost too many lives. This means that this place and this time is important for everyone to know about. Now I'll sing a song which they made up about World War Two. I am glad to say that they made up lots of songs and dances about World War Two in language. We call the custom dances *Naboe*, the songs about World War Two.

Now—and I'll sing it when I've finished—there is something good about the sound of the Noisy Boys String Band when they sing about 'one thousand man Tanna'. The music is good, particularly one phrase in the second verse that says, 'America rose to its full power'. People repeat this song and think the lyrics good because America did rise up to their full power and come. They came to repel the Japanese, and so I am impressed with those who composed this song. They came with all the equipment for fighting, and all the equipment for building the towns of Santo and Vila. They came with their full power because, as some people, such as one man from Paama, said, Japan said that they would win Santo, and after that, make Port Vila suffer. How did they know? How did he say this? Yes, its true, this was the time of fighting, and we were scared that Japan would come into the bush and kill us. Now, let me speak. I'm sorry if I ramble and stray from the topic. This was a frightening time. When the Japanese fought they were cruel, they killed people indiscriminately, including women, in the Solomons.

There is a man, who you may or may not have heard of, called Addison. If you go to the airport in the Solomons you will see a memorial stone outside which says, 'He gave his life for Guadalcanal'. Do you know the story of this man, or not? This man, Addison, gave his life, and after he died America came to fight for the Solomons. America could not overpower its enemy, and the two sides fought on a beach they called 'A Red Fish', because of the blood of both sides that was spilled on it. I've been to this place and I've seen it. After, this man Addison thought he would die, but some miracles happened. He flew high in his plane with many bombs, but the Japanese remained in a place where the bombs could not reach them. And so the Japanese started to build an airstrip there, now called Addison Field, which they did not complete. And the Americans wanted to remove them because if they were able to land planes there they would then be able to come and kill the people of Vanuatu. OK. When the Americans wanted to advance with their infantry, this man went up in his plane with all its bombs and dropped them straight on the Japanese guns and he was killed. There were great explosions, the Japanese were killed, and the Americans were able to advance. That is the story of Addison, of whom they say, 'He gave his life for Guadalcanal'. He gave his life for the cause of all the people of Guadalcanal, and for the Americans too.

But now I've gone too far, to the first fight that came to the Solomons. Just as this man [Lamont] said, Japan made its base in the Solomons to fight the Americans, but did not make it to America. The two only fought in the Solomons. So the fight was both good and not good, and as Solomon Islanders say, it was not the place for either side to fight in. Their places were far away and they didn't fight there, but Japan came and called for America to come.

Do you know why America joined the war? Because the Japanese bombed the *USS Arizona*, a war ship in Hawai'i. After this America declared war. OK, you know, I think on 7 December 1942. I went to see this place—and I'm rambling now—but I do think that everyone should know this memory, and of the memorial at Pearl Harbour. You don't all know this history, and how can I make it clear so that everyone understands? And now I say to you, there are plenty of people who are calling for me, such as the French school here in Port Vila, to talk about this thing called World War Two. And so I can talk for a long time. There are many, many cassettes on which we recorded people. We worked six months on this. Rented a truck for three days here, and rented a truck on Santo for six months. Then, after, we went to Hawai'i. You know, I liked it when I went to Hawai'i, and I went twice. Twice we two went, but I still talk about World War Two. I think I'll become an American because I'm always talking about Americans!

But last time—sorry, but I'm about to say something no good—at the French Embassy here in town, I came across a group of Japanese who were showing some things that Americans threw away. I looked, and I was surprised. One was a woman who spoke Bislama. I said, yes, I work on this, but I can't talk about it. OK, she said that they would make a workshop from 16 to 21 October in town, and she pulled me inside and I saw on the TV the atomic bomb. Did you know that in 1945 America dropped the atomic bomb on Hiroshima? Seventy thousand people died. In Nagasaki, on the ninth, it was two hundred and fifty thousand. So I said this was no good, and now I know. But I told this person, 'But who was wrong?' It was wrong of the boss of the Japanese, but America stopped the war in your place, and if they had not dropped any bombs we wouldn't be here now.

So sorry, I just found out, and I sat down with her for a short while and I looked at the video. But it's not good for children to see this kind of thing. Sorry to say this—I only just saw. I'm surprised at America. I reckon that they've stopped the man who made this bomb from making any again, because it's a rubbish one. If they dropped it on Vanuatu, everyone would perish. So I've talked for too long with all these stories, and now I'll sing a song. I've already sung this song on TV, but I forgot a line. So it would be good if they record it again now. The song of the Americans should be the American National Anthem.

The Americans did not call workers 'boys' at this time. When men worked with them, they were just their friends. One thing that has changed the people of Vanuatu, and that the French and English will never do; all the ni-Vanuatu went to eat on the same table as the Americans. The Americans did it, because—when one took out a packet of cigarettes and opened them, he would give one to everyone. And after he would light it, just like a picture, you would see him lighting and the ni-Vanuatu taking one too. I was always a houseboy. When I was at school I was a houseboy for an English man, and if there was any food leftovers he would tell me to eat it, and if not he would throw it to the dogs. He would never invite people to eat with him, as the Americans would. And they made this kind of life change in Vanuatu.

But sorry, these stories are long. I will sing the song of America. 'Boys', they never called them 'boys'. And it's better as 'friend', because before we said 'master', naturally, and words like this. No, with Americans, when you said 'boy', they didn't like it. And so here is the song. They sang it when they drove trucks and worked.

Okay, this is the last one. There are many that I like, but I will sing only this one. This is a song a man composed about Vila when they came. But the man composed it in three languages; Paama, Ambae and English. You know, at this time women were afraid of the Americans, and so at the end of this story there is a part which is not good, and I won't explain. I will just say that women were afraid of Americans, but they wore the trousers of all of their men. I'll make it short, but after it changes. But now I see that women wear trousers that are different. And that is not at all *kastom*.

Okay, this man composed the song when they came. So he is talking about life at this time, and after that he is talking about the Americans. When they came, they came to the BP Wharf, which is now buried. The passage for the wharf is beside the government building in town. Some women were singing around a fire to get warm, but after that they saw the Americans coming ashore, then sleep, then change into wearing shoes.

Okay, thank you.

6. Diksnari blong Aneityum

Phillip Tepahae

Okei tangkiu tumas olgeta mi gat bigfala hona mo rispek blong stanap long front blong yufala blong kivimaot prisentesen blong mi. Bae mi mas apolojaes long yufala taem we yumi gat tut yumi toktok i stret, be sapos mi no talem samting ino stret, aniwe. Be okei, tangkiu tumas, wan filwoka we nem blong hem Phillip Tepahae, mi blong Aneityum mi papa blong mi i bin go long New-Caledonia long Lifou. So taem we mi bon mi kambak long Aneityum, mi stap longwe hol laef blong mi. Mi long 1992 mi go bak long Aneityum an ating naoia mi gat 75 yias samting olsem. Ale, taem we mi stap long Aneityum mi stap tingting se hao nao bambae olgeta samting olsem kastom. Kirk Huffman wetem Jack Keitadi. tufala i kam long Aneityum, tufala i askem mi blong mi kam long Aneityum, tufala i askem mi blong mi kam mi se 'i oraet, bae mi kam'.

Taem we mi kam mi stap wok long Kaljoral Senta long taon, olfala wan, an mifala i stap long taem lelebet, an taem ia tija blong mifala hemia big man blong yumi ia we hemi kam hemi stap samples ia, Dr. Tryon. Yes, mifala i stap daon an traem mifala blong tijim mifala hao blong mekem diksnari. So taem we hemi talem mi stap mi tingting long hem mi se ating mi save mekem wan. Tat taem ia we kompiuta hemi no plante yet, so hemi katkatem ol eksasaes buk se bambae mifala i mekem oda long ol alfabet mo givim sam sentens, bat hemi had wok tumas long mifala. Ating hemi had long mi from mi no skul. Mi skul long vilej skul nomo. Bat mi traem bes blong mi an wanfala taem oli sendem mifala i kam long USP—olfala USP daon.

Mifala i kam long ples ia mifala i gat tu man i tijim mifala lelebet. Jeff ating hemi tijim mifala long hao blong mekem diksnari, so mifala i mekem i go go hemi had lelebet. Taem Darrell Tryon hemi talem long mi se no tis taem i gud ino mata blong mekem ol oda long ol alfabet from kompiuta i save mekem. Yu save putum eni o olbaot nomo tat bambae kompiuta i save mekem. Mi mi glad mi gohed long wok blong diksnari blong mi mi traem raetem. Mi tingbaot long lanwis blong mi, i gat nem blong wan olsem yumi man wan person i gat ol nem blong evri bodi blong hem, mo ol fis mifala i gat ol nem blong ol fis, mo mifala i gat ol nem blong yam. Mo haos o kraon, mo ston, mifala i gat defren nem, so i mekem mi se ino isi. Mi traem blong raetem olgeta samting ia mi fulumap wan eksasaes buk. Long 1970 mi gohed long hem mi mekem long 1971, taem we mifala i kam long woksop blong mifala daon long Kaljoral Senta olfala Kaljoral Senta. Darrell hemi talem long mi se i gat wanfala man we hemi stap ia nem blong hem John Lynch ating bambae hemi save helpem yu blong mekem diksnari. Mi se, 'oraet, i gud'.

Taem we mifala i kamdaon mi lukim John Lynch hemi toktok long mi. Mitufala i toktok long ples ia nao long 1971. Mitufala i ko-operet long toktok mo mekem diksnari so plante taem mi givimaot ol buk long hem so mi gat tufala, wan diksnari ia mo wan grama blong hem. Mo hemia nao tufala buk ia we mitufala i mekem. Mi faenem ino had tumas from we mi intres long hem an wanem i mekem mitufala i hariap long hem from John Lynch i kam long Aneityum hemi stap wetem mi, hemi mekem wan haos blong hem. Taem we mitufala i stap gohed long diksnari, taem we hemi wantem kambak mifala i mekem smol kakae blong hem. Hemi girap hemi toktok long lanwis, so i mekem bigfala sapraes we hemi save kwik. Mi ting se hemi nao we i wan wei, hemi gud yumi save lelebet lanwis blong aelan we spos yu wantem statem wan diksnari long hem. Mo man we hemi helpem yu hemi mas save evri samting insaed long kastom blong hem olsem nem blong evri samting.

Mi faenem se mitufala i mekem bae hemi no had tumas. Hemi stap long Vila i raetem diksnari. Mi sendem eksasaes buk long hem hemi kopi aot hemi raetem hemi putum long kompiuta, sendem i kambak long mi blong mekem koreksen long hem. Taem we mi luk bae speling hemi no stret mi mekem koreksen long hem, sendem i kam long hem hemi mekem. Mi sendem samfala wod pepa bakegen hemi taepem. Mitufala i mekem olsem. Mi helpem John Lynch hemi helpem mi long wanem samting. Mitufala i wokem go go folem wan diksnari blong Inglis we long 1950. Hemi mekem mi folem, ating mi no save se wanem from olgeta ino save saon blong toktok. Mekem se mifala, olfala baebol blong mifala, taem we mifala ol olfala i ridim mifala i save se wanem insaed we i pronaonsem i olsem. Mi ting se hemi gud from hemi Bislama mo Inglis mo lanwis, so hemi oraet eniwan we sapos hemi lukluk long hem hemi save lukluk long hem bambae mi tekem bakegen.

I mekem se mitufala i mekem kwik wok long diksnari. An taem we mi go bak, long 2000 hemi sendem ol buk i kam. Mi lukluk bae mi no rili hapi. Hemi oraet, be from wanem mi no hapi? From we i mas gat mo wod i go insaed mo nem blong olgeta wod. Taem we wan boe i kam blong askem mi blong i kam wok long ples ia. Mi se i oraet spos yu go, be wanem samting we bae mi talem long yu yu mas raetem ol nem blong ol hil, solwota, ol maonten, ol wota, ol samting olsem long lanwis an bambae yu save kivim long mi blong mi sendem i go. Mo mi talem long boe ia, 'Mi se yu no ting se bambae olgeta i helpem yumifala. Bat yumifala i mas wok festaem, samtaem we oli luk bambae oli save givhan long yumitufala. Mi talem long hem mi se i gud i gat kamera be bambae mitufala i hadwok blong pem, bae i mas pem wan kamera we i gat samting long hem we i save pulum samting we i smol bae i kam bigwan.

Boe ia i wok i go go ating hemi les hemia nao i go. Taem we mi kivimaot diksnari mi talemaot long olgeta se, 'Long wol tede hemi no gat wan aelan lo kantri hemi finisim diksnari blong hem so i minim se diksnari we mi mekem mi soem wan rod bat hemia ino finis. Sipos wan long yufala i wantem i save lukim mi bambae mi helpem hem'. Be until tede mi no luk wan we hemi kam talem long mi se i glad. Sipos wan long yufala i wantem i save lukim mi bambae mi helpem hem antil tede mi no luk wan we hemi kam talem long mi se i glad.

So hemia nao wok blong diksnari blong mi. Mi faenem se hemi isi from hemia nao we mi mi save plante samting long saed blong ol wod, saed blong ol fis, ol wanem. Samfala mi no save bat plante mi save olsem wanem kraon we i stap mo wanem i stap, mo ol krijas, mo plante samting olsem.

Olsem mi save from mi laef long wan taem we ating lanwis blong Aneityum hemi no miksap tumas. Bat tede ating hemi had long yangfala blong oli mekem from tede lanwis hemi miksap tumas, mekem se oli had blong olgeta oli mekem. Bat, eniwe, mi mi ting se eni aelan we sapos hemi ting se i mekem diksnari blong hem.

Mi glad we Richard Leona hemi mekem wan finis. Sapos samfala yangfala oli tingting se jes lukim diksnari blong Richard Leona nomo an faenem wanem wod we oli faenem, oli save kam lukluk insaed blong faenem se i gat o ino gat. I oraet bambae mi listim daon blong sendem diksnari i go mo. Ating hemia nao olsem tingting blong hemia we mi lukluk taem we mi wok long diksnari. Mi save se hemi wan samting we hemi had sapos ino gat ol olfala be spos oli gat bae ino had. Yu save askem. Mo yu gat tingting we yu save hao nao bambae yu mekem hemi save go kwik blong mi save finisim diksnari blong mi. So ating mi no save toktok tumas. Ating smol ples ia nomo mi save talem long diksnari blong mi.

The Aneityum Dictionary Project

Phillip Tepahae

Thank you very much everyone. I have great honour and respect to stand before you and give my presentation. I must apologise to you: when we have teeth we can talk straight, so if I don't say anything that is straight—anyway. I am a fieldworker called Phillip Tepahae, and I come from Aneityum. My father went to New Caledonia, on Lifou. When I was born I came back to Aneityum, I've stayed there my whole life. In 1992 I went back to Aneityum and I think that now I am 75 years old, or something like that. Right, when I was on Aneityum I began thinking how will *kastom* be? Kirk Huffman and Jack Keitadi came to Aneityum, they both asked me to come to Aneityum and I said, 'Alright, I'll come.'

At this time I worked at the Cultural Centre in town, the old one. We stayed for a long time, and at this time our teacher was this big man of ours here, Dr. Tryon. Yes, we were located down in the town and were taught how to make a dictionary. So when he told me, I thought to myself, I think I can make one. At this time computers were not yet plentiful, so he cut up some exercise books and told us to make lists in alphabetical order, and to give some sentences, but it was very hard work for us. I think it was hard for me because I never went to school. I only went to school in the village school. But I tried my best, and at one time we were sent to the University of the South Pacific (USP)—the old USP below.

We came to that place and had two men teach us a little. I think Jeff taught us how to make a dictionary, and so we continued although it was quite hard. Then Darrell Tryon told me that it was now fine if we don't follow alphabetical order because the computer can do this. You can put it in any order you like and the computer will do it. I was glad to progress with my dictionary work I was writing. I thought about my language, that there are names for everything such as the names for all of a person's body parts, or that we have names for all types of fish, and we have names for all types of yam. And houses, land, and stones, we have different names, and this means it's not easy. I tried to write all of these things and filled up a whole exercise book. In 1971 I went ahead with it and I made it in 1971, at the time at which we went to our workshop down at the old Cultural Centre. Darrell told me that there was a man called John Lynch who he thought could help me to make my dictionary. I said, 'Alright, that's good'.

When we came down I saw John Lynch who talked to me. This discussion took place in 1971. We cooperated in our discussions and made a dictionary, and I gave him my books many times, and so he has two, a dictionary and a grammar.

And these are the two books that we have made. I didn't find it too hard because I was interested in it, and what made us hurry was that John Lynch came to Aneityum and stayed with me, and made a house for himself. We went ahead with the dictionary, and when he wanted to come back we'd made a small feast for him. He would get up and talk in language, and it surprised us very much that he did it so fast. I think that this is a way, that it is good that we know a little language of the island if you want to start a dictionary of it. And the person who helps you must know everything contained in its *kastom*, such as the names of everything.

I found that we made it so that it wasn't too hard. He stayed in Vila and wrote the dictionary. I sent exercise books to him which he copied out into the computer, and then sent back to me to make corrections. If I found any incorrect spelling I would make a correction, and then send it for him to do. I would send some pages of words back again which he would type up. We did it like that. I helped John Lynch and he helped me with things. We continued working, and followed a dictionary by Inglis from the 1950s. He made me follow it, and I think I didn't understand it because they didn't know the sounds of the language. In this way we, with our old bible, when us old people read we know how to pronounce what is inside. I think it is good that it is Bislama and English and language, so it is alright in that anyone who might look at it can do so and gain from it.

In this way we made quick work of the dictionary. And then I went back, and in 2000 he sent copies of the books here. I looked up I was not really happy. It was alright, but why was I not happy? Because there needed to be more words in it, including the names of trees. Then a boy came and asked me if he could come and work here. I said, 'It's alright, but what I will tell you is that you must write the names of all hills, sea, mountains, water, all of these kinds of things, in language, and then you can give it to me to send off.' And I told this boy, 'I think that you don't think that they will help us. But we must work first, and then when they see they will help us.' I told him that it is good if we had a camera but it is for us to afford one, so he must pay for a camera that has the ability to make small things become large.

The boy worked for a time and then got tired of it and left. When I gave out the dictionaries I told everyone that, 'In the world today there is an island in the country who has finished its dictionary, and this means that the dictionary I made shows one road, but it is not finished. If any one of you wants you can see me and I'll help you.' But until this day I have not seen one person come to me and say they are glad. If one of you wants to come and see me after and I can help, but I haven't had one person come and say they are glad.

So this is my dictionary work. I have found it easy because of the fact that I know a lot about many things concerning trees, concerning fish, or whatever. There are some things I don't know, but much that I do, such as the location of particular areas of land, and creatures, and plenty of things like this.

I know these things because I was alive at a time in which I think the language of Aneityum was not mixed up too much. But today I think it is hard for young people to do it because today language is mixed up to much, which makes it hard for them to do it. But, anyway, I think that any island can make a dictionary for itself.

I am glad that Richard Leona has made one already. If some young people think to look at Richard Leona's dictionary and find whatever word that they find, they can come look inside to find out if it is there or not. It's alright, I will list them to send the dictionary further. I think that these are my thoughts regarding the time that I worked on the dictionary. I would say that it would be a hard thing if there were no old people, but if there are it will not be hard. You can ask them. And you have an idea of how I was able to finish my dictionary quickly. So, I think I can't talk too much longer. I think I can tell just give you this small account of my dictionary.

7. Discovering One's Past in the Present

Mary Patterson, Koran Wilfred and Ileen Vira

Quite a lot has been written about the nature of fieldwork since I began mine more than 40 years ago. And the world and its institutions have changed. As my entry to the field then was negotiated through the officials of a colonial government, my research now is approved by a committee of ni-Vanuatu who are beholden to no external authorities in their deliberations on its worth or management. Yet George Marcus' comment of more than a decade ago remains valid: 'the regulative ideals and framing presumptions of what it is to do fieldwork very much remain in place in anthropology's professional culture'(1998: 3). Lengthy immersion in a single community, predicated on language acquisition and open-ended agendas, was as much a product of degree time and the institutional context between the 1950s and the 1980s as of unitary models of social organisation that some critics have seen as its driving force. If the *Writing Culture* (Clifford 1986) debates of the late eighties and early nineties did nothing else, they drew our attention to the way in which the epistemological, literary and political are deeply connected. In some parts of the world they also drew our attention to the unexplored history of what came to be seen as novel method in the simplistic way that nuanced debates are often reduced. Multi-sited ethnography in the sense of ethnology in Vanuatu had been established in the work of William Halse Rivers Rivers and even John Willoughby Layard, not to mention the French ethnologist Jean Guiart, well before Marcus extolled a much more complex constitution for contemporary ethnography under this rubric (*ibid*: 14). If in Anglophone universities we now find grant bodies more amenable to shorter periods of fieldwork for our students, and short visits to more places not only more desirable but more likely to enable them to finish their degrees in the ever-decreasing time funded, we are also able to convince such bodies that this is now the method of choice, even if mere proliferation of sites and amended duration is not at all the project advocated by Marcus.

In personalising this piece about the fragmented history of connections to the field, I want to highlight the ways in which issues of representation raised by the 'writing culture' debates form and challenge our notions of how we frame our research, our research methods, and the value of that research through our relationships within and outside the field in apparently mundane ways. I want to talk about the privileged contact I have had in my most recent research in Vanuatu with individuals with whose family I established the kind of emotional bonds that ni-Vanuatu allow us to have with them, even when we are separated for decades and have intermittent contact. Some time ago, Pat Caplan wrote about the way in which her fieldwork experience was formed and directed by alterations to her status as she entered the community in which she worked as a single woman, returned to the field married and a mother, and variously engaged with feminist preoccupations in her own community (Caplan 1992). Where gender overtly influences daily life experience and access to the world, as it does in Vanuatu, the female anthropologist's status has more than a minor role in her research. As an unmarried 23 year old, without the protection or apparent direction of either father or husband, I was both anomalous and in need of a personal family context, and while its provision was not instant, within the first fortnight of arrival in Fona by colonial government boat, I was 'fathered and mothered' by Wilfred Koran, the chief of the village in which I was domiciled, and his wife Sarah who, as it turned out, was the daughter of the then highest ranking man in North Ambrym and sister of its most notorious sorcerer. I had serendipitously been granted access to the domain of an extraordinary man, his feet firmly located in *kastom* as the yam-master of the origin domain of North Ambrym. Chief Koran was at the same time a talented and energetic modernist, skilfully working his connections to both sides of the Condominium government. While he built up his depopulated domain with neighbours who were mostly Anglophone and Presbyterian, he sent some of his children to French Schools, his son becoming a gendarme in the French colonial force.

Whatever I achieved in this period of fieldwork owed everything to Koran's family and initial access to their extraordinary connections across the entire region and beyond. But I was also in some sense a 'problem child'. My anomalous behaviour, in the context of what was expected of young, unmarried women, was frequently challenged by my relatives, particularly the male ones who admonished me publicly for walking about on my own. I was indeed setting a bad example. Nor did I consider that I should modify the kind of autonomous behaviour that young women were claiming at that time in the West. When I returned for a second time after a year and related how I had become ill on the way home from Ambrym it was entirely as my family had predicted. Sorcery and kinship became much more than research topics in my life, and from the point of view of my Ambrym family, the connections between research and life experience needed no esoteric explanation.

After submitting my thesis, my own close personal encounter with its topic, kinship (in the form of three children under five years old), occasioned a departure from the academy for a decade. When I entered another institution after the award of a post-doctoral fellowship, a return to Ambrym seemed a most exciting prospect given that it was a decade after Independence and all of our life circumstances had changed. Now with a husband and three children, from whom I was mysteriously parted, I was welcomed back into village life as a different kind of woman. I found the children I had known were now adults with children of their own, and the turbulent history of the pre- and post-Independence period in North Ambrym had affected the lives of my now vastly enlarged extended family in very different ways.

Coming and going throughout the nineties I was mostly accompanied by my sisters Ileen and Martha. Martha had been a close companion during my early fieldwork but now a widow with grandchildren had become a resident of West Ambrym when her husband returned to his origins in that region after the turmoil of pre-Independence land disputes removed many Northern-born West Ambrymese from their homes. Martha's much younger sister Ileen had been long removed from the north. Educated at a French secondary School in Santo, Ileen had married an Ambaean man and settled with him in Vila. Her husband was in the British Police Force and stationed in Luganville during the Santo rebellion but it was only during my most recent research that Ileen told me the story of her amazing escape with her baby son from Luganville during the violence of the rebellion. Her narrative was prompted by reading the recently-published Condominium Agents' reminiscences, some of which contained accounts of this turbulent period (Bresnihan and Woodward 2002). Ileen's father, Chief Koran, who had been a Nagriamel supporter during my early fieldwork and had lived with his wife at Fanafo for several months, was treated severely in the aftermath of the rebellion when supporters were pursued to their home islands and publicly humiliated. Wilfred was removed as village chief (see Patterson 2002, 2003 and 2006 for a discussion of this period). I also made my first contacts with other family members now living in Vila, and particularly with Koran Jnr., the grandson of Chief Wilfred Koran, whom I had only known as a child when his gendarme father visited the island.

Many anthropologists continue the connections with local communities that they established in their early work, but as the context of our work in distant institutions changes, so too does the kind of work we do. When anthropologists write now about collaborative research they probably mean the kind of collaborations that we are all familiar with through the Vanuatu Kaljoral Senta (VKS) fieldworker program, where a researcher is assigned to a dedicated fieldworker in the area in which they wish to work. They work together on a project and the fieldworker provides access to a network of others who contribute to the project. Or perhaps, as we have seen at this conference, they refer to the kinds of collaborations that anthropologists commonly had before the establishment of the fieldworker program, with particular individuals who acted in much the same way, as navigators in the field terrain. For me, in my early research there were a number of such people; importantly they were both men and women, and indeed children. They were my teachers, nurturers, and usually patient advisors who put up with endless questioning about what were to them everyday facts of life. They directed my research and made it difficult when they understandably grew tired of my attentions. Occasionally I redeemed myself by being able to sew, translate something, tell stories about my place or lend someone some money. However, when I embarked on a different sort of research project in 2003, that was neither village-based nor as open-ended as previous, I needed a different kind of collaboration. The impetus for the research was a growing concern among colleagues in Australia that the Pacific Island states that most of us felt we knew, were becoming characterised in an entirely negative way, driven by the agendas of powerful neighbours and largely in ignorance of the conditions of daily life of the inhabitants, and the context of their statehood. The initial project was a pilot study funded by the University of Melbourne as precursor to an application for Australian Research Council funding that was subsequently obtained for three years (2005–7).

I needed research assistance since the project aimed in a broad-ranging way to investigate a number of themes around the agendas of external aid agencies, their local reception at a variety of levels in rural and urban contexts, and the factors that were influencing peoples' notions of development, governance and what it meant to be ni-Vanuatu in the contemporary Pacific. My research approval by the VKS did not provide fieldworkers for obvious reasons. The research was so broadly based and multi-sited that it required what I initially thought would be a team of enthusiastic young ni-Vanuatu, if not having some training in research methods, then willing to be trained. And although a number of people had worked on urban research projects, no-one was able to suggest where I would find them. Ileen had accompanied me back to Ambrym in the previous year for the pilot study and she had also used her extensive contacts in Port Vila to arrange focus groups with young people, and interviews with individuals from a wide range of backgrounds and life experience in Vila town and several squatter settlements. I had not yet spoken to Koran because I knew that he was employed with the Peace Corps in Vila. The day after I arrived I took a phone call saying that he had resigned from his position the week before, and that he had a few weeks leave before taking up a new government position. At that point I was not fully aware of all his talents. Anthropologists know anecdotally that many of them are drawn to the discipline by their life experience as outsiders of some sort. Forced to learn the 'rules of the game' through immigration or early contact with other cultures, they frequently develop an interest in studying all things cultural and the way in which societies operate. In Vanuatu, of course, exposure to different languages and a variety of cultures *is* part of normal life experience for many people and over a long period of time; much longer than we usually anticipate as our archaeological colleagues point out to us. Change, movement and culture contact has formed the basis of ni-Vanuatu social life since its inception in the archipelago. So, if 'natural' social scientists exist, it is here we are most likely to find them. Koran's background, apart from his personal talents, is a case in point.

Critically aware of his North Ambrym roots and his Ambrymese genealogy, Koran grew up with his family away from the island as he travelled with his gendarme father to various island postings. Always returning for vacations and for extended stays with his family he was ritually initiated with his island 'brothers' when he was a young boy. Both Ileen and Koran were outstanding students but Ileen's early marriage removed her from opportunities for further education as a young woman. Koran became a secondary school teacher and with his talent for language acquisition, learned the languages and cultural mores of the places to which he was posted as a teacher.

As soon as I learned that he was available and interested I suggested that we meet to discuss the project and his involvement in it. The next day I outlined the sort of things that the research hoped to uncover, emphasising that a broad range of contacts was necessary in the urban contexts to represent the diversity of the population. It wasn't until I accompanied Koran down the main street, however, that I realised that the good fortune I had had in ending up in his grandfather's domain so long ago was flowing into the present. The main street in Vila is not very long; it takes about 20 minutes to stroll from one end to the other. Traversing it with Koran Wilfred is another matter. We were unable to go more than a few metres without being pulled up by one of his myriad acquaintances. Vehicles would draw up beside us, people would hail him from across the street or he would wave and indicate that he had to discuss something or other with the person who had just disappeared into this or that building. It took us almost an hour and a half to get from the Kaiviti Hotel to what used to be the Rossi Hotel where we had arranged to meet a politician. By the next day, after a discussion of the project, Koran had produced a comprehensive list of people he thought I should speak to in each of the categories I had outlined to him. By the following day we had worked out a schedule of interviews with government officials, both Francophone and Anglophone, politicians, church leaders, people involved in small business and a variety of NGOs. After a week of interviewing around a series of prompt questions, Koran began to participate in the interviews with questions of his own that followed up on particular points drawing out our interviewees on issues that often I was not aware of. On my next trip we arranged to go to Santo with Ileen for a few days, to conduct interviews, focus groups, extend the school survey and visit Fanafo. I had interviewed Franky Steven on a previous trip and Koran was keen to meet Franky to discuss his grandfather's involvement in Nagriamel in the pre-Independence period. As we walked across the tarmac I saw Koran wave to the pilot in the cockpit of the new large plane that Air Vanuatu had just acquired.

As we took our seats, a voice over the intercom requested that Mr. Koran Wilfred should contact the flight attendant immediately. And that was the last I saw of him until we reached Luganville. The pilot was Koran's ex-student, only too happy to have his old teacher in the cockpit for the flight to Santo. We took a taxi to our hotel from the airport with a taxi driver who just happened to be yet another old acquaintance of my extraordinary research assistant. Our trip to Fanafo was arranged on the spot.

Working with Koran and Ileen raised a number of important issues for me over the kinds of collaborations we anthropologists have in the field. In the 'immersion' kind of fieldwork that we still frequently regard as 'best practice', it is not always clear how collaboration works, particularly when the writing up of a project like a thesis is directed at an audience from which our collaborators are excluded by language and/or academic discourse. This is of course precisely what the designated projects that researchers are given by the VKS are designed to address, but while they do perform a significant counter function in the research process, they do not address the issue of how collaborative our projects can ever be. The lodging of research materials with the VKS contributes materials of historical importance and also reveals how our training and resources have enabled us to access materials that even dedicated VKS fieldworkers may not be able to record. In the case of fieldwork that predates the fieldworker program there are only our records. The task is enormous and of interest to our collaborators as part of their history that we were privileged to witness. The often laborious task of making these materials available in Vanuatu is commonly not assisted by the way in which research is funded and measured in foreign institutions, leaving we anthropologists with a hefty retirement debt.

It is of course a long-standing anthropological truism that projects, however meticulously planned and designed, are inevitably driven in the process of fieldwork by the interests and degree of cooperation of the communities we are working in and of course by our own cultural and academic milieu and training. Anyone who has carried out research in Vanuatu would have noted that language is not all that divides Anglophones and Francophones in our approach to matters cultural; a curious difference in emphasis noted long ago by Mary Douglas, amongst others (Douglas 1975). But even given national predilections, we all like to tell our graduate students that their attachment to a project should always be malleable enough to allow their collaborators to change it. And anecdotes of projects redesigned by field experience are legion. In the contemporary context our project designs, funded not for degree-awarding research, may have very different parameters. It is here that a real collaboration— at the stage of development and implementation of a project—can offer benefits to all sides when we who are institutionally trained are offered the advantages of collaboration with ni-Vanuatu colleagues whose anthropological attitude has emerged from their own cosmopolitan (in the broadest sense) life experience.

I have been more than fortunate in Vanuatu, in the fictive kinship that was established for me so long ago and in the way that those past connections entered into the present of research collaborations that have contributed in a multitude of ways to the research projects I have carried out, and to the way I hope to continue to work in the future. What follows is a translation of the Bislama presentation Ileen, Koran and I gave at the conference. It reflects a partial view of our encounter in this public context with its own context of representation, which I have attempted to flesh out here. My collaborators speak for themselves, but they also speak for us.

Cultural politics and the politics of culture in Vanuatu

Mary Patterson

Toktok blong mitrifala i gat tri pat long hem. Bae mi stat wetem risej we mi bin mekem taem we mi yangfala nomo long not Ambrym. Afta mi givim smol tok blong risej we mi mekem naoia from 2004 kasem naoia wetem Ileen mo Koran. Tufala ia bae i komen long eli risej blong mi tu. Okei long 1968, taem blong tufala gavman mi go fes taem long Ambrym mi go from supavaesa blong mi Michael Allen hemi talem se, 'Intres blong yu long ol samting blong nakaemas long Melanesia, Ambrym hemi wan ples we yu faenem plante i fulap.' Ale taem ia mi gat twante-tri yia, mi go long not Ambrym. Long taem ia ino gat filwoka projek no oli go long Kolonial Gavman and olsem Vila long taem ia ino olsem naoia an oli askem pemisen long Distrik Komisene hemi sendem mesej i go long not Ambrym oli talem se wan stiuden bae i kam i oraet i go stap long Fona wetem yufala long olfala blong Koran ia olsem bubu blong hem, Wilfred Koran. Hemi talem se i oraet yu sendem wan stiuden mifala i lukaotem hem. Ale afta mi go long Lakatoro mi stap mi talem long Darvall Wilkins se, 'Wan samting nomo we mi wantem, mi wantem go long dei laet, yu dropem mi long ples ia long dei laet.' 'Yu no wari i oraet.'

Long eli moning, mifala i go long wof mifala i wet. Mi no save Vanuatu taem yet, bot i gat wan problem, ale afta oli go sakem mi long sanbis long tudak finis. Olgeta oli no save huia woman ia? Huia woman ia? Wehem papa blong hem i tekem hem i kam olsem ia? Oli putum bokis blong mi long sanbis oli lukluk mi, wan stiuden ia ating; yes be ino man ating oli sori lelebet be mi no man olsem mi woman. Bae mifala i mekem wanem wetem woman ia? Ale afta papa Wilfred hemi tekem mi i go insaed long haos blong hem, hemi talem se, 'Yu no wari yu no fraet mifala i lukaotem yu gud.' An i tru. Oli lukaotem mi olsem mi gat wan famle long ples ia, mi gat wan famle long Australia, olgeta ia nao taem we mi go fastaem Koran hemi wan bebi mi no save hemi smol smol nomo, Ileen hemi wan young gel. Nao afta long eli risej ia olsem Ogis go bak olsem long taem ia mi talem se ol kastom i stap strong yet mo i gat ol divisen long not Ambrym olsem ol kristen i stap olbaot long stadi mo insaed long dak bus i gat ol man i stap long kastom yet mo i gat plante oli fraet long posen, o long Ambrym oli kolem *Abio*. So olsem mi mekem stadi long samting ia mo mi mekem stadi long ol samting blong famle. Wan intres blong mi bakegen an olsem olgeta long Ambrym tu bigfala intres long olgeta so long taem ia i defren lelebet an mi talem se *politics of culture*. Kastom i strong mo i gat politik insaed long hem; i gat politik blong man i kam big man i go insaed long *namage* i kam hae jif an luk ia hemia Tain Mal i stap hae jif long not Ambrym long taem ia hemi olfala bubu blong olgeta ia. Mo hemi soemaot olsem divisen blong tufala grup ia wan kastom mared i stap long saed ia mo wan kristen mared. Insaed long hem ol mining blong hemi stap semak be ino gat defren wei blong soemaot, sam oli givim pig sam oli no save givim pig oli kilim wan smol pig nomo an bae oli givim plante samting, ol gift oli givim long famle. And hemia tu pija ia olsem hemia angkel blong Ileen, Tofor, hemi stap go long wan *namage meliun* long taem ia mo long narasaed olsem man ia hemi kam long Fona long wan dei hemi stap slip wan naet mo long moning olsem kastom i talem se yu mas kilim pig an yu mas givim samting long hem so oli stap wari from bae oli faenem pig blong givim long bigfala angkel ia. Oli fraet long hem, Koran mo Ileen bae i komen long eli risej ia.

Koran Wilfred

Tangkiu tumas mi nem blong mi Koran mi stap long Ministri blong Intenol Afea ating bae yufala i luk se hemi kam stap mekem wanem long ples ia. Bifo mi stap kolem anti Mary nao bikos risej hemi mekem se mifala i kam wan famle nao, bifo mi wok wetem Mary mi bin wok wetem hem long 2004 bae mifala i tokbaot sam risej mifala i kari aot hemi kam karem mi olsem riseja asisten bat olsem mi talem bae mi traem go bak lelebet long wanem we hemi talem long taem blong visit blong hem taem hemi yangfala gel olsem hemi kam. Mi stil rimemba wan taem mifala i stap an ten olfala grandfata blong mi we mi mi karem nem blong hem, Koran Wilfred, hemi wan bigfala jif long not Ambrym hemi bin talem long mi se yangfala woman ia hemi pat blong famle nao yufala i kolem hem anti from mi karem hem olsem dota blong mi. So hemi wan samting we mi stil rimemba long taem ia we mifala karem Mary i kam insaed long famle olsem pat blong famle blong mifala long Ambrym. Narafala samting we mi wantem mensenem long ples ia, long taem ia hemi veri intresting bikos ol pipol long not Ambrym long taem ia oli no save wanem nao woman ia bae hemi kam mekem, i gat tumas kwestin oli bin askem se, 'Be i kam stap wetem yufala from wanem? Yufala i faenem hem olsem wanem? Hemi kam olsem wanem? Papa blong hem wia?' Yu save yumi long Vanuatu i gat tisfala famle tae so oli stap traem blong kwestinim mi se, 'Waet woman ia i kam stap wetem jif Wilfred hemi faenem hem olsem wanem?'

So blong talem nomo olsem blong kipim wan bigfala pija se long taem ia risej hemi bin veri veri difikel blong ol pipol oli andastanem yu olsem wan riseja olredi yu gat defren skin an ten yu gat defren kalja taem yu kam yu liv insaed long wan komiuniti olsem hemi bin liv long hemi no bin isi blong hem. Bat wan veri gud samting we mi mas talem long ples ia is long taem ia olsem olredi wetem tufala koloniel paoa we i stap, ol jif oli bin gat samfala actif rol blong luk afta long ol strenjas we oli kam. Hemia hemi wan, bae mi talem olsem wan strong paoa we hemi bin holem ol jif tugeta long ol vilejes oli luk afterem ol pipol we oli kam aot saed. So hemia nao hemi mekem se taem we anti Mary hemi kam insaed long famle blong mekem stadi blong hem olsem hemi mensenem i faenem tat famle blong mi, hemi obei long hem so hemi mekem se hemi helpem wok blong anti Mary long taem ia blong hemi kari aot risej. Narafala poen we mi wantem mensenem long ples ia long taem blong risej is tat hao ol pipol oli koperetif taem oli andastanem rol blong Mary olsem wan stiuden long taem ia. Mi rimemba taem oli stap go aot long ol vilejes hemi stap go aot long, oltaem bae abu blong mi bae hemi talem se, 'Yutufala i folem Mary from posen'. Olsem hemi stap talem, oltaem bae tu o tri boe i akampaniem Mary i go olbaot long ol vilejes blong hemi go mekem stadi blong hem. So blong givim wan big pija long yumi nomo olsem se long taem ia hemi risej hemi bin had we pipol long tat taem oli no andastanem tumas objektif mo wae nao ol waet pipol ia oli kam stap long vilej bat olsem mi talem hemi bin wan samting we later on smol, wan yia afta oli kam blong andastanem, 'Yes hemi kam blong mekem wan samting ia an ten nao yu save luk ol man oli save kamaot'. Taem yu askem kwestin, ansa i kam i sili bat bifo tat oli holem bak ol tingting from oli no rili andastanem jes bikos kalja hemi defren mebi skin hemi defren so hemi mekem se task o responsabiliti blong ol pipol we oli kam blong mekem risej hemi bin difikal. So mi glad tumas we famle blong mi hemi bin pat long tatfala risej mo mi tink se mi praod long ples ia. Famle blong mi long aelan mifala i pat long tatfala divelopmen blong risej i kam kam kasem tede bikos mifala i bin akseptem wan yangfala ledi we hemi from Nowei, hemi kam hemi stap wetem mifala antil tede tisfala famle relesensip hemi stap iven sipos hemi go long Australia i kambak i mas go visitim ol famle blong mi long aelan.

Mary Patterson

Okei long risej we mifala i mekem i stat long 2003 wan pailot projek blong wan bigfala risej long wan grant we mi holem long Australia mi kambak long Vanuatu an mi faenem Wilfred we i jes finis long Peace Corps hemi avelebol blong helpem mi long risej ia an hemi wan rili kolaboreta wetem risej blong faenemaot ol samting we mifala putum long ol kwestin we mi askem long risej. Risej ia nem blong hem *Modernity and Governance in Melanesia*. Kes blong Vanuatu i kamaot long sam konsen blong ol koligs blong mi long Australia, we olgeta politisen long Australia oli stap representem ol aelan long Pasifik long negativ we. Oli tokbaot wik stet, oli tokbaot *The Arc of Instability* oli tokbaot ol samting we negativ samting long Pasifik aelan oli lukluk long plante samting we ino gud long ples ia.

Projek ia, i wantem save wea ol negativ samtingia i tru o no. Mi wetem koligs blong mi i go wok long PNG mo Solomon mo hemia long Vanuatu. So risej ia wan defren kaen risej i veri defren from eli risej we mi mekem long aelan nomo. Koran mo Ileen i mekem kolaboresen ia wetem mi long pailot projek afta mifala i mekem ol fasen blong mifala olsem inteviu mo fokes grup olsem yu save filwoka ating yu save finis we yu faenem sam yangfala o olfala o olsem wanem sam grup blong olgeta yu tekem hem yu inteviu hem long wan ples and mifala inteviu plante defren kaen pipol politisen, olgeta long sivil sosaeti, NGOS, VANGO mo i fulap long ol defren samting we mifala i mekem. Mo wan samting tu mifala i mekem long wan kes stadi long Nagriamel from divelopmen blong hem afta long independens i veri intresting from i gat insaed long hem sam influens blong aotsaed an wan pat blong projek ia i askem kwestin se ol polisi blong aed dona we oli gifem aed, oli putum bigfala intres long hem i stret long Vanuatu o ino stret, i stret long ol sosaeti long Pasifik o ino stret. Hemia nao mifala i wantem se mining blong sivil sosaeti mo gud gavanens oli andastanem olsem wanem. Mifala i wantem lukluk long resistens long sam polisi we maet ino stret long aelan komiuniti so ino gat plante risej we i lukluk long ol samting ia; i gat sam be ino plante. Hemia nao mi givim bak long Koran mo Ileen from oli storian mo long kolaboresen blong mifala blong wokemaot difren kaen projek ia.

Ileen Vira

Gud moning evriwan mi nem blong mi Ileen, mi tu wan memba blong famle we olsem Koran i talem finis yufala i harem. Mi, Mary Patterson we i stap long ples ia hemi kam tru long New-Hebridis bifo mi bin gat ileven yia. Taem hemi kam mi mi stap skul long Santo mi go holidei afta mi stap wokbaot wetem hem long ol risej blong hem afta mo tan twenti yias naoia hemi kambak blong mekem risej. Hemia nao olsem mitufala mo Koran mitufala i travel plante wetem hem go bak long Ambrym mo Santo blong mekem inteviu. Olsem hemi talem finis ol pipol we long ol defren sosaetis mifala i mitim olgeta long aelan mitufala i go long Ambrym las yia mitufala i go mitufala i givimaot fom olsem risej blong hem hemi dil menli wetem sivil sosaeti hemia nao mifala i wokbaot plante long hem mifala i mitim ol lida blong ol komiuniti. Mitufala i jes pas raon long olgeta skuls long Ambrym distribiutim sam foms long ol prinsipol blong ol stiuden blong oli save fulemap blong yufala i save luk long pija antap ia mifala stap wetem ol tija blong Ranon sekonderi skul we fulap i stap harem an long pija antap ia i gat wan Nagriamel tu we Mary hemi bin inteviu hem Olsen Kae we stragol blong indipendent yumi stap kasem, man ia tu hemi stap insaed. So ating mi no gat samting mo blong talem. Mi stap wok long *Secret Garden* olsem wan Franis tua gaed. Ating mi dil plante wetem turis long saed blong kastom we mifala i save eksplenem an blong kolaboret mo long saed blong famle hemia Mary i bin talem finis mi mi wan angkel blong wan big jif longwe hemia jif Tofor we evriwan i save long hem. Mo mi wantem tu se taem Mary hemi kam mifala i helpem long saed blong kastom blong mifala from mifala nao mifala i save go klosap long kastom vilej ia we hemi Fanla i gat strong kastom i stap long hem be tru long mifala nao Mary i save kasem mo samting mo histri long Fanla vilej. So ating hemia nomo tangkiu blong lisin.

Koran Wilfred

Ating bae mi, mi go on smol bakegen long risej we mifala i bin kari aot olsem risej assistant long taem ia hemi long 2004 spos yu luk long pija ia ating hemi wan projek we VKS hemi givim long Mary blong hemi risej long hem. An mi talem long hem se hemi wan veri veri intresting projek we mi bin involv long hem bikos hemi tokbaot wanem nao role blong kastom hemi kam insaed long divelopmen blong Vanuatu an long kwestin we mifala i stap askem blong talem lelebet pipol long Vanuatu oli tisfala wod nomo 'kastom' olredi i gat fulap definisen blong hem we wan i givim defren wan, wan i givim defren wan. Yumi no tokbaot ol fren blong yumi we oli kam ova sis, definisen blong olgeta long kastom tu hemi olsem wanem so hemi mekem se mi talem risej ia hemi veri intresting long mi bikos mi stap traem blong luk wanem role nao kastom hemi plem long divelopmen blong kantri blong mi olsem wan Ni-Vanuatu.

Bifo mi go long hemia mi tokbaot lelebet hemia mi jes givim niu bref deskripsen nomo long wanem hemi bin hapen taem Mary hemi kam taon i stap lukaotem wan risej asisten ten mi askem hem, mi se mi mi gat koneksen lelebet long ples ia. Mi save sam man long gavman, mi save sam man long jos sam man long komiuniti long Port Vila. Hemi se, 'Okei mi nidim yu blong yu kam yu helpem mi blong wok blong mi blong yumitu kari aot risej ia.' So wetem asistens blong mi mo samfala koneksen we mi gat long Vila i mekem se mifala i kari aot wan gudfala risej long ples ia spos yu bin luk long ol privius pija we i go mifala inteviu ol politisen, mifala inteviu ol daerekta generol sam gavman ofisas i kam taon kasem sam yut mo mifala i go long skul ol sekonderi skul mo mifala i toktok tu wetem ol prinsipel so hemia nao lelebet long ol pipol we mifala i traem blong toktok long olgeta ating long metod we mifala i bin yusum.

Mifala i yusum intaviu, kwestin ia long ol skuls mifala i mekem sam rikoding an ten tu mifala i jes kam an diskas, toktok storian jes storian mo mifala i go bak putum ol tingting tugeta. So hemia nao samfala metod we mifala i yusum wea ples mifala i mekem risej. Well mifala i doim fastaem long ples ia long Port

Vila an ten mifala i go aotsaed lelebet long Port Vila olsem Sisaed, Freswota etc an ten mifala i go long Santo blong mekem tu samfala storian long Santo an long Santo mifala i mitim samfala pipol tu longwe, mifala i toktok wetem olgeta blong oli givim tingting blong olgeta long tisfala topik. Mifala i go kasem long Fanafo mo yu save luk pija ia hemi mi wetem Franky Steven an spos yu lukluk gud han blong mi, mi holem ino tufala eg blong faol ia hemi tufala koen we mi stap karem. Mi wantem talem smol long ples ia se bubu blong mi Koran Wilfred oli veri veri klos wetem jif Jimmy Steven oli bin veri klos i kam a taem i gat smol rao bitwin ol pipol long aelan ten mekem se Olsen Kae wetem abu blong mi Koran Wilfred oli go bak long aelan bat tingting blong olgeta se tisfala koen we yu stap luk long pija long ples ia se koen ia taem yumi karem indipendens koen ia nao bambae yumi yusum an veri intresting, bubu blong mi hemi bin stap talem mi ol storian ia an long taem ia long 2004 mi bin gat janis blong holem tufala koen ia long han blong mi so hemia nao bae yu luk Franky Steven hemi stap long nakamal blong hem hemi stap toktok and mi mi gat janis blong askem tufala koen spos mi save holem an hemi bin givim. Tingting blong hem long saed blong kastom in komiuniti divelopmen long Vanuatu sipos ripot i kamaot bae hemi wan veri intresting ripot blong luk wanem nao rol we kastom hemi plem?

Olsem mi stap talem lelebet i gat toktok ia kastom fulap mining hemi kamaot. Samfala ansas we mi stap karem we i stap wetem mi long ples ia se sam ni-Vanuatu i talem se, 'Kastom hemi wei blong laef'. Okei narafala tingting oli talem se, 'Kastom hemi Melanesian wei, hemi minim olsem nomo se hao yumi rispektem pipol, hao yumi helpem pipol etc'. So lelebet hemia long olgeta definisen we oli stap givim taem mifala i stap karemaot risej ia. An taem yu luk long hao nao yumi ol koligs blong yumi long aotsaed oli defaenem toktok ia kastom bambae hemi defren lelebet long wanem we yumi stap traem blong difaenem long tingting blong yumi ol ni-Vanuatu, nao long risej ia mifala i faenem se fulap defrens long ol opinions long topik ia we mifala i stap kari aot risej long hem an insaed long Vanuatu yumi gat olredi ol defrens, i gat defrens blong inta-aelan, yumi gat defrens blong lanwis, sam oli tok Inglis sam oli tok Franis so i gat ol defrens ia finis plas kastom bakegen insaed.

Yu luk hemi no isi se pipol oli faenem hat, traem blong luk wanem rol nao kastom hemi pleim insaed long wan komiuniti o insaed long Vanuatu. Okei ating fulap we mifala i interviuem olgeta oli talem se kastom hemi wan samting we hemi divaedem, i divaedem komiuniti mo mi no save givim ansa blong hem sipos i raet i rong mi no save. Be hemia hem i wanem we mifala i karem from ol pipol we mifala inteviuem olgeta. Nao ating majoriti nao oli talem se kastom hemi wan gud samting bikos hemi yunaetem yumi an wetem yuniti ia nao divelopmen i save go.

Insaed long Vanuatu, Vanuatu hemi wan yunik kantri we kastom blong hem hemi stil strong mo hemi help blong givim divelopmen long nesen ia. Ating hemia nao long big tingting we mi mi olsem wan asisten riseja, mi luk olsem nao se yumi yunik long Pasifik iven wetem kastom we yumi gat yumi save helpem yumi blong yumi save mekem divelopmen long kantri ia an ating las toktok nomo mi wantem talem olsem se mi glad long toktok blong daerekta hemi talem olsem se hemi bildim kapasiti bilding mi mi no ekspektem nating se bae mi mi save mekem wan risej olsem be mi sapraes long mi taem we Mary i givim long mi ol aotlaen ol samting olsem wanem blong mekem i jes kam fil, long Franis oli talem 'à l'aise' nomo blong mi kari aot samting ia. Bikos nomata mi no gat skil long hem bat wetem smol we mi bin lanem hemi helpem mi spos long fiuja wan riseja i kam long Ambrym bambae mi hapi blong wok wetem hem from mi gat smol skils ia finis so ol risej we yufala i bin mekem long pas i kam i stap helpem ol risejas blong mekem wok blong olgeta long kantri. Tangkiu tumas.

Cultural politics and the politics of culture in Vanuatu

Mary Patterson

There are three parts to our introduction. I will begin by talking about the research I began when I first came as a young student to North Ambrym. Then I will briefly discuss the project I have been involved in since 2004 with Ileen and Koran. Both of them will also comment on my early research and on our subsequent collaboration. In 1968, in the Colonial period I first went to North Ambrym because my supervisor Michael Allen said, 'If you want to pursue your interest in sorcery in Melanesia you should go to Ambrym because it is notorious for it.' I was 23 years old when I first went to North Ambrym. Research permission then, was dictated by the colonial government who, if they approved your presence contacted the District Agent in the area you wanted to work in. A message to inquire if a student could come and carry out research was sent to chief Wilfred Koran of Fona village in North Ambrym, the grandfather and namesake of Koran. The Chief agreed and said the student would be looked after. I left Vila for Lakatoro, the headquarters of the colonial district of CD2 where the British District Agent was an Australian named Darvall Wilkins. I had one request—'Please can we arrive in Ambrym in daylight,' I said. 'That's fine,' he replied.

Early the next morning I headed for the wharf to wait for the boat that would take me and Paul Binihi, a colonial government official to Fona. I didn't yet understand 'Vanuatu time' so the wait was much longer than expected and when we reached the shores of Ambrym it was already nightfall.

There were people on the beach who had come to see who was arriving. None of them knew who I was. What is this young woman doing here and how has her father allowed her to come here? My belongings were put on the beach while everyone inspected me. A student perhaps? But why hadn't they sent a man! Whatever are we going to do with this woman? Chief Wilfred took me to his house and said 'Don't worry or be anxious, we will look after you well.' And indeed this was true. I was cared for as a member of Wilfred Koran's family.

When I first arrived Koran junior was just a baby and Ileen was a young girl. At this time *kastom* was very strong and there was a division between Christians and those who maintained *kastom* restrictions. Many were afraid of sorcery that is called *abio* in North Ambrym. I did make a study of sorcery but at the same time I also studied kinship and family. Another interest that I had which was also an interest of Ambrymese, was the 'politics of culture'. *Kastom* was strong but it had its own politics, which was a bit different from the situation today. The politics was around competition between men in the *mage* (this is the North Ambrym word for *namange*) about who would have the highest rank. At this time, Tain Mal of Fanla was the highest ranking Chief and he is Koran's great grandfather (his father's mother's father) and Ileen's grandfather (her mother's father). There were other ways that the division between Christians and *kastom* people made life complicated at times, especially in family relations and weddings where there were differences over the exchange of valuables like pigs. Ileen's uncle Tofor (Tain Mal's son) took the grade of *Meleun* during this period. An example of the difficulty caused by the division between Christians and *kastom* people is illustrated by an incident that happened when Ileen was a girl. Tofor slept in Fona one night, the village of his brother-in-law Wilfred who was married to his sister. According to *kastom,* his presence dictated that a pig should be killed and the pork presented to him. Everyone was worried about where they would find a suitable pig at such short notice. Another factor was that Tofor was feared for his reputation as a sorcerer.

The following picture shows the family standing around the gift of vegetables and meat given to Tofor that morning in 1968.

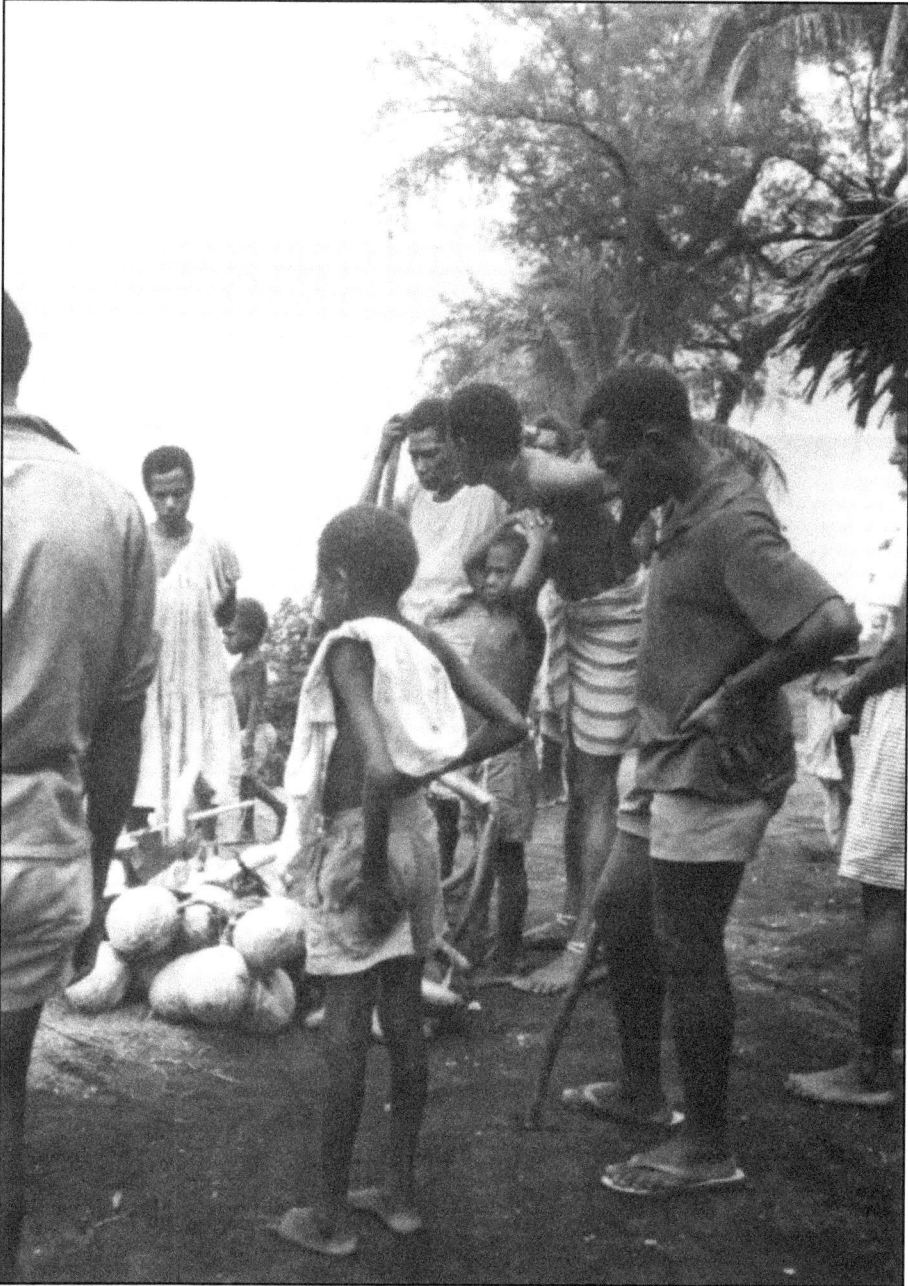

Figure 7.1. The unexpected discovery that Chief Tofor has spent the night in the village requiring presentation of food and meat caused consternation. Koran's father Jonsen stands on the right, Tofor, facing away from the camera is wearing the striped calico over his *nambas*. Fona Village 1968

(Mary Patterson, photographer)

Koran Wilfred

Thank you. My name is Koran and I am employed in the Ministry of Internal Affairs. I expect you will wonder what I am doing here. I call Mary 'Aunty' now because research has turned us into a family. I worked with Mary in 2004. Before I talk about the research I did with Mary in 2004 as her research assistant I want to go back a bit to what she has said about the research she did first as a young woman. I still remember when my grandfather whose name I carry, Koran Wilfred, who was a big Chief in North Ambrym, said this young woman is part of our family now and you should call her 'Aunty' because I will treat her as my daughter. This is something I remember from the time Mary became part of our family in North Ambrym. Something else I would like to mention is that the people of North Ambrym at that time had no idea what this young woman was doing and asked lots of questions. 'Why has she come to live with you?' 'What is she like?' 'How does she come to be here?' 'Where is her father?' In Vanuatu we have strong family ties so there were lots of questions I was asked to answer, 'What does Chief Wilfred think of this white woman who is living in his village?'

To put this in perspective, during this period research was very, very difficult for people to understand; to start with, your skin is different and then you have a different culture. It was not easy to live in a very different community. But one thing I would like to note here is that during this period, the chiefs with the colonial powers of the time had an active role in looking after any strangers who might arrive on their shores. She is an example of the way that the chiefs were held together by this ethic of hospitality to outsiders. So when 'Aunty Mary' arrived, as she mentioned, she found that our family was very helpful in carrying out her research. Another point is that at this time when people found out that Mary was a student they were pleased to cooperate. I remember when she used to visit lots of different villages and my grandfather would say 'you go with Mary to protect her from sorcery'. So, just as he directed us, each time two or three boys would accompany her to the villages as she carried out her research.

So to mention the context again, during her research, people didn't have much of an idea of research objectives or why white people came to live in villages with them, but as I've said it wasn't long before people gained an understanding. 'Yes, she has a project and now you see how others will follow on.' When you asked questions, you might get silly answers but initially people held back their real thoughts because of lack of cultural understanding, making the task of researchers difficult at this time. So I'm really glad that my family was part of that research and I can say here that I'm proud of that. Because we accepted a young lady from an unknown place, my family in the island is part of the development of research that has emerged today. She came and stayed with us and our relationship remains so that whenever she goes back to Australia and returns she must visit the family in Ambrym.

Mary Patterson

The research that we began in 2003 was a pilot project for a bigger study that was supported by a research grant from Australia. I found Wilfred just as he had finished working for the Peace Corps and he was available to help with the research. He was truly a collaborator on this project helping formulate the research questions. The name of the project was Modernity and Governance in Vanuatu. The research came out of concerns shared by many Australian colleagues that in Australia, Pacific Islands were represented as 'weak states' which were part of an 'Arc of Instability' producing a very negative depiction of the region.

This project was designed in collaboration with colleagues working in PNG and Solomons, with my research in Vanuatu and a short period in Solomons. An edited volume based on this work is in preparation for publication next year (Patterson and Macintyre n.d.). This project was very different from the early project that was just focused on North Ambrym. Koran and Ileen collaborated in the pilot project where we used interviews and focus groups. Focus groups consist of asking questions of a group of youths or older people or whatever is appropriate to the information you want to discover. We also carried out interviews with representatives of many different interest groups, politicians, NGOs, peak bodies like the Vanuatu Association of Non-Government Organisations (VANGO), representatives of 'civil society' with a number of different approaches. We also carried out a case-study of Nagriamel and its development after Independence which offers a very interesting demonstration of external influences. One part of this project was to discover how the policies of Aid donors are viewed in Vanuatu, as appropriate or not to local life. Are external policies appropriate in the Pacific or not? We wanted to discover how the policy of promoting 'good governance' and 'civil society' was locally understood. We wanted to investigate resistance to such policies because there has not been a great deal of research in this area.

And now over to Koran and Ileen to discuss in more detail our collaboration on this different kind of project.

Ileen Vira

Good morning everyone. My name is Ileen and I am also a member of the family Koran has talked about. Mary Patterson arrived in the New Hebrides when I was eleven years old. At this time I was at School in Santo but during my holidays I often accompanied her as she did her research. After more than 20 years she returned to carry out more research. Koran and I travelled around a lot with her doing interviews in Ambrym and Santo. As she said, we met many representatives of different parts of society and people in the islands. Last year we went to Ambrym to do a survey of peoples' views mainly about civil society. We interviewed a lot of community leaders. We also went to schools in Ambrym where we distributed a survey form to principals to give to students. You can see me in the picture at Ranon Secondary School (Figure 7.2). We also interviewed Olsen Kai a Nagriamel leader involved in the struggle for Independence. That's about it from me. I work now in the Secret Garden (Mele) as a French-speaking tour guide where I have to do a lot of explanation about *kastom*. In relation to the collaboration Mary was speaking about with our family, the famous Chief mentioned, Chief Tofor, was my uncle. We were able to help Mary because we had access to the *kastom* village of Fanla where *kastom* was extremely strong. Mary has been able to document the history of Fanla village.

Thank you for listening.

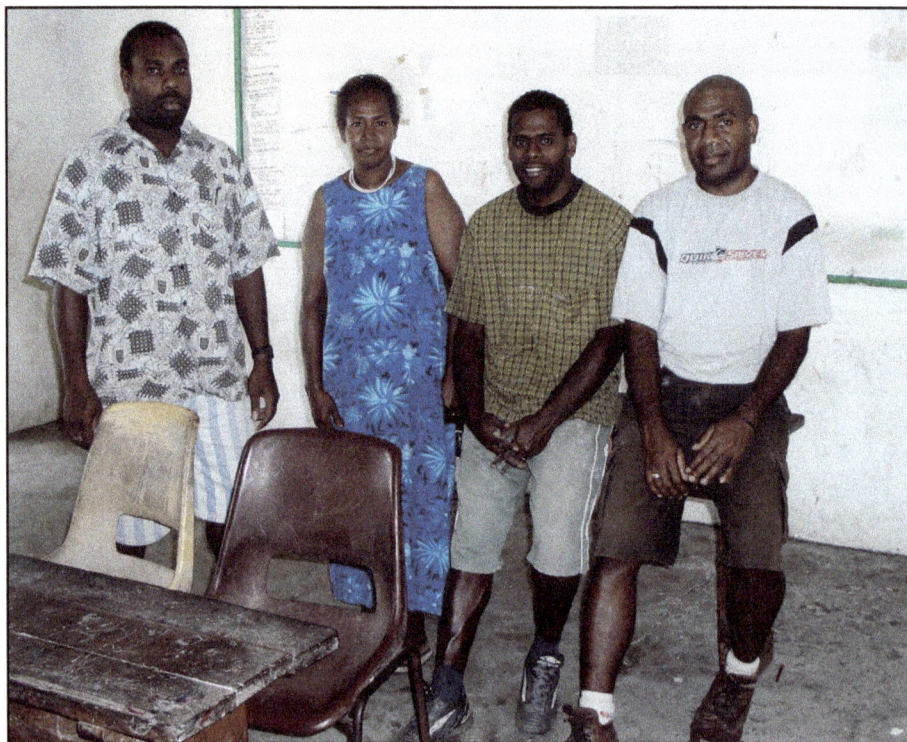

Figure 7.2. Ileen Vira with three of the teachers at the Ranon Secondary School North Ambrym

(Mary Patterson, photographer)

Koran Wilfred

I would like to say something more about the research we carried out where I was the research assistant in 2004. The picture below is from the project that the VKS gave Mary as a research project. I said to her 'this is a very interesting project that I'm involved in because it is about discovering the role that *kastom* has in development in Vanuatu.' The questions that we asked made us realise that for the people of Vanuatu, the word *kastom* already carries many different meanings for different people. I'm not talking here about our overseas friends but what was interesting for me was finding out, as a ni-Vanuatu, what people thought the role of *kastom* in development was all about.

Before I take this any further I want to talk a little bit about how I came to be the research assistant on this project. I told Mary, 'I have a few connections round here.' I know people in government, in the Churches and in the communities of Port Vila. She said, 'OK I need you to work on this research project with me.' So with my help and my connections in Vila we did some really good research as you will see from the previous pictures of interviews with politicians, director generals, government officials, youth groups, secondary school principals and students.

We used various methods, interviews, some recordings were made at schools, and sometimes we just had discussions and got people talking, after which we would go back and put it all together. First of all we worked in Port Vila, then outside the centre a bit at places like Seaside and Freswota and then we went to Santo where we had the same sort of discussions on the topic. We went as far as Fanafo and you can see the picture of me with Franky Steven (Figure 7.3). If you look closely at my hand, you will see that I am not holding two eggs, but two coins (Figure 7.4).

I want to tell you a little bit about this place. My grandfather Koran Wilfred was very close to Chief Jimmy Steven until there came a time when there was a dispute with the island people (of Santo) which meant that Olsen Kai and my grandfather Koran Wilfred went back to their island. But they knew that these coins that you see in the picture would be used one day when it was time for Independence. This is very interesting to me because my grandfather told me this history and then in 2004 I got the chance to hold these two coins in my hand. We were talking to Franky in his *nakamal* about this period and I asked him if I could hold the coins and he agreed. His opinions on the role of *kastom* in community development will make very interesting reading in the report on this issue.

I want to talk a little about the many meanings of *kastom*. Some of the answers I got from ni-Vanuatu were '*kastom* is a way of life'; others said '*kastom* is the Melanesian way, meaning how we respect people, how we help them and so on.'

These were the sorts of definitions we got when we were carrying out this research. If you examine now how our overseas colleagues define the discussion of *kastom*, we will find that it differs a bit from the meanings given by we ni-Vanuatu. And in this research we already found many differences on this topic in this country: inter-island differences, language differences, those of English and French and so on.

Figure 7.3. Franky Steven with Koran Wilfred at Fanafo October 2004

(Mary Patterson, photographer)

Figure 7.4. Koran holds one of the coins minted for Nagriamel (left) and another for Solomon Islands

(Mary Patterson, photographer)

It is no easy task to discover what role people think *kastom* plays in a community or in Vanuatu. Many of the people we interviewed said that *kastom* is something that divides people, it divides communities. I cannot say myself whether this is the case or not. But this is something that we took from the people we interviewed. The majority however, said that *kastom* is a good thing because it unites us and with unity development is able to proceed.

Vanuatu is a unique country in which *kastom* remains strong and assists in developing the nation. As a research assistant this was the central idea for me. I see now that we are unique in the Pacific; even with the *kastom* that we have we are able to help ourselves go forward in the development of this country. Finally, I want to say that I am pleased by what the Director (of the VKS) said in his speech about building capacity. I had never ever expected to be doing research but I was surprised at myself when Mary gave me the research outline that it felt quite comfortable, in French we would say 'à l'aise', that I should do this research. It did not matter that I wasn't trained but what I have learned will enable me to collaborate should a researcher come to Ambrym in the future. Having acquired some skills, I would be pleased to assist. The research that all of you have carried out in the past remains to help all future researchers in their endeavours in this country. Thank you.

References

Bresnihan, Brian and Keith Woodward (eds), 2002. *Tufala Gavman: Reminiscences from the Anglo-French Condominium of the New Hebrides*. Suva, Fiji: Institute of Pacific Studies, University of the South Pacific.

Caplan, Pat, 1992. Engendering knowledge: the politics of ethnography. In *Persons and Powers of Women in Diverse Cultures*, ed. Shirley Ardener, 65–87. Oxford: Berg Publishers Ltd.

Clifford, James, 1986. *Writing Culture: The Poetics and Politics of Ethnography*. Berkeley: University of California Press.

Douglas, Mary, 1975. 'If the dogon....' In *Implicit Meanings. Essays in Anthropology*, ed. Mary Douglas, 124–41. London. Routledge and Kegan Paul.

Marcus, George, 1998. *Ethnography through Thick and Thin*. Princeton New Jersey: Princeton University Press.

Patterson, Mary, 2002. Moving histories: the dynamics of place and movement in North Ambrym, Vanuatu. *Persons and Powers of Women in Diverse Cultures* 13(2): 200–18.

Patterson, Mary, 2003. Leading lights in the 'Mother of Darkness': perspectives on leadership and value in North Ambrym, Vanuatu. *Oceania* 73(2): 126–42.

Patterson, Mary, 2006. 'Finishing the land': identity and land use in pre and post colonial North Ambrym. In *Sharing the Earth, Dividing the Land: Territorial Categories and Institutions in the Austronesian World*, ed. Thomas Reuter and James Fox, 323–44. Pandanus Books, Canberra.

Patterson, Mary and Martha Macintyre (eds), n.d. *Managing Modernity: Capitalism, Cosmology and Globalization in the Pacific*. St. Lucia: University of Queensland Press (forthcoming 2011).

8. Ol Woman Filwoka

Jean Tarisesei

Tangkiu long yufala evriwan we i stap, olsem ol big big man blong ol risejas we oli bin stap finis an ol filwokas an evriwan we i stap long ples ia ol staff. Mi talem tangkiu blong mekem se mifala tu mifala i save tek pat long sam toktok o sam risej blong mifala ol filwokas. Mi wantem talem smol nomo olsem se Richard hemi bin toktok finis olsem hemi talemaot wanem nao wok blong ol filwokas an ol woman filwokas olsem netwok blong olgeta i jes stat nomo. Long 1994 we fes woksop blong olgeta i bin stap olsem Richard i bin talem finis an hem nao hemi bin helpem aot helpem mifala blong soem mifala wanem nao mifala i sud mekem o ol woksop blong mifala i sud go olsem wanem an olsem smol toktok nomo long saed blong hao hemi bin kam antap olsem long taem ia kaljoral senta hemi gat bod blong hem finis, bod blong hem i stap finis. So long mi ting blong bod ia oli bin diskas long taem lelebet blong faenemaot se hao nao bae oli karem ol woman tu olsem filwokas. Ating long taem ia ol man we oli bin stap ia oli no tingbaot se ol woman tu oli pat blong ol wok blong kastom we oli stap mekem long ol aelans oli tinkabaot olgeta nomo. So toktok i kam se man hemi mekem wok i gud be sam samting we oli no tokabaot we woman hemi kontribiut long hem we hemi bigwan long ol wok blong olgeta tu long saed blong kastom. An so oli kamap wetem tingting se i gud blong gat ol woman tu from woman hemi mekem se wok blong kastom hemi balans from sapos man nomo i tokabaot wan samting be i gat woman tu i gat pat blong hem we hemi tokabaot mo hemi plei long hem blong mekem se kastom hemi ful hemi balans.

So let Grace Molisa hemi bin stap long tat taem ia so hemi bin toktok strong se hemi mas gat network blong ol woman filwokas an tu long taem ia yumi save se Dr. Lissant Bolton hemi bin stap long Australian Miusium mo hemi stap kam long Vanuatu Kaljoral Senta blong stap helpaot blong lanem olgeta staf blong mekem katalog ol samting olsem. So long taem ia hem wan i bin mekem risej blong hem long Ambae long saed blong mat blong Ambae.

Mi bin stap long taem ia mi wok klosli wetem netwok blong VNCW an tat taem ia hemi bin wok wetem narafala woman be i kam long wan taem se mi bin wok wetem hem festaem hemi no save mekem so mekem se mi mi stap long risej wetem hem. Olsem long taem ia tu mi lanem tu hao blong mekem risej an mi no save se kastom hemi olsem wanem be hemi stat an ten mi go tru mi save se yes kastom hemi olsem. So mifala i talem tangkiu long Dr. Lisa Bolton wetem long taem ia tu. Dr. Darell Tryon hem tu hemi stap kam long woksop blong ol man hemi bin helpem mifala tu hemi kontribiut an hao Kirk Huffman hem tu hemi bin kontribiut plante long woksop blong mifala ol woman. I save gohed an mi gat wetem mi long ples ia tu ol woman we oli bin stap olsem filwokas. Long fes woksop blong mifala long 1994 mifala i bin gat ten woman nomo an as mifala i go along an ten mifala i stap tekem ol narafala oli kam nao ia mifala i gat abaot foti woman filwokas. An olsem mifala i bin wok, olsem ol topiks blong mifala we mifala i jusum hemi menli long saed blong wok blong ol woman olsem hao blong lukaotem pikinini taem hemi smol i kam antap an hao ol woman oli tekem rang blong olgeta olsem ol erias we mifala i luk se i nid blong ol woman oli save ol samting ia an wok hemi blong mifala ol woman an mifala i tokabaot kastom mared from hemia kontribiusen i bigwan long saed blong ol woman an tu ol woman long sam erias oli gat rang blong olgeta. So i gat ol topiks blong mifala we i kam kasem tede olsem mifala i luk se wanem we i stap go blong lus mo wanem nao i impoten long laef blong mifala ol woman.

Ating bae mi si smol smol se risej long samtaems hemi isi mo samtaems hemi had olsem bae mi talem wan tingting se mifala ol woman mifala i gat fulap netwok olsem ol organaesesen mekem se sam oli go long ol komiuniti oli talem difren toktok an ten sam oli go talem difren toktok an samtaems mifala i go olsem long wok blong mifala an mekem se hemia nao i had tu blong go tru long ol komiuniti. Ating long mi, mi faenem olsem samtaems i had sam taems hemi isi bat wok blong ol risejas wetem ol projeks we mifala i karem tru long netwoks blong mifala ating hemia nao hemi help bigwan blong mekem se wok blong mifala i save kam antap an ol woman filwokas taem riseja i go stap wetem hem hemi mekem se hem tu i save hao blong mekem wok blong hem ol risej blong hem. So long saed blong mi, mi faenem se i olsem nao se projeks wetem ol risejas we oli kam stap long aelans wetem olgeta hemia nao oli promotem wok blong olgeta bigwan.

The Women Fieldworkers

Jean Tarisesei

Thank you to everyone here, including all the senior researchers, all the fieldworkers, and staff. Thank you especially for making it possible to take part within the same forum, researchers and fieldworkers together. I would like to describe briefly, following on from Richard Leona, what the work of fieldworkers and especially the new women's fieldworker network is. The first women's fieldworker workshop was held in 1994. At this time Richard Leona helped to show us what we should do, and how our workshop should proceed. He also explained how the idea of a women's fieldworker network arose within Vanuatu Kaljoral Senta board meetings.

The issue of how to create a women's fieldworker program had been discussed for some time in Vanuatu Kaljoral Senta board meetings. I think that at this time the men who sat on this board hadn't thought about the idea that women, too, are a part of the work of *kastom* that occurs throughout the islands, but they only thought of themselves. However it became clear that while men perform good work, there are some things that women contribute that men don't talk about, and these are also a part of this work relating to *kastom*. As a result, they came up with the idea that it would be good to have women involved too, because women make the work of *kastom* balanced. If men are talking about something, and women also take part in the conversation, and play with it, this makes *kastom* full and balanced.

The late Grace Molisa was around at this time, and she spoke strongly about the need for a network of women fieldworkers. Also at this time Dr. Lissant Bolton was working at the Australian Museum, and would come to the Vanuatu Kaljoral Senta to help staff members learn how to do such things as make catalogues. At this time she was the only foreign researcher in the country, and was working on the topic of mats on Ambae. Meanwhile, I was here in Port Vila and working closely with the networks of the Vanuatu National Council of Women (VNCW), and while Lissant originally worked with another woman, that didn't work out, so I assumed the role of being her research counterpart. So at this time I also learned how to perform research, and although I didn't know what *kastom* was about, the more I worked the more I realised its importance. We therefore need to thank Dr. Lissant Bolton for her work at this time. Dr. Darrell Tryon was also coming to the men's workshops, and he also contributed to the instigation of the women's workshop, as did Kirk Huffman.

Here with me today are some of the first women fieldworkers. At our first workshop in 1994 we had only ten women. We have now grown to having about 40 women fieldworkers. The topics that we have chosen have mainly related to women's work, such as childrearing, *kastom* marriage, and how women acquire rank. These are all areas that we believe women have a need to know about. The topics we have covered so far relate to practices and knowledge that we believe are being lost, and things that are important to our lives as women.

I would like to add that sometimes our work is hard—sometimes easy, but also sometimes hard. For example, we women have many networks and organisations, and this means that some of these go into particular communities and say one thing, while some go and say another. As a result, sometimes when we arrive to work as fieldworkers we find it is difficult to enter these communities. I think that for me, while it is sometimes easy and sometimes hard, the work of researchers and the projects that we carry through our networks contribute greatly to the development of our work. It is also important that when researchers come to stay with women fieldworkers they have particular skills which help them with their research. I have found that projects involving researchers that work with women fieldworkers are more successful.

9. Women Fieldworkers' Collaborative Research: On the History of House-Girls in Vanuatu

Margaret Rodman, Leisara Kalotiti and Numalin Mahana

This chapter describes a unique, collaborative project with contributions from twenty-one indigenous and four expatriate women. It led to a book, called *House-Girls Remember* that was launched in spirit at the Port Vila Conference in November 2006, and published in 2007. At the conference the three of us collaborated in anecdotally presenting material from our research. Here, in a more formal way, we offer some excerpts from our respective sections of the book, edited and summarised to reflect what we talked about at the conference. Margaret Rodman spoke about, and has revised here, material she co-authored with Daniela Kraemer, Lissant Bolton, and Jean Tarisesei. While the conference presentation was in Bislama, this chapter, like our book, is in English with text boxes in Bislama.

Margaret Rodman

While women's history is a popular topic globally, Pacific Island women have had few opportunities to conduct research and publish in this field. A 2001 workshop in Port Vila on the history of house-girls in Vanuatu provided such an opportunity. The goal of our workshop was to record the recollections of indigenous women who had lived and worked as house-girls during the Anglo-French Condominium of the New Hebrides, before Vanuatu gained independence in 1980.[1] This was a special workshop for selected women fieldworkers with an interest in moving beyond training workshops to conduct historical research. Lissant Bolton and Jean Tarisesei convened the workshop for which I had obtained funding as part of a larger study of gender and race in Vanuatu's settler history.[2] The results of this collaborative research project were so interesting and important for ni-Vanuatu and other Pacific islanders that we decided to publish them as a co-edited book.

In addition to our contributions as editors, the resulting book includes workshop reports by eleven ni-Vanuatu women fieldworkers and ten others

1   For historical context regarding the Anglo-French Condominium of the New Hebrides see MacClancy (1981) and Bresnihan and Woodward (2002).
2   For financial support of this project, we are grateful to York University, the Social Sciences and Humanities Research Council of Canada, and the Rockefeller Foundation.

who spoke about their personal experiences as house-girls.[3] A York student, Daniela Kraemer, contributed the results of her research with Port Vila-area house-girls in 2001, and co-edited the book. Jean Mitchell contributed a piece on a Vietnamese orphan who became a house-girl.

Employers of house-girls discussed in our workshop included English or French government officials, missionaries, and settlers (planters, traders, and small business people). Most of the employers were considered to be white (mainly English- or French-speaking), but the women identified some employers in Bislama as *Sinwa*, which literally means Chinese (from the French *chinois*), but includes Vietnamese and other Southeast Asians. The cost of labour was low enough that virtually every expatriate had the option of hiring a house-girl in the colonial period. Domestic workers were essential to maintaining even a fairly simple expatriate lifestyle. The climate, the kind of housing employers lived in, and the lifestyle to which they aspired required constant defence, waged with brooms and buckets, against ants, rats, cockroaches, mosquitoes, spider webs and mud.

A few house-girls worked for ni-Vanuatu women who lived with white men, and one in our workshop worked for a white woman married to a ni-Vanuatu man, but all had western lifestyles. Today, many house-girls work for ni-Vanuatu couples (see Ch. 9), but before independence this was rare. The workshop recorded one such experience from the early days of the independence movement in 1970, as Leisara Kalotiti describes in the next section.

Working for a leader of the independence movement

Leisara Kalotiti

I was born on 17 May 1956. I finished school in 1969 and I wasn't doing anything in particular. In 1970, Peter Taurokoto (from Lelepa Island off North Efate) was transferred to Santo as Assistant Education Officer. He was married to Nelly (from Tongoa) and they had one daughter at that time. So I went to work for them as their house-girl. That's what they called me. I was afraid on the flight to Santo; it was the first time I had been on a plane. I knew nothing about being

---

3   The fieldworkers participating in the workshop were: Numalin Mahana (Tanna), Mailie Michael (Tanna), Lena Kalmat (Pango), Leisara Kalotiti (North Efate), Lesaruru Tamearu (North Efate), Sinlemas Kalo (North Efate), Lewia Charlie (Tongoa), Lucy Moses (Ambrym), Tanni Frazer (Malakula), Siaban Denison (Pentecost), Kate Ruth (Banks). The former house-girls were: Edna Albert (Pango), Eva Kaltapan (Pango), Netty Joseph (North Efate), Lonnette Tasale (North Efate), Lepakoa Dick (Tongoa), Rachel (Ambrym), Estelle (Malakula), Robin Ken (Malakula), Françoise Molwai (Pentecost), Jocelyn Kibi (Banks).

a house-girl. I didn't know how to use an electric iron or anything like that. Nelly showed me how to use the settings on the iron—steam, cotton, delicate. Nelly taught at Sarakata Primary School. They lived in the British Paddock (headquarters for the British District Agency, Northern District) on the edge of town.

I still remember that on 26 March, Donald Kalpokas, who was teaching at Hog Harbour, went with Peter to Malo Island to hold a discussion about the government taking over the education system. They wanted to know what the Malo people thought about this and they found out! The Malo people were so angry about this news that they refused to feed Donald and Peter. After that, the two men stayed up very late talking. That's when they decided to form a Cultural Association (that led to the formation of the Vanua'aku Pati). The District Agent asked them to come to his house, not his office, and he loaned them a truck. They drove to the Rarua family's place to talk more about their plans. They concluded that all land should come back to ni-Vanuatu, and they decided to press for independence.

So I worked as a house-girl for a man who was part of the beginning of the independence movement. I looked after the firstborn, Nancy (who became a nurse) and then I looked after the second daughter, Amy (who became the first ni-Vanuatu woman to train as an airplane pilot). My salary was $12 Australian every two weeks. Peter and Nelly opened a savings account for me. After I married I stopped working for them, but they would give me gifts of sugar when they saw me in town. They were kind to me.

> *Having trained as a house-girl with the Taurokota family, in 1972 Leisara went to work for an Australian pastor in Paton Memorial Church named John Casey, a man she remembers for his kindness.*

Working for kindly Pastor Casey

Leisara Kalotiti

When my father, who was an elder, went to a Presbyterian meeting, Pastor Casey told my father that he wanted a house-girl. So my father came back to our island, and told me to think about whether I wanted to work for Pastor Casey, or not. I thought that he would be all right, and that if he didn't find another house-girl, I would be happy to go and work for him.

I worked for Pastor Casey for one year. Pastor Casey had five children, two boys and three girls. The two boys lived in Australia, and the two girls lived in the

New Hebrides, as Vanuatu was called before. They gave me a room, and so I slept in the house with them. They ate in the morning, and in the afternoon, and we shared the food. Whatever they ate, I also ate.

Figure 9.1. Women fieldworkers at the conference in 2006, including Leisara Kalotiti (far right) who contributed to House-Girls Remember

(John Taylor, photographer)

You all know what we black people eat, but the white people, some of the white people's food we don't know. So sometimes when the food came to the table, I would look at the food; I wouldn't know what it was, and I would be frightened. Some of their food I knew but I remember one food that I didn't know. It came in a tin, the mushroom I think. When we wanted to eat, I felt like I was going to throw up. I tasted a little, that's all. But I tried it anyway because my boss said that I had to eat, that if I didn't eat I'd be hungry. And so I ate.

I didn't think about going home on the weekends. Only one time did I go home on the weekend. I slept with them in the house, and I saw that their ways were good. The food that we ate, we shared it together. So I didn't really think about going home. I only went home one time. The time that I did go, I came back Sunday afternoon, because Monday I had to start work again. So I didn't go back to the island too much, just one time that's all.

I was glad to work for them. The *misis* and the master, their ways were good. They paid me $5 Australian every two weeks. I swept the house, I washed the plates, I cleaned around outside, I washed the bathroom and the toilet. Sometimes the *misis* would send me to the market to buy vegetables. Sometimes the *misis* would make a list for me to go down to the store to go shopping. I would go and make the shopping at the Burns Philp, now it's called the General Store, it's close to the market house. So that's the place where I would go to make the shopping.

Their ways were good, and their children were also kind to me. Whenever they would come back from school they would bring back some chocolate. And when I finished doing one thing, they would sing out to me, 'Stop your work and come and we'll eat some biscuits or some chocolate.'

I was happy to be with them. The pastor took care of me. He knew that being on the island was different, that life was different. That when you come to town, life is different, town is different. When I stayed with them in Vila, he took care of me. He would tell me that if I wanted to go out I would have to tell them where I was going and when I would come back to the house.

I worked for them for one year then I went back to my island. I was married in 1977. My husband was a teacher who lived on Tanna. So we went to Tanna, and stayed there until I was about to give birth for a second time in 1982. That year, we all came back to Efate for the Christmas holidays. When we were back I went by the hospital. Pastor Casey saw me in town, and said to me, 'You know where we live, that we're at the Paton Memorial Church, so why did you wander around town like this, and you didn't come and say hello to us in the house where we all ate together?' That is what he said to me. I was frightened. He said, 'Next time you go to the hospital, you have to come to the house.'

So when I went to their house, he and the *misis* said we had to go to the office. And when we went to the office, they put a sewing machine on the table and told me that they were giving the machine to me. It's a second-hand machine from an Australian man. An Australian man brought it with him and left it at the church office. That man had paid for it, but they gave it to me for free. I took it. I used it on Tanna, I still use it today. Once it had a small problem, but I managed to fix it. So I still use it today.

In January, I went to the hospital to give birth to my baby. Pastor Casey was there visiting a friend of his. He saw me at the hospital. At the hospital, the food is not what you and I black people like to eat. So the time when he came, he passed by and saw me. He asked me what time I had come to the hospital. I told him that I had come yesterday. He looked at the plate of food that they had given me. It was on the little cupboard that they give you at the hospital to put your things inside. My plate had two bananas that weren't ripe at all, and this soup. He came and said, 'Leisara, is this your food?' I said, 'Yes.' He said, 'How is it possible for a woman to give birth to a baby when all they give her to eat are unripe bananas?' He told me that he wasn't happy with the food they had given me, that I shouldn't eat it, that when they come in I should tell them to take the food away. He said that he was going to tell his wife to prepare some food and he would bring it. So I didn't eat the hospital food. He went to his house. The *misis* prepared some food for me, and he brought it in a container. Later he brought me some fruit, some apples, pears and oranges. He came and gave it all to me. That day was Saturday. In the afternoon I started feeling some small pain. At about midnight I gave birth to my baby.

On Sunday morning, he came and visited me. He came by, and he said that he had gone to the ward, and he had asked the nurse. So he had found out that I had given birth to twins, two boys, but that one was alive, and one was dead. When he came in, he was sorry that I had lost one of the twins. He came and prayed. And he gave me some encouraging talk. When he went back to his house, he told the *misis* that Leisara gave birth to twins, but sadly, only one lived.

So, in my opinion, this master, his ways were good. He was very good. I remember he told me to call him 'papa', and her 'mama'. Our friendship was very good. Our relationship was strong. I liked them, and they too liked me.

Collaborative research in practice

Margaret Rodman

The history of house-girls project has methodological significance for anthropological fieldwork. Part of our intent was to produce a book that: 1. shows how unwritten histories of women's experiences can be documented in Pacific Island contexts; 2. demonstrates ways in which indigenous women can write their own histories of gendered experience in colonial contexts; and 3. suggests what collaborative roles indigenous and expatriate anthropologists can play in this process. Indigenous fieldworkers are central to this collaboration, yet foreign scholars are not excluded. In sum, the collaborative approach demonstrates possibilities for redefining post-colonial research in Pacific anthropology and beyond. Leisara Kalotiti clearly contributed to achieving these goals, as did Numalin Mahana, a fieldworker from Tanna, who used the metaphor of a house to put into words the sense of shared involvement with a project bigger than any one of us:

[This research] is like a house which has a treasure inside—you have to open the doors to see this treasure. I don't know if the metaphor makes sense, but it is as if you have to open a door or a window, and when you do you see instructions telling you where to go. You open another door, and then you see an arrow pointing in the direction you should follow next. What interests me so much about fieldworker research, is that the more research you do, the more you find that the work is without end, it goes on and on.

Numalin went on to comment on the diversity of kinds of white people who employed house-girls:

The topic of this workshop, house-girls, seems to me to be an especially large one, because if you classify white people, then you have traders of many nationalities, there are many kinds of missionaries, there are the nuns, the hospital matrons. These people don't do the same work; there are doctors, district agents, teachers, many different professions. I'm talking here from the perspective from my island: there were many different kinds of people who worked on Tanna, which was a centre like Santo, Malakula and Vila. That is why I think this is no small subject.

She offered recollections from her Tanna childhood when she lived with her grandmother who was a house-girl for a missionary family and later with an aunt who worked for a trader. Numalin was curious about the white people and a keen though covert observer of their customs and culture.

Studying white people's ways as a Tanna girl

Numalin Mahana

When I lived with my grandmother, I was able to see how she worked for the missionary. She worked, but I just played. I went to watch her do her master's ironing. The missionary did the washing, but the washing was done in a kind of washing machine. I can't describe the machine now, my memory isn't clear, but I remember a big iron thing, when it was turned on all the clothes flew around in it. All of us used to hide so we could watch it—me and all the village children. When we heard the truck coming we used to run away, we'd hide. Or if the missionary turned up, we would take off and hide. Eventually we discovered that the missionary was kind and wasn't going to chase us, and then we began to feel free to come out of our hiding places.

When a child was sick or one of us fell down, we used to go and ask for medicine, because when the missionaries came—I don't know if this was true in other places too—when they came, they were well-equipped, they had medicines. In those days there was no hospital, they treated people in the village. So they worked as doctors too. Anybody who was sick used to go to them; we always used to go to them.

At the time I'm talking about I wasn't yet going to school, the bigger children went to school. I used to follow them, I used to go and watch. Sometimes I used to watch the trucks. Two or three trucks would come, with lots of white people inside. We would go and hide and look through the window, or through the holes, to see what the white people were doing. Our parents told us about the war, how in the past men had fought and raced around. When we looked at the white men like this we were trying to find out what they would do. Would they bring guns, or would they bring tinned fish or tinned meat or something else? We couldn't communicate with them. It was hard to talk. Eventually the missionaries learnt our language and talked to us, and then we went closer to them, we mixed together and played.

They gave rice and tinned meat to my grandmother, and she cooked it in a special style. She would boil the rice and then turn the tinned meat into it and stir it, mixing it together. I don't know if you're familiar with this style of cooking or not, but that was the kind they made. When they shared out the food, many of us there lined up for it. They didn't share it out on plates, they served it on newspapers that they had finished reading. My grandmother would put a small helping on some newspaper, and pass it to us. We felt pretty pleased that we'd done better than other children by getting to eat some of the missionaries' leftovers.

That's about as much as I remember. Once I started going to school I learned that they were missionaries and that we must respect them. So I stopped going to their house, and I didn't eat their food any more. I kept away. I kept away because I knew that it was important to be respectful towards them. So that's the first experience I remember.

My second experience was when I stayed with an aunt of mine who also worked for a white man. He was a businessman, an Australian. He came by himself, without a wife, and he made his station near our village. Someone in our family gave him the land and he built a house on it. He called his house Newcastle. I imagine that is the name of the place in Australia that he came from. He built a big house, a store, a cinema and a copra shed.

As far as food goes, I never knew what food the Master ate. He wasn't the sort of person whose place was easy to go near. Sometimes we used to go and collect tins or plastic from his rubbish heap. Some of us who remember things as they were, remember crawling carefully. When the house-girl threw out the rubbish, we would go and get things for ourselves. We would get newspaper, tins, and bring them back. If we heard the door slam we'd say, 'Oh! The master will shoot us now!', and then we'd race for our lives. We really were frightened that he would shoot us.

Their rubbish dump was on the path to the sea, so it was close by. I would creep to it. The Master's house was a little bit away from it. So when we saw them throwing rubbish away and walking away, we would come from the other side and pick up the rubbish. We might see a tin, and keep it as a good container for collecting water. Some of our mothers didn't actually tell us not to this, and I never heard my grandmother speak about it, but I felt that they disapproved. So I would hide these things initially, so that she wouldn't see them straight away. I'd hide things and then I'd bring them out gradually. I thought if I brought them out immediately she'd know I'd been to the rubbish heap. So I made a point of hiding them. But I wanted to look at the newspaper, so I'd take it.

The tins, tins that held fruit and tins that held fish, we would bring back. They were very useful for us children. We'd break them, and make small trucks, or we'd tie ropes to them and make them into shoes to walk about with. You might call it rubbish, but when we took these things and transformed them they became great toys for us.

Concluding themes

Margaret Rodman

Themes underlying stories that the fieldworkers and other women told resonate with the experiences of domestic workers around the world. Some of these themes include:

Work

Fieldworkers and former house-girls talked about 'work' as a colonial concept, in effect a new way of ordering space and time. The idea of working hours, starting at 7:30 a.m., breaking at midday, then resuming work from 1:30 or 2 p.m. until late afternoon, was strongly associated with the world of expatriates' churches, schools and workplaces, and was a major adjustment for women used to more flexible rhythms of village life.

Washing clothes was a dominant topic in the workshop reports. Boiling, bluing, starching, and ironing were tasks described in detail. The clothes themselves were often different to what the house-girls wore at home; the fabrics, styles and ways of washing and ironing them were of interest to the workshop participants. Food and cooking also received a lot of attention. In particular, clothing and food stood out as markers of cultural difference. The fact that one former house-girl had a collection of saucepans in her bamboo house as an old woman was taken as a sign that she had worked for white families.

We noted the short periods for which women worked as house-girls. For many, working as a house-girl was a transitional occupation between school or childhood and marriage. Working for a few months or less was not uncommon. Some women, as fieldworker Tanni Frazer put it, refused to consider working as house-girls because they would not be any man's 'slave'. Many others left employment when the *Misis* shouted at them, or the pay was too low, or the equipment they had to use was too baffling, or because they wanted to do something else. In the pre-independence world where subsistence agriculture remained an ever present option—something less available to current urban ni-Vanuatu—working for wages was not a necessity and house-girls could generally go back to their village and garden.

Figure 9.2. Tanni Frazer, Netty Joseph, and Francoise Molwai at the house-girls' workshop in 2001

(Lady Patricia Garvey, photographer)

Money

Every workshop report mentioned money. If the presenter didn't say how much a house-girl was paid, it would be one of the first questions asked. Much discussion ensued about the relative purchasing power of money. While two pounds in the 1950s did not sound like much, the women agreed that two pounds once bought a lot of goods. Occasionally, a woman said the money she was paid was irrelevant. For others, the lack of money in their household prevented them from continuing their education and led them to seek employment as house-girls. The 'bad old days' before independence when wages were low and colonial employers could be arrogant and even racist, were sometimes seen as the 'good old days' because money went so much further and employers provided payment in kind—especially, housing, food, and transport.

Communication

Some employers were fluent in Bislama and a few whites born in the islands were native speakers of a local language; others, notably some missionaries on Malakula, waited until they had learned the local language to hire house-girls. But many employers knew little Bislama when they first hired house-girls and, especially in recollections from before World War II, the house-girls sometimes had limited knowledge of Bislama. Workshop reports included some very funny stories about miscommunication, about joking behaviour that played with language, as well as some skilful imitations of English, French and Chinese employers' speech and body language.

Vanuatu's linguistic diversity as well as its geography—many islands with rugged volcanic terrain—have made communication throughout the group problematic. While this posed, and still poses, difficulties for administrators and for the economy, communication gaps could work to the advantage of women who wanted to escape from an intolerable, local situation. One story in our book tells of an Ambae woman seeking refuge on a settler's ship in the early 1900s. The woman was unhappily married to a chief with ten wives, and seemed— although we will never know for sure—to prefer life working on the Whitford's Islet of Pakea in the Banks Islands. As the fieldworker reported, such women were glad to know that when they ran away they were unlikely to be found. 'People in those days did not know how to speak Bislama or English. And when a woman went away on a ship, the men were afraid to call out or to ask after her because they were afraid of the white men. It was like that. They couldn't do anything about it.'

Perceptions of women

Received wisdom in Vanuatu suggests that men were the ones who travelled and that women did not move much outside their own areas. Movement to a husband's village at marriage might be the only move a woman made. Yet the workshop showed how those who worked as house-girls moved a lot, even in the colonial period. Some paddled from one island to another to go to work, as one workshop participant did when she was still a child. Others moved to Santo or Vila towns. Some house-girls left their home island to follow a relocating employer, as Jean Tarisesei described in her workshop presentation about Tongoan house-girls who moved with Stan and Olive Breusch to Ambae.

Much of the house-girls' movement was not simply from one physical location to another but into white spaces that were out of bounds for other ni-Vanuatu. In their employers' homes, house-girls had a chance to acquire their own perceptions of the women for whom they worked. They developed notions of domesticity, of how women from other cultures (notably French, English/ Australian, Chinese/Vietnamese) prepared food, cleaned house, washed clothes, sewed, and how they cared for infants and children. These activities provided much to talk about in the workshop, as participants explored the practices of everyday life in colonial times, some of which continue to influence the way island women live their lives today.

Relationships

Perhaps not surprisingly, given the topic of the workshop, relationships with expatriates were central to participants' reports. Male employers worked, that much seemed clear, but what the *Misis* did was often mysterious to the former house-girls. In other research, Margaret Rodman recorded many stories from white women about the hard work they did on plantations, but the stories that came out in the workshop often concerned female employers who had the time to be very critical of their house-girls and who seemed less kind than male employers. Why this is so bears reflection. Possibly male employers had less to do with house-girls and being more remote, as Robin Ken's story in the book suggests, could afford to seem more soft-hearted than the *Misis*? Male employers, too, were always possible sexual partners, even if that possibility was only theoretical, and this may have coloured house-girls' assessments of them as at once more frightening and more attractive than their wives.

Even ni-Vanuatu women came off worse than men as employers. Ni-Vanuatu women who were settlers' mistresses, as stories from Ambrym and Malakula suggest, seem to have asked more work of house-girls—including vegetable gardening, for example—than expatriate employers, even though some of the mistresses in question started out as house-girls themselves.

In one story in the book, a ni-Vanuatu man is reported as being angry that his wife has (forced) sex with the Master, but there is little he can do about it. Few ni-Vanuatu men appear in these stories to defend their women or to get angry at them, though in contemporary life jealousy is a major spark for domestic violence. While some ni-Vanuatu women married or lived in long-term relationships with their employers, others found themselves on their own and pregnant. Much of the talk about sex with employers was expressed in the workshop as talk about babies, such as the many illegitimate children whom various expatriate men (including black American soldiers) were alleged to have fathered in the islands.

Several reports spoke of deep affection for the children in the house-girls' care. Leisara Kalotiti reported a former house-girl, Leimala, as saying, 'I was fourteen years old and I looked after [the Chinese employer's] children like they were my children. I was happy to look after them. I bathed them in the afternoon, I changed them. And they too, they liked me.' Many reported that grown children kept in touch with the house-girls who had helped to raise them, sent them letters and presents, and looked them up when they visited Vanuatu. A few house-girls had visited former employers' children overseas.

House-girls do not denigrate paid domestic work

One of our most intriguing research findings is that ni-Vanuatu women themselves do not denigrate paid domestic work. On the contrary, they value washing, cleaning, and looking after other people's children. While expatriate employers, ni-Vanuatu employers and members of the general community seem to denigrate paid domestic work and paid domestic workers, most of the past and present house-girls told us that paid domestic employment is important and useful work. This finding is in contrast to that of anthropologist Judith Rollins, who has suggested that 'paid domestic work is universally despised and those who do it universally dehumanized' (1985: 58).

Despite their employers' denigration of paid domestic workers and paid domestic work, most ni-Vanuatu house-girls seem to have a strong and resilient sense of self, and are able to retain a sense of dignity and self-respect even in exploitative working conditions. Historically and in the present, it is not paid domestic work or housework that house-girls find problematic, rather it is the conditions under which house-girls work that they find difficult.

Many house-girls expressed an awareness that their employers' perceived sense of difference affects the way they and their work are treated. They recognise that the greater their employers' perceptions of difference, the more negative their employers' interactions are likely to be with their house-girls, and the poorer the conditions within which they will have to work. The most successful relationships, those in which the house-girl enjoyed her work and felt like she was one of the family, were those in which differences were transcended through curiosity (e.g., cuisines or languages), 'love' or generosity of spirit, and mutual respect.

What do house-girls want? Respect

Given this context, it is interesting that what house-girls want from their employers is not equality. The house-girls in the workshop and in Daniela Kraemer's research on contemporary house-girls accept the fact that because they are employees they will never be equal players in their interaction with their employers. Historically, even a house-girl who became a settler's wife remained aware of the inequalities in her relationship. She ate and slept separately. Today, many house-girls still accept the central role inequality plays to the functioning of paid domestic service. They realise that equality in their workplace would actually destroy the industry in its present form. And while some social activists might celebrate the elimination of paid domestic service because it perpetuates the devaluation and denigration of women, ni-Vanuatu paid domestic workers themselves argue that such work gives them an opportunity for financial and social freedom that they might not otherwise have.

Similarly, house-girls in Vanuatu seem not to be concerned with narrowing or de-emphasising race, class and/or cultural differences between themselves and their employers. In the workshop, the expatriates expressed discomfort with the ni-Vanuatu participants' insistence on referring to themselves as Black and to the expatriates as White; why not use ni-Vanuatu and expat instead? But such objections elicited shrugs from the ni-Vanuatu women and no change in terminology. The ni-Vanuatu participants saw no reason to deny that racial differences are labelled in their ordinary speech. That did not mean, however, that they or the women in their reports felt all whites were alike. House-girls framed their employers' different behaviours or different mannerisms, not in terms of race, class or cultural identity, but in terms of character or what they thought of their employer as a person.

The central issue for house-girls, then, is not one of inequality/equality, nor one of 'difference'; rather, it is an issue of respect. What house-girls want, and what house-girls need, is for employers to respect their feelings and their dignity as human beings. This is evident in every chapter in this book. House-girls in the past and today often find themselves belittled, demeaned, berated, taken advantage of and ignored. Although physical violence against employees was more tolerated, and probably more common, in the colonial period, it occurs even today.

Indeed, the need for respect is one shared by paid domestic workers all around the world. As Bonnie Dill suggests about paid domestic workers in the United States, 'making the job good meant managing the employer-employee relationship, so as to maintain their self-respect. [Paid domestic workers] insisted upon some level of acknowledgement of their humanity, [and] actively fought against their employer's efforts to demean, control, or objectify them' (1988: 50).

Figure 9.3. Two unidentified house-girls from the 1950s

Certainly, in Vanuatu, part of the reason for insufficient respect, is that house-girls and employers are involved in a complex relationship of understanding and misunderstanding. Arguably, communication was better in the colonial period when house-girls had frequent interactions with their employers, often living on the premises. House-girls knew where they stood within the exploitative practices of colonialism. Stories in our book show that they knew when to hide in the closet and when to expect gifts of chocolate. However paternalistic, colonial employers' relations with their resident house-girls had more possibilities for sociable connection than relations with urban daily domestic workers. Today, although house-girls and employers intersect in the physical realm—house-girls work in the space in which employers live—house-girls and employers often spend little time talking to each other and do not intersect in terms of understanding and communication. Such a situation invariably results in tension. Very little is being done to try and bridge the miscommunication and misunderstanding between house-girls and employers.

We hope that our work will remind employers of the importance of respectful understanding and communication in order to bridge cultural differences. Misunderstandings and miscommunications can make for funny stories, but too often they make the house-girl-employer relationship fraught with tension. A key to better house-girl-employer relations is improved understanding and communication; without this, neither house-girls nor employers feel they are being respected and treated right.

References

Bresnihan, Brian and Keith Woodward (eds), 2002. *Tufala Gavman: Reminiscences from the Anglo-French Condominium of the New Hebrides.* Suva: Institute of Pacific Studies, University of the South Pacific.

Dill, Bonnie Thornton, 1988. Making your job good yourself: domestic service and the construction of personal dignity. In *Women and the Politics of Empowerment,* ed. Ann Bookman and Sandra Morgen, 33–52. Philadelphia: Temple University Press.

MacClancy, Jeremy, 1981. *To Kill a Bird with Two Stones.* Port Vila: Vanuatu Cultural Centre.

Rodman, Margaret, Daniela Kraemer, Lissant Bolton and Jean Tarisesei (eds), 2007. *House-Girls Remember: Domestic Workers in Vanuatu.* Honolulu: University of Hawai'i Press.

Rollins, Judith, 1985. *Between Women: Domestics and their Employers.* Philadelphia: Temple University Press.

10. Myths and Music of Futuna, Vanuatu: Past and Present in Dialogue

Janet Dixon Keller and Takaronga Kuautonga

I wish to speak to a book project entitled *Nokonofo Kitea/We Keep on Living This Way*. Taking its title from the opening line of a customary Futuna song, the project aims to present, translate and understand aspects of the wisdom of Futuna elders and ancestors as embodied in traditional lore.[1] The goals of the volume are twofold: first to challenge the idea of a narrative archive as a static repository of past knowledge with the idea that collections of narrative constitute resources for dialogue and negotiation of both past and present; and second to discuss the Futuna theory of narrative meaning as one path to dialogue.

I note first that this is a collaborative project co-authored by Takaronga Kuautonga who has taken a lead in retelling oral narratives in written form in ways we hope will be accessible to the people of Futuna familiar with the stories, to young people from Futuna who may be less familiar with them, to the people of Vanuatu more generally in their search for lines of connection across communities, and even for those from outside Vanuatu who have much to learn from local *kastoms*. The work has been a collaboration since the 1970s when islanders first helped me to acquire some of the traditional narrative and musical repertoires. Popoina Magau has been a long term advisor for over 30 years, assisting in transcription and translation again and again. Numerous elders and community members have contributed wisdom, wit and biting commentary through their narrative versions and interpretive discussions. I think especially of Napause Teifisou and Naparau Naora who opened my ears to *furi fesao* or turned words so that I could hear the messages. Some who helped with this project are no longer with us and perhaps the book to come can be a tribute to their memory.[2] I think especially of Iawoi Sore, Vaega Liji and Liji Sore, of Teikona Nuaita, Breisa Tamalua, Naparau Naora, Napause Teifisou and Nawali Sore. Some have criticised the work as it developed and their critiques have helped us to improve.

---

1   This article draws on jointly authored work and grows out of collaborative reflection. It was originally written and delivered by the first author and reflects her perspective. The second author followed this presentation with his own oral commentary and both of us engaged the original audience in dialogue to follow (which explains the use here of first the person singular in what is acknowledged as a jointly authored paper (editors' note)).

2   The Keller and Kuautonga work, *Nokonofo Kitea: We Keep On Living This Way* (2007), is now available in published form through Crawford House Publishing, Belair and the University of Hawai'i Press, Honolulu.

This project is oriented by Futuna theories of meaning and metaphor. We begin from the perspective that stories are structured by *ata* and *hkano. Ata,* the surface words of tellings, lead listeners to *hkano,* deeper meanings derived from ancestral wisdom. This dynamic means that telling (and singing as well) are ways of cueing listeners to important understandings. Listeners, themselves, must reason from the spoken cues to realise hidden significances. Such reasoning can be a process of thinking to one's self, but it can also involve conversation and negotiation over meanings. Such processes of reflection essential to the understanding of any Futuna narrative, insure that a collection of tales and songs from the island, or possibly from any ni-Vanuatu community, must combine words, spoken or sung, with dialogues of their audiences.

In addition, people of Futuna recognise that stories are told in a moment and cues vary as tellers adapt to current purposes. The same tale or lyrics may cue an audience toward one set of meanings in one context while being elaborated to cue listeners to different messages in another. As the Western cultural psychologist, Jerome Bruner, argues 'the impetus to narrative is expectation gone awry' (2002: 28). When troubles or novelties emerge new stories may be told, and familiar tales may be reshaped to address the unanticipated. Transformations of the familiar are interesting for these have the potential to articulate enduring values with unpredicted developments. In such re-tellings, narrators have the power to restore order to the narrated world by reconstructing principles from myth and *kastom.* Such resolutions, by extension, may cue listeners to novel perspectives on real world problems. However, neither the author nor the text dictates possibilities, it is those who listen to narrative who must grasp connections and make relevant inferences. It is in discussions among audience members from where insight must emerge and applications to the present develop.

The process of collaboration for *Nokonofo Kitea: We Keep on Living this Way* builds on this core perspective to join in a critique of common Western approaches to oral literatures (Bauman and Briggs 2003) by pointing out that establishing written collections as national or community archives—is a process that stifles the cultural negotiation of meaning that should occur with storytelling and musical interpretation. With Takaronga we have indeed produced a written collection, yet we have done so with the expectation that the text will engender dialogue. The volume includes dialogues that surrounded narratives we recorded and later wrote down. These conversations are critical to interpretation as speakers index events and experiences in a dynamic process of uncovering the unsaid (Basso 1996; Kulick 1992; Tyler 1978), but they are not the last word. Dialogue promotes dialogue in a process that should stir still more (re)assessment with time.

Nokonofo Kitea takes up a notion of 'reaccentuation' from the Russian scholar Mikhail Bakhtin (1989), to elaborate on the Futuna ideas regarding interpretation. 'Reaccentuation' recognises that the process of talking together to assess meaning implies that written collections of oral literatures can maintain and promote 'fluid and context-specific' cultural processes required for establishing relevance and importance over time in a manner that mirrors *kastom* talk (Regenvanu 2005). A text, whether spoken or written, is only half of a story or song. The other half resides in listeners' reflections. As long as people continue to read, perform out loud, and transform the words of a written document to address new circumstances, a collection stays alive and grows in the ever changing present (Goldman and Ballard 1998).

A native Hawaiian navigator, Nainoa Thompson, who has been involved in a reconstruction of Pacific canoes and navigational voyaging, argued to other islanders participating in one project: 'A culture does not remain alive unless it is practiced. To keep your voyaging tradition alive, you have to keep sailing' (Finney 2003: 53). Building a canoe is a start, but it is not enough to keep traditional wisdom alive. In the same way customary narratives can be constructed as oral or written texts, but in order to stay alive they need to be practised—spoken, performed, discussed, critiqued, and transformed (Micarelli and Gomez 2002). I offer some examples here of the lively interpretation of Futuna tales witnessed during the building of the *Nokonofo Kitea* collection. These interpretations are a part of what is written there, *ano pito*, bits and pieces, of the creative dialogues that surround these narratives and should continue to grow and serve as inspiration for new roads addressing community heritage and national independence, conservation and waste, modernity and the dilemmas created by globalisation.

I start with a great myth (Bonnemaison 1994) of Majihjiki and the Pasiesi. For those of you who might not know him, Majihjiki is a culture hero and trickster. Pasiesi are monsters, goblins that inhabit the hinterland of Futuna. The great myth is an ancient tale harkening from at least the nineteenth century. But it is also an allegory for today. In this story Pasiesi sets out to rid the land of its human occupants so that it will be his alone. Majihjiki's intervention allows the survivors to escape the monster's hold, eventually dispatch him, and to resettle the land recreating an original circuit of villages. Majihjiki's stated aim is to recreate the excitement and hum of human interaction that rests on independent individuals, couples, or villages interdependently enmeshed in reciprocal social exchange.

The story is told as a fantastic series of events with characters of mythical proportions who do mythical things—searching for lost children, for example, from an upside down posture. But it can be read as a critique of individual autonomy, gluttony, and selfish excess—dangerous behaviours of real situations today as in the past. This critique is articulated in arena after arena by members of the Futuna community. To start somewhere, take the Western and Christian ethic of forgiveness. In a community that is unquestionably Christian, Futuna voices still point out the need for shaping this idea to local norms of respect, encompassing both notions within local cultural logic. Christianity it is said is ni-Vanuatu. The values and norms of Christianity precede its religious introduction from the West. Yet the foreign forms in which it is returned to the islands may threaten local life ways. Forgiveness applied without limit undermines the mosaic of interdependence among people of an island community—the very mosaic of reciprocity that Majihjiki aimed to recreate. It is the Pasiesi's lack of respect, a respect that would by custom be demonstrated in asking permission for the harvesting of fruit or the use of land, that threatens to destroy island life as much as his literally murderous acts. If 'stealing what belongs to others' can be forgiven, how will the orders of kinship, age and leadership that maintain community persevere? The Majihjiki story is a starting point for just this discussion.

The Pasiesi himself might be seen as modern life, an evil ogre who disrupts contentment and sociality, for self interest. One who devours everything. The consequence, if he has his way, is the destruction of community. But this destruction can be overcome by the logic of *tufa,* gift giving, and *vaea,* sharing, among simultaneously independent and interdependent villagers. Such logic builds on the arrangement of villages and neighbourhoods established as separate residential sites but in proximity to one another—often in a circle that facilitates mutual support and exchange. Modernity and urbanisation, as pasiesi, destroy that logic replacing it with single individuals who compete for and then hoard wealth, while residence is transformed into a landscape that scatters citizens across space, isolating community members from one another. Again the Majihjiki story encourages reflection on such transformations asking the listener to envision ways to keep community alive even as modernity progresses.

Another story is referred to in *Nokonofo Kitea* as Majihjiki and *Fafine Tonga* and it is about women from afar who fly to Futuna to swim in the clear waters at Sinou. Majihjiki appears here as a trickster who hides a woman's wings so that she might stay with him as his wife. Together they have a child, but Majihjiki's own trickery becomes a stumbling block as his wife discovers the hidden wings and returns home to her own island. The tale raises questions about honesty and it poses the dilemma of homesickness when one lives far from one's homeland. Also questioned and not resolved are issues of residence—should women live with their husbands' families or should men live with the families of their wives? How should a couple decide? Majihjiki eventually takes his son and follows his wife and they continue to have children and raise a family far from Majihjiki's home. Successfully so; and as the generations pass one son, Jiverau, returns to find a Futunese bride, Sina, who in another tale leaves her Futuna homeland to live with her husband. What might be learned from these tales about the blessings and heartaches of interisland marriages? How might they help to assuage the pain of border crossings today and celebrate the openings for exchange introduced by coming to know *maivaka,* strangers, from other places?

This story too creates another talking point. Similar tales are frequently told in Vanuatu (Bonnemaison 1994; Jolly 1999; Thieberger 2000). In each case episodes and events differ but some elements are shared. Discussions of the possibilities for understanding commonalities of heritage that bind together peoples of Vanuatu might focus on comparisons that would yield shared cultural values as well as contrasting modes of reason. Such discussions might contribute to debates on *kastom* and national identity by suggesting that *kastoms* may offer both common ground and signs of community differences, simultaneously posing ways to think about foundations for ni-Vanuatu identity as well as the uniqueness of individual communities (cf. Tonkinson 1982).

A final example might be taken from a song about lobster trapping, *najehji,* a fantastic activity to be sure that engages all of the senses, strengths, and patience of the trapper to provide for family, for community and perhaps even to offer a tribute to the heavens. But in a Futuna song *najehji* becomes *furi fesao* (metaphor) and is used to characterise nineteenth-century evangelical missions. In this nineteenth-century song, a local voice hidden in the language of lobster trapping speaks to the dangers of being caught by foreign ideological traps. Again the issue of respect arises as the singer invites the interlopers to learn the wisdom of his land of Futuna. The situation with evangelism is very different today, but perhaps the caution urging a wariness of foreign ideas is still relevant as Vanuatu negotiates an international presence, yet aims to avoid the traps set by foreign politicians and developers. How are such traps to be recognised? How avoided? Is capture by foreign entreaty ever acceptable, and if so, when? These are some puzzles the *najehji* song might offer for consideration.

And in each retelling, each discussion, some new wisdom may become apparent. Tradition is at its best when it inspires a new song, a new story, or a new insight that wrestles with novel circumstances while keeping the tradition alive not only in the words of the past but in the processes for shaping new allegories and musical lyrics that open conversations about contemporary situations. A new public building, the spread or cure of foreign disease, and election results are the kinds of events that Futuna narrative can celebrate, ratify or lament leading one to puzzle over or clarify the present.

These insights, emerging from the collaborative processes resulting in and, we hope, continuing beyond *Nokonofo Kitea*, resonate with other discourses of custom and nation current in Vanuatu (Regenvanu 2005). Our hope is that narrative heritage may have the potential to open roads for productive engagements within communities, and across communities, and thereby play a role in envisioning the future of the republic.

Rather than narratives serving as icons of the past, as Western scholars have often heralded folklore, the Futuna tales can be seen to represent dynamic wisdom offering insight into community values, contemporary circumstances of migration, urban life, and international relations. This heritage offers ni-Vanuatu ways to challenge and reshape modernity and rethink the dilemmas created by globalisation. Whether as the foundation for a parent's instruction to a child on the right ways of living, a chiefly edict to resolve a conflict, a lesson in a classroom, or a sermon, these narratives can convey valued principles and generate productive discussion. The narratives can participate in a cyclic dialogism as they constitute resources from which new lifeways can be patterned while those new lifeways inspire still more narratives addressing constantly emerging ways of life. The narratives are a tradition that is in flux. What is written, in this hybrid Futuna-Western view, is neither authoritative nor fixed, but a custom resource that may be strategically employed, rewritten or retold, and transformed as occasions require, as politics demand, or as people desire. In this way the past informs the present and offers those engaged in dialogue surrounding narrative a resource for envisioning a continually evolving future.

References

Bakhtin, Mikhail M., 1989. *The Dialogic Imagination, ed. Michael Holquist, trans. Caryl Emerson and Michael Holquist*. Austin: University of Texas Press.

Basso, Keith H., 1996. *Wisdom Sits in Places: Landscape and Language among the Western Apache*. Albuquerque: University of New Mexico Press.

Bauman, Richard and Charles Briggs, 2003. *Voices of Modernity: Language Ideologies and the Politics of Inequality*. Cambridge: Cambridge University Press.

Bonnemaison, Joël, 1994. *The Tree and the Canoe: History and Ethnogeography of Tanna*. Honolulu: University of Hawai'i Press.

Bruner, Jerome, 2002. *Making Stories: Law, Literature, Life*. Cambridge: Harvard University Press.

Finney, Ben, 2003. *Sailing in the Wake of the Ancestors*. Honolulu: Bishop Museum Press.

Goldman, Laurence R. and Chris Ballard, 1998. *Fluid Ontologies: Myth, Ritual and Philosophy in the Highlands of Papua New Guinea*. Westport, Conn: Bergin and Garvey.

Jolly, Margaret, 1999. Another time, another place. *Oceania* 69(4): 282–300.

Keller, Janet Dixon and Takaronga Kuautonga, 2007. *Nokonofo Kitea: We Keep On Living This Way. Myths & Music of Futuna, Vanuatu*. Belair, Australia: Crawford House Publishing and Honolulu: University of Hawai'i Press.

Kulick, Don, 1992. *Language Shift and Cultural Reproduction: Socialization, Self and Syncretism in a Papua New Guinean Village*. Cambridge: Cambridge University Press.

Micarelli, Giovanna and Hernan Gomez, 2002. *The Body of Memory: Theater Anthropology as a Tool for Cultural and Linguistic Reaffirmation in Indigenous Amazonia*. Proceedings of the Sixth FEL Conference. R. McKenna Brown.

Regenvanu, Ralph, 2005. The changing face of 'custom'. Vanuatu people and culture. *People and Culture inOceania* 20: 37–50.

Thieberger, Nicholas, 2000. Walking to Erro. Paper presented to a cross-disciplinary conference: Walking About: Travel, Trade, Migration and Movement in Vanuatu. Canberra: The Australian National University.

Tonkinson, Robert, 1982. National identity and the problem of kastom in Vanuatu. *Mankind* 13: 306–15.

Tyler, Stephen A., 1978. *The Said and the Unsaid: Mind, Meaning, and Culture*. New York: Academic Press.

Projects

11. Welkam Toktok

Ralph Regenvanu (Daerekta: VKS mo NKK)

Tangkiu tumas long *Jif Murmur* long nambawan toktok blong yu. Mi wantem talem olsem Daerekta blong Kaljoral Senta mo Nasenel Kaljoral Kaonsel welkam bakegen long yufala long tis rum tede long nasenal miusiem mo tu long Port-Vila Vanuatu. Mi aknolejem presens blong Jif mo Presiden blong Malvatumauri, Nasenel kaonsel of Jifs we i stap wetem yumi, mo tu Jif Murmur, Presiden blong Efate kaonsel of Jifs mo tu Representatif blong Ministri blong Intenol Afea we i stap, wetem tu ol olfala filwoka blong yumi we oli stap speseli Jif Richard, James mi no luk sam bakegen long ples ia yet. Wetem ol woman filwokas blong yumi we oli stap ia wetem presiden blong olgeta, presiden blong ol man filwokas yufala ol distinguis riseja, frens blong yumi long ovasi we yufala i stap wok long ples ia long taem, i gat yufala tumas we yufala big bigfala impoten pesen so bae mi no save talem nem blong yufala wetem ol narafala frens we yufala stap, ol staf blong Kaljoral Senta welkam long yumi evriwan long tede long tis opening seremoni. Mi glad tumas se Vanuatu Kaljoral Senta hemi save provaedem ples we yumi mit tis taem long Vanuatu wetem konfrens ia from fulap taem ol risejas we oli stap wok long Vanuatu oli stap mit long ol narafala kantri araon Vanuatu. So hemi gud tumas se naoia yufala i save mit long Vanuatu an yufala i stap tokbaot Vanuatu mo risej blong yufala long ples ia. Mi wantem talem tangkiu long oganaezing komiti we yufala i bin pulum samting ia i kam wan ples, tangkiu long yufala we yufala i putum tingting se bae konfrens i stap long Vanuatu. Mo tangkiu tu long yufala we yufala i save kam, sam long yufala i kam longwe tumas blong stap long ples ia. Hemi gud tumas se konfrens ia hemi stap long medel blong tufala fildwokas worksops blong mifala blong ol woman i jes pas, i finis long last Fraede mo blong ol man bae i jes stat long next Mande. So hemi gud tumas from hemi givim janis long ol filwokas tu blong oli save stap long ples ia we olgeta tu oli stap mekem ol impoten risej projek long raon erias blong olgeta an bae yumi gat janis tede mo tumoro blong harem sam long olgeta bae oli givim toktok abaot risej blong olgeta.

Hemi impoten blong konfrens i stap long ples ia, long taem ia from hemi soemaot tim blong konfrens we hemi 'collaboration' fasin blong wok tugeta, ol risejas blong ovasis wetem ol lokel pipol long ples ia wetem ol filwokas wetem ol komiuniti blong save mekem risej. From yumi save witaot ia bae eksasaes blong risej bae hemi no save wok gud. Mi glad tumas tu se long konfrens long tis wik bambae i gat trifala lanwis oli kamaot: Bislama, Inglis mo Franis. Hemia tu hemi impoten blong soemaot se hemi wan konfrens blong Vanuatu, abaot Vanuatu. Kaljoral risej polisi we Kaljoral Senta mo National Kaljoral Kaonsel we i bin endosem long yia 1994 mo hemi stap wok kasem tede hemi wan impoten stamba blong fulap risej we i stap mekem naoia and hemi wan model yet long Pasifik rijen mo long wol. UNESCO i stap yusum risej polisi blong yumi long Vanuatu olsem wan model we i stap promotem mo tu hemi stap long wolwaed wol oganaesesen i stap long websaet blong olgeta olsem wan wan model risej polisi. An mi glad tumas se mifala i stap kontiniu blong promotem long Vanuatu mo ol risejas we oli stap wok long ples ia oli kontiniu blong wok wetem mifala antanit long gaetlaen we hemi provaedem. Hemi wan polisi we i talemaot klia wanem nao wanem mifala i wantem long risej blong Vanuatu, mo wanem nao ekspektesen blong gavman wetem Kaljoral Senta wetem Kaljoral Kaonsel mo tu wetem ol filwokas, ol lokel komiuniti blong yumi. Polisi i talemaot se i sud gat kolaboresen mo hemi askem ol risejas blong trenem wan wan man o wok wetem wan wan man o woman blong mekem risej blong olgeta blong mekem se taem oli aot long Vanuatu ol skils we oli gat oli save stap wetem ol pipol long ples ia.

Mo tu hemi gat fulap narafala samting we hemi askem long ol risejas: fo eksampel evri samting we oli mekem, ol rikoding, ol fotos, ol films, ol samting we oli raetem, mifala i askem se kopi i kam stap long ples ia. An long bilding ia nao ol kopi i stap long hem. I gat Nasonal Film mo Sand Akaev narasaed ia, i gat Nasnal Laebri antap ia, i gat Nasonal Heritej narasaed, detabes i stap. So evri infomesen i kambak mo i stap mo i yus long divelopmen blong Vanuatu we hem nao i sud bi wan long olgeta men grups of pipol we hemi tagetem risej i go long olgeta. Yumi askem tu se bambae ol risejas oli mas mekem wan samting blong komiuniti we oli stap long hem blong benefitim komiuniti. Samtaem hemi ol buks blong skul long lanwis mo samtaem hemi abaot wan samting long Inglis, Franis we hemi abaot komiuniti ia.

Be sam taems ol komiuniti oli askem wan samting olsem wan wota tang ol samting olsem ia, hemia tu wan samting we i save benefitim komiuniti. Mo tu long kaonsel, Nasonal Kaljoral Kaonsel mo long Vanuatu gavman, mifala i stap askem tu sam seveses blong ol risejas blong mekem wanwan samting we oli stap mekem blong helpem ol risej we mifala i stap mekem, o go tuwods helpem wan polisi we gavman hemi gat. Polisi hemi rikognaesem se spos yumi no putum in ples ol samting olsem ia, fulap taem risej we yumi, we oli stap long yunivesiti ol institusen ol akademik institiusen fulap taem risej we yumi mekem hemi rili no benefitim ol man Vanuatu. From wanem? From ol man Vanuatu fulap long olgeta oli no save rid kasem standet we yufala i raetem ol samting blong yufala long hem. An fulap taem ol risejas oli kam long komiuniti oli karem infomesens be hemi impoten blong oli luk save se i gat samting i kambak long olgeta tu.

An hemi wan obligesen long mifala olsem institiusen we i lukaotem risej long Vanuatu blong mekem sua se ol komiuniti oli luk save se i gat tu wei relesonsip from hemi fasin blong kastom blong yumi—taem yu givim samting i mas gat samting i kambak. So tats wae mifala i askem, askem long yufala ol risejas mo ol koligs blong yufala we maet oli tingting blong kam wok long Vanuatu anta long Kaljoral Risej Polisi we yumi gat. From hemi traem setemaot ia mo hemi traem blong sekiurim risej i go long fiuja, from taem ol komiuniti oli luk save se risej hemi benefitim olgeta bambae oli glad blong mekem mo akseptem ol narafala risejas long fiuja i kam. So hemi no wan samting jes blong benefitim blong Vanuatu, hemi wan samting we i save benefitim risej long Vanuatu as a hol, mo hemi wan samting bae yumi save luk long konfrens long tis wik. Bae yumi save luk ol benefit blong kaen koloboret risej we yumi stap traem blong inkarejem naoia.

Mi wantem talemaot tu long ples ia se long las yia gavman hemi bin establisem, wetem wan act blong Parlamen, Nasonal Lanwis Kaonsel. So Nasonal Lanwis Kaonsel hemi tekem tugeta ol impoten bodis long Vanuatu oganaesesen long Vanuatu, fo eksampol: USP i stap insaed wetem Kaljoral Senta wetem SIL wetem ol narafala oganaesesen olsem Lanwis Ofis blong Praem Minista mo tu sam taem Dipatmen blong Lanwis Seves mo Malvatumauri. So Lanwis Kaonsel wan wok blong hem tu hemi blong apruvum risej long saed blong lanwis, an naoia taem Nasonal Kaljoral Kaonsel hemi wok hemi blong apruvum ol risej, apruvum ol risejas long Vanuatu hemi tekem advaes long Nasonal Lanwis Kaonsel nao abaot wanem nao ol lanwis blong yumi we i nid blong mekem risej long hem.

Naoia we i stap ol wok long lanwis blong Vanuatu we ol linguis we oli stap, ol ovasis linguist wetem linguist blong yumi long ples ia long Pasifik Lanwis Yunit oli stap help blong pripem venakiula edukesen blong Vanuatu. So olredi yumi gat klosap twante skuls long Vanuatu we oli tij finis long lanwis long kindegaten. So hemi wan ajivmen we hemi soemaot hao pipol blong Vanuatu oli save benefit long ol kaen risej we yufala i stap mekem we yufala i kam long ovasis mo tu ol filwokas we yufala i stap wok wetem ol lanwis blong yumi wan wan komiuniti blong yumi.

Mi wantem talemaot tu long ples ia se long next yia bambae gavman hemi establisim Nasonal Saentific Risej Kaonsel. So bae hemi fes taem we gavman i luk save regulesen mo ol i moniterem ol risej long saed blong saens. From naoia Kaljoral Risej Polisi blong yumi hemi no kavremap ol samting olsem ia: ol risej long saed blong ol kaen plant blong yumi o samting we i stap long bus we i save provaedem meresin fo eksampol ol kaen animal o insek we yumi gat—ol samting olsem ia.

Olsem mi talem finis yumi luk fulap finis, fulap gudfala samting i kamaot long ol risej we i stap hapen finis long Vanuatu ol koloboresen we i stap hapen finis long saed blong risej. Mi talemaot finis tijing blong lanwis long skul hemi wan impoten benefit. Ating fulap long yufala i harem nius blong Teouma Lapita Saet, we hemi stap kolosap long ples ia nomo. Hemi kam wan long olgeta top Lapita Saet long Pasifik we hemi save soemaot hao nao ol man long Pasifik i bin setel long ol kaontris blong Solomons, Vanuatu kasem Tahiti. Hemi wan saet we hemi diskava tru long kolaboresen ia tru long wok blong ol filwokas we oli risivim trening long ol akiolojis. An yumi gat filwoka we hem nao i tekem trening ia mo hemi faenem, luk wan pis Lapita we wan man ples blong hem and ten hemi go faenem saet ia. So witaot tat kaen of kolaboresen bae yumi neva faenem tat ples.

Mo tu yumi luk se naoia ol filwokas blong yumi oli stap wok wetem ol raetas blong ol musiums we oli benefit long ol save blong ol filwokas oli givim bak blong mekem se ol koleksen blong olgeta oli save gat mo valiu, blong oli save gat mo abaot koleksen blong olgeta tru long wok blong ol filwokas mo ol man we kolaboret mo ol risejas. So yumi tu, yumi benefit long kolaboresen ia.

An blong talem nomo se fulap long ol filwokas blong yumi we oli stap wok long Vanuatu naoia oli gat bigfala ekspiriens long saed blong hao blong mekem risej tru long help blong ol risejas we oli wok wetem olgeta and oli soem long olgeta wanem oli stap mekem and givim sam tingting long olgeta long saed blong wanem kaen projek oli stap mekem. An mi glad se naoia long Vanuatu ol filwokas oli mekem fulap ol defren kaen projeks long ol erias blong olgeta. Ol projeks long saed blong diksnari, long saed blong ol Ats Festivals, long saed blong ol seremoni we long taem oli no mekem bae oli mekem bakegen, long saed blong givim givhan long ol man oli askem ol kwestin long olgeta, olsem ol risejas, mo tu long saed blong save pasem kastom i go long yangfala blong oli save lanem bakegen, blong tijim olgeta long saed blong kastoms.

Mi glad tumas se long konfrens ia bae yumi gat ol filwokas oli givim tingting blong olgeta long wok blong olgeta we oli stap mekem mo tu yufala we yufala kam long narafala kaontris, yufala i save talemaot wok blong yufala. Mo yumi evriwan yumi save harem hopfuli bae hemi save jeneretem mo kaen prestij olsem long fiuja an hemia nao yumi luk fowod long hem. So mi wantem talem tangkiu tumas long yumi evriwan blong save stap long ples ia, hemia nao hemi end blong smol toktok blong mi.

Welcome Speech

Ralph Regenvanu (Director: VCC and NCC)

Thank you very much chief Murmur for your excellent speech. I wish to say, as the Director of the Cultural Centre and the National Cultural Council, welcome once again everyone today to this room in the National Museum, and also to Port Vila, Vanuatu. I acknowledge the presence of the chief and President of the Malvatumauri National Council of Chiefs who is with us today, and also Chief Murmur, the President of the Efate Council of chiefs and also the representative of the Ministry of Internal Affairs, and also all of our older fieldworkers who are with us, especially Chiefs Richard, James, and others who have not yet arrived. Also all of our woman fieldworkers who are here with their President, the President of the male fieldworkers, distinguished researchers, friends from overseas who have worked here a long time. There are too many of you important people so I won't be able to say all of your names, or the names of our other friends who are here, however with the staff of the Cultural Centre I welcome you all today during this opening ceremony. I very glad that the Vanuatu Cultural Centre can provide the venue for this meeting and conference, especially since many times when researchers from other countries who work in Vanuatu meet in those other countries around Vanuatu. So it is very good that now you are able to meet in Vanuatu to talk about Vanuatu and the research that you undertake here. I want to say thank you to the organising committee who pulled this event together, and thank you to those who decided that this conference should be held in Vanuatu. Thank you also those of you who have been able to come, as many of you have come from very far away to be here. It is very good that this conference is situated between the two fieldworkers' workshops—the women's workshop that just passed, and finished last Friday, and the men's which will start next Monday. This is particularly good in that it will also give the chance for the fieldworkers to attend, who also run important research projects in their areas, and you will have a chance today and tomorrow to hear some of them give presentations about that research.

It is important that this conference is held here, at this time, because it shows the theme of the conference: that is 'collaboration', or ways of working together; of researchers from overseas, local people from this place, fieldworkers and communities who can conduct research. We know that without this, the exercise of research would not work well. I am glad also that at this week's conference there will be three languages represented: Bislama, English and French. This also is important in showing that this is a conference of Vanuatu, about Vanuatu. The Cultural Research Policy that was endorsed by the Cultural

Centre and the National Cultural Council in 1994, and that is still working today, is an important foundation to much research that is now undertaken, and it is an ongoing model across the Pacific region and the world. UNESCO is promoting Vanuatu's research policy as a model, and this is demonstrated worldwide on their website as a model research policy. And I am very glad that we continue to promote it in Vanuatu, and all of the researchers who work here continue to work with us underneath the guidelines that it provides. It is a policy that states clearly what we want of research in Vanuatu, and what are the expectations of the government and the Cultural Centre and Cultural Council, with the fieldworkers, and with our local communities. The policy states that there should be collaboration, and asks researchers to train a man or a woman or work with a man or a woman in making their research to ensure that when they leave Vanuatu their skills may remain with the people of this place. There are many other things that are asked of researchers: for example everything that they make, recordings, photographs, films, written material, we ask that copies are made to remain here. All of these copies are kept in this building. There is the National Film and Sound Archive on the other side here, there is the National Library upstairs, National Heritage is on the other side, and there is the database. In this way all information comes back and may be used for the further development of Vanuatu, as should be the main purpose of research.

We also ask that all researchers must do something for the benefit of the community in which they reside. Sometimes this is books for learning language, or sometimes it is about something in English or French concerning that particular community. Also, sometimes communities ask for something specific such as a water tank, or something else that can benefit the community. Also, in the council, the National Cultural Council and the Vanuatu Government, we ask some services of researchers to contribute something of what they do to help the research that we are doing, or to go towards helping a government policy. The policy recognises that if we don't put these things in place, often the research that we do, that takes place in universities and academic institutions, often the research that we do does not really benefit the people of Vanuatu. Why? Because many people in Vanuatu can't read up to the standard that you use in your writing. And often researchers come into communities and take information but it is important that they understand that something comes back to them too.

It is also an obligation of ours, as the institution that looks after research in Vanuatu, to make sure that communities understand that there must be a two-way relationship, because it is the way of our *kastom*—when you give something, there must be something that comes back. That is why we ask you researchers, and your colleagues who may be thinking of coming to work in Vanuatu, to do so under the current Cultural Research Policy. This is because it attempts to set out and secure future research, because when communities understand that research benefits them, they will be happy to participate and accept the arrival of other future researchers. This is not something that merely benefits Vanuatu, it is something that benefits research across Vanuatu as a whole, and this is something that we will see across the conference this week. We can see the benefits of the kind of collaborative research that we are now trying to encourage.

I also wish to say here that last year the government established, by Act of Parliament, the National Language Council. The National Language Council brings together all the important bodies of Vanuatu, for example: the University of the South Pacific (USP) is there along with the Cultural Centre, the Summer Institute of Linguistics (SIL), and all the other organisations such as the language office of the Prime Minister and also the Department of Language Service and Malvatumauri. One function of the Language Council is to approve research about language. At present the Cultural Council approves such research and takes advice from the National Language Council about which of our languages require what kind of research done.

As it is now, with regard to work on present languages, foreign linguists with our own linguists at the Pacific Language Unit help to prepare vernacular education in Vanuatu. We already have close to 20 schools in Vanuatu that are teaching in vernacular languages in kindergarten. This is an achievement that shows how the people of Vanuatu can benefit from the kinds of research that you carry out, you who come from overseas, and also the fieldworkers who work with our languages across our various communities.

I also wish to say here that next year the Government will be establishing a National Scientific Research Council. This will represent the first time in which the government recognises the need to regulate and monitor scientific research. As it stands, the present Cultural Research Policy does not cover these things: research about different kinds of plants, or things in the bush that may provide medicine, for example, or different species of animals or insects that we have— these kinds of things. We don't yet have a location, but we can say that work is currently going ahead to establish a National Science Council next year, and this will encompass every kind of research that is currently taking place in Vanuatu.

As I have already said, we have seen a great many good things come out of the research that has taken place in Vanuatu, all the collaborative research projects that have already been undertaken. I have already told you about teaching language in schools, and the important benefits of this. I'm sure that many of you have heard news about the Teouma Lapita Site, which is located close to where we are now. This has become one of the top Lapita sites in the Pacific, showing how Pacific peoples settled in the countries from the Solomon Islands, Vanuatu to Tahiti. This site was discovered through collaboration, through the work of fieldworkers who received training in archaeology. And we have a fieldworker who undertook such training who looked at a piece of Lapita pottery that a local man found; then he went and found the site. Without that kind of collaboration we would have never found that place.

Also, we are now seeing that our fieldworkers are working with museum writers who are benefitting from the knowledge of fieldworkers to make sure that their collections are more valuable, and that they may know more about their collections through the work of fieldworkers in collaboration with researchers. So we, too, benefit from this collaboration. I would also like to point out that many of our fieldworkers who are working in Vanuatu have gained a great deal of experience in how to make research through the help of the researchers who have worked with them, and who show them what they are doing, and give some ideas to them regarding their particular projects. And I am pleased to see that, in Vanuatu, fieldworkers are carrying out many different kinds of projects across many different areas. There are dictionary projects, arts festivals, projects concerning the rejuvenation of ceremonies that haven't been performed for a long time, projects that help people ask the right questions and pass on *kastom* to young people so that they can learn it again, and to teach them about their *kastom*.

I am very pleased that at this conference we have many fieldworkers presenting their thoughts about their work, and you who come from other countries; you too can present your work. And as we hear about these, hopefully this will generate prestige in the future that we look forward to. So I want to say thank you very much to everyone who is able to be here. This is the end of my small speech.

12. Vanuatu Nasonal Film Unit

Jacob Kapere

Gud aftenun long yumi evriwan mi gat bigfala hona blong stanap long fes blong yufala ol hae woman, man we oli harem nem blong yufala bifo mo yufala i mekem plante wok long Vanuatu mo i gud tu blong luk yufala evriwan yufala i kam joen olsem wan famle blong ol riseja we oli joenem grup blong ol filwoka mo ol man blong Vanuatu film unit. Mi mi bin joenem film unit long 1986 taem Kirk hemi faenem mi long rod long taon ating hemi bin faenem mi long nakamal hemi faenem se mi mi bin gat smol skil long saed blong video kamera. Nasonal Film Foto mo Saon Unit hemi olsem wan nasonal dipositri blong plante samting long saed blong film, foto mo saon mo hemi olsem wan kastom bang hemi olsem wan ples we i stap long hat blong miusium long ples ia we yumi stap risejem ol kastom save blong kantri ia long hem. Ples ia hemi olsem hat blong hemi stap yet be ol branj ol aktiviti blong hem i stap olbaot long ol aelan we hemi minim se stamba wok blong olgeta nao ol man oli bin setemap ples ia nao hemi olsem ol filwoka ol fes riseja we oli bin stap long kantri. Taem yu tokbaot film unit olsem plante taem ol man oli harem long saed blong filming o rikoding be long bifo mi gat plante man blong yumi oli bin fraet lelebet long taem bifo from ating oli luk ol fes riseja we oli bin go long sam aelan blong yumi oli bin rikodem ol man oli plem oli harem voes blong olgeta an oli go oli nomo kambak plante oli nomo kambak oli bin stap long taem. Afta oli ating, putum wan nem we hemi olsem se ol masin we oli yusum hemi ol masin we oli stilim voes mo oli stilim man oli minim se olsem olgeta oli no save tumas se. Mo oli no bin save se i bin gat wan seksen olsem we i stap long Kaljorol Senta we oli save ron i kam olsem naoia. Oli ron i kam blong faenem plante samting an bifo ino bin gat, mekem se wok we oli bin mekem long kantri spirit i bin stap long hem oli tekem yet oli stap olsem se hemi propeti blong Vanuatu. Wan dei hemi mas kambak long Vanuatu an mekem se taem olgeta we oli bin setemap seksen ia oli bin traehad blong karem ol samting ia tu i kambak.

So wan long olgeta fes man we mi mi bin joenem wok blong olgeta long taem lelebet mi olsem kolosap nomo be mi stap kam olfala. Mi no stap luksave be taem mi luk ol olfala filwoka mi save ol man we oli stap long ples ia olsem fes filwoka we yumi bin harem nius blong olgeta long moning James Gwero we hemi stap mo Richard Leona olgeta nao oli bin stap blong bildimap bang blong save ia blong kastom so James Gwero hemi wan long olgeta fes man we hemi stap rikodem ol samting mo hemi bin aot blong trenem olgeta blong hao blong oli yusum ol kaen ekwipmen olsem ia blong rikodem ol samting. An James ino long taem tumas hemi stap ia hemi kam long hem be hemi talem se, bifo solda blong hemi bin so lelebet from ol ekwipmen blong bifo i bin hevi. Hemi talem long mi se, 'Man yufala naoia yufala ino stap wok had tumas ia mifala bifo mifala swet gud ia!' We ating hemi kam hemi luk se i gat plante man an ino gat inaf blong yumi go aot long aelan blong rikodem.

Be hem wetem ol narafala koligs blong hem blong oli stat mekem wok from tingting ia nao olsem ol man ples i talem se sam waet man oli bin kam stilim voes blong mifala finis, oli kam stilim mifala oli kam stilim foto blong mifala bakegen ale yufala bakegen yufala i kam blong wantem mekem ol wok ia. So mekem se wetem help blong Kirk Huffman hemi bin traehad mi sua se sam long yufala ol riseja we oli stap naoia ol olfala riseja i bin helpem hem blong aedentifaem sam samting olsem ol foto we yufala we oli wok long defren institiusen ovasis i bin save sam foto wetem sam audio wetem sam film we oli bin karem long bifo. An wan long olgeta bigfala wok we oli bin traehad blong karem ol samting i kambak hemi olsem wok blong risej ia nao we Kirk hemi bin faenem long ovasis an hemi manej blong karem fes film blong yumi long 11 minit long vilej blong Matantua long 1917 we man ia hemi bin kambak bakegen 1919 blong mekem ol film blong Vao, Malakula mo sam nara ples bakegen hemi bin mekem longfala film.

Be long risej long Kirk hemi faenem aot se bigfala pat blong film ia hemi bin lus, oli bin distroem so yumi laki tumas blong gat 11 minit ia we hemi pat blong Solomon tu i stap insaed long hem. Mo ol fes foto we oli bin stap tu long taem ia olsem long ripot blong Tepahae i stap givim naoia se 1852 sam samting long Aneityum hemi no longtaem. Wan yia afta hemi 1853 hemi ol fes foto we Kirk hemi bin karem blong kambak long Kaljoral Senta. Fes koleksen ia nao we i olfala i blak an waet we i kam i stat blong bildimap kastom bang blong yumi. Sem taem hemi stat blong leftemap intres blong pipol taem we oli stat blong karem i go bak long aelan blong soem long ol pipol bakegen mo ol fes rikoding.

I gud blong yumi traem karem ol samting ia i kambak ovasis fastaem so long tabu rum i gat plante plante blak an waet foto we oli bin kolektem long plante defren miusiums wetem yunivesitis. Mo plante long ol foto ia mifala i stil stap traehad blong faenem ol infomesen blong olgeta yet blong go wetem so ol foto oli stap wetem ol rikodings. Ol rikodings long taem ia oli bin stap long defren fomat mekem isies wei we long taem we Kirk olgeta oli bin stap manij blong holem taet ol sikistin o ol rikoding olsem ol riliz ol fes film oli stap long sikistin milimita film olsem sinema be oli bin transferem olgeta oli go long VHS. Nao stamba wok blong ol filwoka mo ol man ples hemi blong go aot blong kolektem ol infomesen. Ol infomesen long aelan, rikodem ol samting, filming ol samting blong kam putum long fiuja jeneresen from oli luksave se lanwis i stap jenis folem laef we yumi stap go long hem. Ol man oli stat muv i kam long taon plante oli luksave se lanwis bambae hemi jenis mo lanwis hemi stamba blong plante samting we oli stap mekem long aelan. Olsem long lanwis nao hemi mekem se i gat wan kastom i kamaot long wan eria oli pefom long wan wei from we lanwis nao hemi talem oli save se sipos ino gat lanwis bae kastom ia ino save gat wan mining we mufmen blong tanis o ol samting we i go insaed long tanis bae ino gat. So hemi mekem se film unit hemi gat stamba wok blong oli traem blong kolektem plante infomesen bifo ol samting oli stat blong lus. Taem we mi mi stat mi bin foldaon long sem spirit we mi blong go aot nomo blong karem o filming ol samting blong karem bak blong putum long akaef an plante plante long olgeta oli talem se olsem ol samting we oli rikodem ol samting we yumi rikodem blong kasem we oli blong fiuja jeneresen. Yumi traem blong putum i go long narafala institiusen bakegen blong hemi yusum so hemi olsem ol samting blong olgeta we i stap we oli save se wan dei oli ded be ol pikinini blong olgeta oli go long ples ia bae oli save faenem plante samting we oli save divaedem sam samting bakegen.

James Gwero hemi stap blong yusum smol muvi kamera we hemi 8 milimita film hemi wan smol muvi film we i bin gat sam we oli bin transferem be plante oli no transferem yet i stap. Nekis fomat we i bin kamaot long taem ia long maket hemi Video 8 an Video 8 Viane hemi bin yusum, Viane hemi olsem wan filwoka hem tu i bin yusum mo Alben Ruben, hem blong South West Bay we Kirk hemi bin spendem plante taem long eria ia blong mekem ol stadi blong hem an hemi faenem se ples ia hemi nidim wan kamera so hemi bin askem James Gwero i kam karem smol trening. Alben oli sendem hem i go long Fiji i karem smol trening bakegen i kambak saye oli karem wan video kamera mo bifo oli sendem video kamera wetem hem blong go long aelan hemi sendem toktok i go long aelan se bae kasem aelan wetem wan video kamera. Be ol man aelan oli no save gud tumas mo oli no bin luk pija blong olgeta bifo. Samfala oli harem oli spretemaot nius mekem se ol jifs oli bin oganaesem wan bigfala seremoni long dei blong ol jifs long namba 5 maj we oli stap selebretem oltaem mo oli bin gat wan seremoni oli bin blesem Alben wetem video kamera blong hem bifo hemi stat blong yusum long fil so hem tu hemi gat wan koleksen. Bigfala koleksen i stap mo long taem ia nao we mi mi kam blong go joenem olgeta an ten mifala yusum video 8, mifala yusum hai 8 we hemi nekis fomat i aot long afta long video 8. Mo mifala yusum ol defren fomat we yu save faenem ol kaset blong hem oli stap long tabu rum hemi i gat 16 milimita, i gat 8 milimita, i gat video 8, i gat hai 8, i gat VHS, i gat SVHS, i gat DV, i gat DVC Broadcast. Evri koleksen we mifala i gat most long olgeta oli transferem olgeta long VHS an ten mifala i traehad blong transferem olgeta bakegen yu putum i go long fomat we hemi DVC Broadcast mo olsem mi talem i gat plante we oli no transferem olgeta yet naoia.

Olsem i kam long wan taem we yumi stat blong luk save se tabu rum hemi olsem wan kastom bang. Be kastom bang ia hemi gat hemi olsem mani we i gat intres blong hem an intres blong yu mas benefitim komiuniti so yumi mas yusum. Mekem se long 1990 samting mifala i stat blong mekem ol fes program blong mifala long kastom mo kalja long TV kasem naoia. Naoia mifala stap kontiniu yet blong mekem an oli givim taem long mifala blong mifala i stap yusum tu haoa long wan wik i mekem se i gat tu taem long wan manis we mifala i save yusum koleksen blong mifala o go aot blong filmim wanem blong kam blong mekem program blong hem blong putum long TV sendem kopi long aelan blong ol man oli save luk.

So naoia olsem ol man oli wantem, yumi wantem mekem se ol man oli get yus long ol samting we yumi gat blong promotem kastom blong promotem lanwis blong karem bak intres blong bringim intres blong pipol i kam antap. Mo long saed blong radio mifala i stap gat ol kastom mo kalja radio program long evri Satede blong afanaoa hemi stap kamaot long af pas sikis i go long seven klok. Mifala i bin raetem blong ekstendem taem tu blong oli pasem ol program blong Paul Gardissat we hemi bin stap long radio long taem blong New Hebrides i kam long Vanuatu mo hemi bin stap mekem ol program long saed blong kastom. Program ia tu mifala i stat blong mifala i iven toktok long olgeta long radio oli glad blong putum so i minim se mifala i traem blong winim mo taem long radio blong pasem ol samting blong yumi i go long hem.

Ol foto blong yumi mifala i stap i gat wan kolum long *Daily Post* niuspepa we evri wiken i stap go long hem mo mifala i traehad blong mekem se i traem kamaot tu long evri dei so mifala i yusum ol foto ol olfala foto ol blak an waet foto blong putum i go. I gat ol pablikesen tu we i stap kamaot we oli yusum ol storian we oli bin rikodem we i stap long tabu rum blong mekem ol buklet blong kastom stori mo hemia we oli kolektem so hemia tu olsem hemi pat blong wok blong yumi traem blong mekem se pipol i yusum wanem we yumi gat.

Mifala i gat wan nasnal polisi blong filming tu we i stap we mifala i stap moniterem ol defren film kru we oli stap kam long ples ia hemi minim se spos wan film kru i wantem mekem wan film long saed blong kalja long Vanuatu hemi mas aplae i kam blong mifala i in advans an hemi no wan bigfala kampani nomo be i save kam olsem wan wan man so i gat plante i respektem samting ia be plante ino respektem an mifala i save se i gat plante long ol wok ia tu oli stap long ovasis yet. Evri taem we oli kam i mas gat wan ofisa blong kaljorol senta i mas folem olgeta i go long aelan blong kontrolem olgeta blong mek sua an sapos we oli save se olsem polisi i stap nao. Mi wantem putum long ol riseja we oli bin mekem wok bifo se sapos sam long yufala ino bin givim wok long yufala yet olsem ol rikoding ol foto i save kam putum olsem tabu rum i gat ol rul blong hem hemi stap long Kaljoral Senta hemi blong fiuja jeneresen mo mifala i gat databes blong hem mo ol foto i gat databes blong hem blong putum ol infomesen blong mekem se ol man oli save kam blong yusum ol samting ia tu isi. Tangkiu tumas.

The Vanuatu National Film Unit

Jacob Kapere

Good afternoon everyone, I have great honour to stand in front of all of you important women and men whose names I have heard before, who have done lots of work in Vanuatu, and it is good to see you all coming together like a family of researchers joining with the fieldworkers and the staff of the Vanautu Film Unit. I joined the film unit in 1986 when Kirk found me on the street in town, maybe it was in a *nakamal*, and he saw that I had some skills in using a video camera. The National Film Photo and Sound Unit is a national repository for anything on film, or photos or audio recording and it is also a *kastom* bank, like the heart of the museum here where we can research *kastom* knowledge from Vanuatu. This place is like a heart in that it branches into different activities on all the islands, and the main work is done by the fieldworkers and the first researchers who worked in the country. When you talk about the film unit now everyone knows about filming and recording, but before there were many ni-Vanuatu who didn't trust filmmakers because of their experience before with the first researchers who came in and recorded people, they played the recording and they heard the voices, but they never came back. Then the old people called these machines 'voice-stealers' and they thought that they stole the people too, because they didn't know too much about such things. And they didn't know that there was a special section at the Cultural Centre which keeps all these recordings. They can come and find lots of recordings made in the past, the spirit of the country is there; it is kept as the property of Vanuatu. One day it must come back to Vanuatu and so all those who set up the National Film and Sound Archive have been trying hard to bring back all of these recordings.

I was one of the first ones to join this section and now I am becoming an old man. It doesn't seem like that to me, but when I look at the older fieldworkers, I can see that the ones who were here as the first fieldworkers, who we heard from this morning, James Gwero and Richard Leona, they are the ones who built up the knowledge bank about *kastom*. James Gwero is one of the first to have recorded all this and he went out to train others in using the equipment to record all these things. As he told us, his shoulders were sore because the equipment in those days was heavy. He said to me, 'Today you don't work so hard, not like us before, we used to sweat hard!' He can see that while there are plenty of fieldworkers there are still not enough for us to go to the islands to record.

But James, together with his colleagues, started this work because people were saying the white men had come and stolen their voices, they stole their photos, and now you have come to do the same thing. So, with the help of Kirk Huffman, James and I'm sure others of you researchers who are here helped to identify these things, like photos, that you who work in overseas institutions knew about, also films and audio recordings. It was a lot of work to get this material copied and sent back to Vanuatu. Kirk managed to find the first film made in Vanuatu, an 11-minute film from Matantua village in 1917, and the filmmaker came back in 1919 to make a longer film about Vao in Malakula and some other places.

But Kirk also found out that most of the film had been lost, so we are lucky to have eleven minutes with some footage from the Solomons in it too. And we also found the first photos, as Philip Tepahae's report noted; they are from somewhere around 1853 from Aneityum. This first collection in black and white started building up our *kastom* bank. At the same time it began to build up people's interest as they started to take these things back to their islands.

We have tried to bring these things back from overseas and in the *tabu* room there are lots of black and white photos collected from many different museums and universities. We are still searching for information about the photos we have so they can go together with recordings. The films in those days were in a different format, usually sixteen millimetre, but they were transferred to VHS. Now the main job for fieldworkers and other ni-Vanuatu is to collect information. Information from the islands, record everything, film everything and preserve it for future generations so that they can understand that language changes with the new life we are moving into. Many people are moving into town and they recognise that their language is changing and that language is the basis for lots of cultural activity on the islands. So in the language there is a way of performing a *kastom* ceremony in a particular area because the language tells them. If there was no language then the *kastom* would have no meaning, like a dance movement or other parts of a dance would have no meaning.

So that is why the film unit's basic work is to collect lots of information before it is lost. When I started I also went out and filmed and put the films in the archive and many people say that the things we recorded are for the future generations. We also put copies in other institutions so they can be used, so that it reflects the people who are there today who know that they will be gone, but their children will be able to go to this archive and find these things again.

James Gwero used a small 8 millimetre camera and some of his films have been transferred to VHS, but many have not yet been transferred. The next format to come out was Video 8 and Viane used Video 8. Viane was a fieldworker, and so did Alben Reuben, from South West Bay, a place where Kirk spent a lot of time doing his research and he thought the area needed a camera so he asked James Gwero to do some training. They sent Alben to Fiji to do some training then they had a small video camera and before he went to an island they sent a message saying they would come with a video camera. People on the islands didn't really understand and they hadn't seen pictures of themselves. Some of them spread the news and the chiefs organised a ceremony on Chiefs' Day, March 5, and they blessed Alben with his video camera before he started using it. There is a big collection of films and then, when I came, we used Video 8 and High 8 which was the next format. We used all the different formats which you can still find in the *tabu* room, there is 16 millimetre, 8 millimetre, Video 8, High 8, VHS, SVHS, DV, DVC Broadcast. Most of the collections were transferred to VHS, then we transferred to DVC Broadcast, but there are many that aren't transferred yet.

So now we come to a time where we look at the *tabu* room as a *kastom* bank. But it is a bank where the money has interest and the interest has to benefit the community, so we all have to use it. In 1990 we started to put programs about *kastom* and culture on television. Now we are still making these programs and they give us a timeslot of two hours per week so twice a month we can use our collection or go out and film something to put on television and send copies to the islands.

So now we want everyone to get used to the collection to help promote *kastom*, language, to raise people's interest. And on the radio we have a *kastom* and culture program every Saturday for half an hour from 6.30 to 7.00 p.m. We asked them to extend this time to replay all the programs that Paul Gardissat made long ago in the time of the New Hebrides, about *kastom*. We talked to the radio people and they were happy to put these programs on again.

Our photos are in the *Daily Post* every weekend and we could even put one in every day to use all the photos in the collection. There are publications that have come out which use stories that were recorded and are in the *tabu* room, booklets with *kastom* stories, so that is also part of our work to get people to use the material that we have.

We have a national film policy so we monitor all film crews so, if a film crew wants to make a film about culture in Vanuatu they must apply to us in advance— not just big companies, even just some one who wants to film—lots of people respect this, but lots also don't respect this policy so we know there is lots of film overseas. Every time a film crew comes it must take an officer from the Vanuatu Kaljoral Senta (VKS) with them to the islands to control what they do and to make sure they understand the policy.

So I want to ask all researchers to deposit their work, like photos or recordings, in the *tabu* room and there are rules at the Cultural Centre so they will be there for future generations. There is a database of all of this and there are photos in the database so it is easy to find information there.

Thank you very much.

13. The Digital Archive and Catalogues of the Vanuatu Cultural Centre: Overview, Collaboration and Future Directions

William H. Mohns

The Vanuatu Cultural Information Network (VCIN) is an on-going initiative of the Vanuatu Cultural Centre (VCC) to organise, manage and protect its digital archives.[1] These archives include those of Vanuatu's National Library; Public Library; National Museum; National Photo, Film and Sound Archive (NFFSA); Vanuatu National Heritage Register; Women's Culture Program; Young People's Program; Traditional Resource Management Program; and Sand Drawing Project. Together these sections comprise the Vanuatu Cultural Centre.

The VCIN, known internally as 'the database project', is a collaborative process among all sections of the VCC that began in December 2004 with the placement of a Canadian CUSO volunteer (the author) at VCC and was managed by a 'database committee' of representatives of the various sections of the Cultural Centre. The project is indebted to, and builds on, previous work in cataloguing and documentation at VCC.

This paper focuses on six aspects of the Vanuatu Cultural Information Network: 1. vision and guiding principles; 2. primary components of the project; 3. impacts of the project; 4. unique features and innovations; 5. role of researchers; and 6. planned and potential future directions.

Vision and guiding principles for the VCIN

Vision

The vision of the VCIN is to make it easier to find information in the Cultural Centre Archives, where a particular individual has the right to access the information, and to preserve the knowledge held in the archives (in the form of catalogue records and digital objects in the archives) through local and offsite backups.

1   The author and the Vanuatu Cultural Centre would like to thank CUSO-VSO, AusAID, the U.S. Ambassador's Fund for Cultural Preservation and the Baillie Family for their support of this project.

Central to the first part of this vision is providing a single platform that will connect information across the various sections of the Cultural Centre. For a given cultural event in Vanuatu or for a given village or language group, there may be relevant information in different forms of media spread throughout the archives of the different sections of the VCC. For example, there may be relevant photos, audio and video recordings in the NFFSA; artefacts in the National Museum; text, audio and video in the archives of the National Heritage Register; as well as books and newspaper articles in the National Library.

A goal of the VCIN is to be able to understand how all of these items are connected—to each other, to language, to individual people and to place. As a result, if a user researches a particular cultural ceremony, for example, they will not only find all publicly-accessible information in the archives, but it will also be clear to them how the various objects in the archives are connected. The user will be able to see, for example, that an object that is in the National Museum was used in a particular ceremony that was recorded by the National Photo, Film and Sound Archive (NFFSA), and that documentation on this ceremony is available from the National Library. Moreover, the user should be able to view digitised photographs of the object from the Museum collections, read relevant electronic documents from the National Library, listen to audio recordings and view photographs and video footage of the ceremony from the NFFSA. As a result the user will be able to understand the museum object in a more appropriate cultural context. In addition, they will be able to navigate through the archives in this way in any of Vanuatu's three official languages: Bislama, French and English.

This vision for the VCIN is reflected in the following six guiding principles: make it easier to find things; respect *tabu* restrictions; understand social and spatial connections; function trilingually and translingually; be easy to use and accessible; and integrate digital content with the catalogue records.

Make it easier to find things

This initiative is about making it easier to locate holdings in the Cultural Centre Archives: easier to find books, artefacts, information about cultural and historical sites, photographs, videos and audio recordings, and traditional knowledge. At the same time this system must respect the structure of *tabu* restriction that is critical to the integrity and functioning of the archives.

Respect tabu restrictions of the archives

The VCIN incorporates differing levels of secured access to the objects and information stored in the network, respecting and reinforcing the existing access structures employed by the Cultural Centre. As such, the VCIN will only make it easier to find things that one has a right to access, and therefore has differing levels of secured access to the information stored in the network. Currently the system relies on sixteen different levels of *tabu* restriction based on gender, family, village, *nasara* and island.

Understand social and spatial connections

We want to create a system that understands the connections between the items in the archives, and the people, places, languages and cultures associated with them. In effect the goal is to be able to map these social and spatial contexts and relationships into digital relationships.

Arrange trilingual and translingual connections

The typical user of the archives is competent in multiple languages and wants to be able to access any material related to their interests, regardless of the language of either the archived object or its catalogue record (its metadata). As such, the VCIN needs to be trilingual in the sense that the user can choose to navigate the archives in any of the three official languages, but also trilingual *and* translingual in that the user can find what they want in the archives by entering search terms in any of the three languages and find what they are looking for without the item necessarily having to be fully catalogued in the three languages (due to the time constraints and expertise that is required to do so).

Easy-to-use and accessible interfaces for cataloguing and searching

The system needs to facilitate greater access to the archives, rather than be a barrier, regardless of the computer skills of the user. It must be easy to use for both the cataloguers and for those searching the catalogues, and to be appropriate for people with differing computer and language skills.

Fully integrate and manage our digital archives with the catalogue records

The system needs to integrate our digital archives with the catalogue information so that the digital objects (full-text document, photo, audio and video recordings) are directly accessible to users alongside the object's detailed catalogue record. Additionally, from a system management perspective, these digital objects and their catalogue records need to be well-organised, easy to manage, and easy to backup. This is a key part of both the Vanuatu Cultural Information Network and of the broader conservation strategy for the archives.

Primary components of the project

The work of realising the vision of the VCIN can be broken down into four main areas of work: cataloguing, digitisation, developing or acquiring appropriate software, and the development of a cultural thesaurus.

Cataloguing the archives

The biggest and most crucial component of the project is the cataloguing of the information in the archives. This has involved most staff of the Cultural Centre and is dependent upon their expertise. As of late 2006, over twenty thousand items from the VCC archives have been catalogued, albeit to varying degrees and not all of which are (as yet) fully integrated into the network.

Digitisation

Another major area of work is the digitisation of portions of the archives. Digitisation is more important and more appropriate for some formats than others. Museum artefacts, for example, do not lend themselves to digitisation very well, while for photographs, audio and video recordings, digitisation is much easier and more appropriate. As such, our digitisation efforts are focussing primarily on photographic, audio and video recordings in the archives, and on incorporating digital texts where already available.

Software: cataloguing and content management applications

The VCIN requires computer software to catalogue and retrieve information as well as to manage our digital content. This software must be capable of meeting each of our goals and principles mentioned above. These requirements are unique, particularly our approach to trilingualism and translingualism, our system of *tabu* restrictions, and our need for a system to manage and integrate our digital files. Moreover, we need a system to do all of this in a way that would be accessible to a wide variety of users.

Typically, commercial cataloguing software packages focus on one particular area: there are library packages, museum packages, photographic archiving packages, but we require a system that does all of this, as well as meeting the other requirements outlined above. At the time that this project was initiated we could not find an appropriate commercial off-the-shelf solution, so we decided we would develop our own applications.

The software we are developing, our Content Management System (CMS), uses a combination of web technologies, including: Coldfusion (an application development framework), Extensible Hypertext Markup Language (XHTML), Cascading Style Sheets (CSS), JavaScript and Structured Query Language (SQL). The use of these web technologies has the benefit of making the system easily deployable over our internal computer network (our intranet) and suited to future deployment over the internet (via an internet website or as a secure extranet), if desired.

Developing our own software is allowing us to ensure that we get a system that precisely meets our needs, and it will allow us to modify and update that system as we require. However, there are challenges and drawbacks to developing our own software, most notably the time and expertise necessary.

The Vanuatu Cultural Thesaurus

A fourth area of work has been to develop a thesaurus to be used in cataloguing. A thesaurus is a word or subject list used in describing and categorising items in cataloguing and to assist in generating relevant search results for users. In this case, the aim is to develop a thesaurus that can broadly encompass all relevant areas of culture in Vanuatu and thus, the vast majority of the holdings of the VCC. The majority of the holdings of the Public Library are a notable exception to this. As much of its holdings come from overseas and are not necessarily concerned with Vanuatu, the Public Library uses the Sears List of Subject Headings, an international English-language subject list used by many special libraries. The National Library uses both the Vanuatu Cultural Thesaurus and the Sears List of Subject Headings in cataloguing its Vanuatu and Pacific Collections.

The thesaurus is used to provide additional description to items in a manner that is consistent, so as to allow for users to find all items on a certain topic. As every cataloguer would presumably describe some items differently from another cataloguer, a thesaurus or subject list is intended to standardise description. It provides a controlled vocabulary and represents an agreement among cataloguers on whether to use the term 'family' or 'kinship', for example. But the standard subject lists that are used by libraries internationally are quite large, yet not necessarily appropriate. They contain many terms that are irrelevant to the Cultural Centre, and yet do not contain many words that are crucial to describing cultural knowledge in Vanuatu.

Consequently, we decided to develop our own subject list specific to Vanuatu, but we also needed to make it trilingual, which meant deciding upon appropriate translations and spellings of words. The challenge is in keeping the list as short as is reasonable, so that cataloguers can come to know it very well in a short period of time. Also different words are of importance to different sections of the Cultural Centre, so a lot of discussion and compromise has been necessary in the development of the cultural thesaurus. And it is the thesaurus that facilitates the trilingual functioning of the catalogue without each of the items in the collection needing to be fully catalogued in each of the three languages. The Vanuatu Cultural Thesaurus currently contains approximately 250 words in each of the three languages.

Unique features and innovations

The Vanuatu Cultural Information Network is unique in the Pacific, if not the world for its integration of multiple media and archival institutions, and for its approach to multilingualism and translingualism.

A system such as the VCIN can only be as valuable as the content it promotes and manages. As such, what really makes this initiative unique is what makes the Vanuatu Cultural Centre itself unique: very rarely do you find a nation's primary cultural institutions so well integrated and cooperative at the national level. As a result we are able to create an incredibly rich and valuable resource for Vanuatu.

The project is also unique in being trilingual and in its approach to multi- and translingualism. Not only is the catalogue able to make the most (multilingually) out of the Cultural Centre's limited cataloguing resources, and cater to and take advantage of the multi- and translingual skills of the typical user of the Cultural Centre, but the project also leaves open the possibility of adding additional languages in the future with relative ease. By translating the Cultural Thesaurus into another language, the catalogues would gain basic search functionality in that language.

Role of researchers

The project should make it much easier for researchers to access the archives, just as it makes it easier for staff, fieldworkers, and the general public. In addition, the project should give researchers a better understanding of the relationships between items in the collections. The system we are creating should also make it easier for researchers to contribute to the archives, both in terms of contributing knowledge and digital files, particularly in the case of photographs.

The potential exists for our photographic archives in particular to grow very quickly. Very simply, it is easier for researchers, fieldworkers, staff, public and tourists to generate digital photographs in much greater number than they generate audio or video recordings, or books. So plans for the network include setting up a system whereby, if a researcher, fieldworker, visitor or member of the public comes to the Cultural Centre with photos to contribute, they can be given a password that will allow them to login to the Content Management System, upload their photos, and enter into the catalogue any information they can provide about them. Then the Cultural Centre's photo archivist would only need to review the uploaded photos and the information provided, and add any additional information required, in order for the photos to become part of the archives. This will save the archivist time in data-entry, and takes advantage of the specific knowledge of the collector/photographer.

This has the potential to allow our photographic archives to grow quickly while reducing the resources and expense required by the Cultural Centre. We are also looking to add a similar feature to allow approved staff, researchers, and fieldworkers to add comments to catalogue entries in a style similar to a 'wiki'. Further to this though, we have begun to include more biographical information in the catalogues. As such, if one contributes photographs, for example, we will ask that they provide biographical and contact information about themselves, as well as for the people appearing in their photographs and this information will be linked to all relevant catalogue entries, leading to the creation of a bibliographic database.

Impacts of the project

Conservation and accessibility through digitisation

In this project, digitisation is a tool in the conservation of the archives because digital copies (where appropriate): provide backups which are more easily transported off-site for protection against damage from natural disasters, fires and theft; are potentially more easily transferred to new media formats; make the creation of additional backups quicker and easier; can be more easily checked for data integrity; and reduce the need to access the original copies, thus reducing the chance of damage to the originals.

Furthermore, digitisation, and the ease of access to digital records created by the Content Management System (CMS), allow for greater access to the archives by the public. Through the CMS, digital archives can be accessed, where appropriate, without the need for staff or users to access the original items or the rooms which hold them, saving time for both staff and user and protecting the original objects. Further, the VCIN allows for the potential of remote access to the archives in the future.

Impacts on the ways in which users interact with the archives

The VCIN makes the archives more accessible to cultural research by helping VKS/VCC staff to locate and access the archives of their section and the archives of other sections of the Vanuatu Cultural Centre with relative ease. The VCIN also permits users to access the archives directly, where appropriate, and it facilitates more detailed documentation of information about the archives and the relations between objects.

However, the VCIN not only changes the way in which VCC staff and users interact with the archives, but also how users interact with VCC staff and with the archives via staff. Such a system makes some information accessible without the need to interact with staff, and thus changes the role of staff as gatekeepers of the archives. Staff still control the level of accessibility of information stored in the archives, but once the appropriate staff member assigns a level of accessibility, then anyone who is granted that level of access can potentially access that information without interacting directly with a staff member. In short, while VCC staff control the CMS, setting the parameters for access to individual objects, some of the role of keeper and gatekeeper of knowledge is transferred from the staff member to the CMS as the user interacts with the CMS to retrieve cultural information, rather than the staff of VCC.

This approach can potentially save VCC staff time in locating and retrieving objects while also ensuring that knowledge is not lost through staff turnover or damage to the archives. However, it also changes the role of the staff member and the dynamic between staff and users changing the transfer of knowledge from an oral to a written process and potentially reduces personal contact between VCC staff and users of the archives. What effect will this have on the relationship between VCC staff and users of the archives? What impacts will any changes in these relationships have on cultural research?

More effective integration of information from multiple media forms from different sections of the Cultural Centre

The system promises the ability to relate various types of media and information from across the Cultural Centre. Again, this means that users can quickly and efficiently access data from various sources and in various media forms: listening to a radio program, viewing photos and reading cultural information retrieved from newspapers or scanned documents, or in databases included in the Network.

Making relationships explicit

The VCIN attempts to make pre-existing relationships among data explicit, drawing connections between objects, catalogue records, place, language and people. These are relations that in some cases would otherwise appear invisible. This is, in effect, a re-contextualisation of objects in the archives into their social, spatial and archival contexts.[2]

Planned and potential future directions

Disseminating information from our catalogues

Up until this point, the focus of the project has been on developing the software, developing the cataloguing practices across and within sections of the VCC, cataloguing objects, and making the catalogues useful to relevant staff of VCC.

The next step envisaged is to make portions of these catalogues available to all staff in the Cultural Centre and to visitors to the Cultural Centre. Following this, the next step would be to consider making the catalogues and possibly part of our collections accessible beyond the Cultural Centre. This could be nationally or internationally via the internet or by setting up the catalogues at a few select institutions (offline or using an extranet).

Disseminating software and exchanging information

A further step would be to exchange collection information with other institutions in Vanuatu in order to expand our collections and allow the VCIN to provide information about holdings elsewhere. This would be particularly useful for the National and Public Libraries to be able to direct users to information held elsewhere and to find out about publications on Vanuatu which are not yet held by the libraries. This would be to make progress toward a broader, national information-sharing network.

One way in which this could be facilitated would be to share the software that we are developing for this project. This would require VCC to support these libraries and provide training and installation assistance. While VCC does not currently have the staffing resources to offer that, there would be a number of advantages to disseminating the software, particularly in facilitating the exchange of information and creating a broader national information sharing network. As such, this is a potential future direction for VCC and the VCIN.

---

2   For a detailed analysis of the links between digital and social relationships in the VCC database, see Geismar and Mohns, (2011).

Costs of supporting and expanding the VCIN

Another important element to consider is the cost involved in maintaining the system and in continually adding content to the VCIN. At the same time, it is important to recognise that good electronic digital content—which the Cultural Centre definitely has—is a valuable commodity. As such, an important consideration in future directions may be to assess the potential for recovering some of the costs of providing services at the national or international level and to expanding the scope of the project. A further question is whether or not there is interest in making portions of our digital archive available overseas, via the internet or otherwise.

Requirements for success

The project is currently at a crucial stage in its development, and its continued success will depend upon substantial investment in the development of VCC's in-house expertise in electronic cataloguing, digitisation, and web development.

Final thoughts

The Vanuatu Cultural Information Network is an ambitious and groundbreaking project of the Vanuatu Cultural Centre. A great deal has been accomplished already, particularly in the cataloguing of the Cultural Centre archives, and the development of a unique Content Management System to run the Information Network. The results of the VCIN are greater accessibility and therefore increased use of the Vanuatu Cultural Centre Archives; increased knowledge stored in the archives; and an increase in the security of the archives. Yet a great deal of work remains on the project, and there is considerable flexibility in what directions the project will go and how much of its potential it will be able to achieve.

References

Geismar, Haidy and William Mohns, 2011. Social relationships and digital relationships: rethinking the database at the Vanuatu Cultural Centre. In *The Aesthetics of Nations: Anthropological and Historical Approaches*. Special Issue of the *Journal of the Royal Anthropological Institute*, vol. 17, issue supplement s1: 133–55, ed. Christopher Pinney and Nayanika Mookherjee.

14. Risej Long Ejukesen blong olgeta Pikanini long Saot Ambae

Roselyne Garae

Long saot Ambae, long Penama provins long toktok we bae mi toktok long hem tede hemi pikinini mo papa. Olsem wanem bae mi statem toktok blong mi olsem bae mi no putum pikinini fastaem bae mi putum se papa mo mama hemi diuti blong tufala blong lukaotem pikinini long home. Taem papa mo mama we tufala i stap, tufala i fes karem pikinini blong tufala taem tufala i karem pikinini blong tufala olsem taem pikinini i bon oli no save se hemi wan pikinini boe o gel. So tat taem ia ol anti blong olgeta oli sakem ol ting long rod blong mekem se hemi soemaot se hemi wan pikinini boe o gel. Taem oli mekem se ol anti blong olgeta oli luk ol hafhaf pandanas we oli stap sakem long ol rod ol pisis we oli stap sakem long ol rod olsem, hemi soemaot se hemi wan gel we hemi bon long wan smol haos we neva wan man hemi luk. So taem oli luk olsem pikinini blong brata blong mi hemi bon hemi wan pikinini gel, hemi soem se pikinini ia bae hemi gru ap bae hemi mekem wanem we hemi stap olsem papa hemi bin telemaot finis we, o anti blong hem i bin lemaot rol blong hem finis se bae hemi gru ap bae hemi mekem.

Taem hemi gru ap bigwan papa hemi putum nem blong hem blong mekem se bambae hemi kam wanem kaen pikinini o wanem kaen gel o boe bambae hemi wok olsem wanem. Bae hemi putum nem blong hem hemi olsem spesel nem we mifala long Ambae mifala i singaotem 'Garae' o 'Gmweta' o 'Tambe' o 'Waileleo'– hemi minim wan samting. Mifala ino gat wan samting blong hemi spesel blong mifala i mekem olgeta i spesel be folem toktok we hemi stap hemia olsem papa hemi mas putum long pikinini blong krim blong kokonat blong mekem se hemi wan boe o gel bambae hemi olsem wanem. Taem hemi gru ap hemi folem wanem we papa o mama blong hem tufala i mekem.

Wetem hemia tu oli mekem seremoni blong bildimap pikinini. Taem papa hemi mekem seremoni so hemi mas givim ol samting long ol anti blong hem tu blong olgeta i pakemap hem tu long strengtenem hem tu long toktok we hemi sud lanem long hom. Taem hemi wan bebi hemi no save wan samting yet so mama hemi stat blong singsing, Lanem kastom, singsing long hem blong mekem se hemi save muvem han blong hem mo muvem leg blong hem mo hed blong hem blong hemi mekem se taem hemi gru hemi kam wan helti pikinini. Hemi mekem wan singsing blong mekem se hemi muvem han mo hemi mekem wanem hemi laf afta long hemia bae pikinini i luk afta hemi traem blong hem tu i mekem olsem papa mo mama blong hem tufala i mekem. Taem hemi wantem talem ol kaen kaen toktok olsem hemi stap saonem ol sot sot toktok olsem papa oli talem lanwis so hemi statem blong lanem pikinini blong hem long lanwis nao. Hao blong singaotem 'papa', olsem mifala i singaotem se 'tata', hemi stat blong lanem fes lanwis blong hem blong singaotem 'papa'. Taem hemi kam blong save stori papa mo mama tufala i lanem kastom stori long hem. Taem tufala i lanem kastom stori long hem taem hemi gat save smol tufala i soemaot famle blong smol boe. Tufala i soem se hemia sista blong yu hemia mama blong yu, tufala i stat blong talem ol toktok olsem blong pikinini hemi tok mo folem, singaotem brata blong mo angkel blong hem long lanwis blong hem. So tat taem ia hemi stat blong toktok mama mo papa blong hem tufala i mekem san droing be tufala i raetem long kraon blong mekem se tufala i stat blong lanem pikinini blong tufala. Taem mi kambak long hom mi kam be mi luk yu no gat be yu stap raon long vilej blong mi so i gat saen we papa i lanem hem taem hemi smol, taem hemi kam papa hemi nogat hemi luk saen long kraon mo hemi save se hemi olsem. Taem papa hemi stap lanem olsem hemi stap tijim hem tu long san droing blong mekem se hemi stat long smol samting, hemi kam antap i gat plante samting bae mi sotem nomo olsem. Taem hemi kam antap blong hemi karem rispek papa blong hem i mas talem long hem se yu no mas mekem samting olsem, yu no mas mekem samting olsem long taem bifo toktok hemi no plante oli, toktok olsem oli putum saen long ol lif o neija, oli no toktok. Blong lanem pikinini blong wokbaot long wan rod soem hemia hemi talem se tabu, yu no mekem olsem tabu yu no mekem wan samting i olsem yu mas mekem olsem yu mas mekem olsem. So oli tokbaot long lif nomo oli putum long kraon taem yumi wokbaot yumi pas yumi no askem yumi jes luk ol mining blong ol lif oli stap yumi save se hemi talem olsem. Taem mifala i gru antap olsem ol papa blong mifala oli lanem evri samting we mifala i save blong mifala i protektem mifala mo mifala i save go long wanem we mifala i wantem blong mekem rod mo ol mama oli mekem ol kakae oli mekem olsem wanem.

Mi traem blong putum long pepa blong olgeta i rid mo tu oli luk mo sem taem oli luk pija. Sem taem tu oli lukim wanem hemi tokbaot long lanwis blong mifala, olsem mi stap tij tu long skul olsem ABC hemia long alfabet blong mifala nomo, mifala i mekem nomo long lanwis blong mifala mekem se wanem we mi tijim long ol pikinini long skul hemia nao long Wenesde mo Fraede, ol samting ia mi stap tijim ol pikinini long hom.

Tangkiu tumas mi bin gat wan riseja we hem i kam stap wetem mi, nem blong hem hemi Catriona hemi blong Australia. Hem nao hemi kam stap wetem mi hemi helpem mi plante long lanwis so hemi stap wetem mi hemi raetem lanwis blong mifala mo hao blong mekem ol smol smol buklet. Hemia olgeta long SIL oli bin trenem mi long USP hao blong mekem ol smol smol buklet olsem. Taem mi stap olsem mi gat ol woksop we oli bin kamaot, ol konfrens olsem mekem se oli leftemap wok blong mi blong mekem wan samting we mi no save mekem olsem naoia mi save mekem blong helpem ol pikinini blong mi long hom. Tangkiu.

Researching Childhood Education in South Ambae

Roselyne Garae

In south Ambae in the Penama Province regarding what I am about to talk to you about today, that is children and parents. How will I start my talk? I won't begin with children, I will begin with the father and the mother, for it is their duty to look after children in the home. Where there is a father and mother, when the child is newly born, people do not know whether it is a boy or a girl. So, their Aunties will throw things about on the road to show whether the new child is a boy or a girl. When they do this, their aunties see all the bits of pandanus that they're throwing on the roads, and this shows that a girl that has never been seen has been born in a small house. So, when they look, like the daughter of my brother who was just born, it shows that this child will grow up and do whatever it is that the father has already foretold, or that an aunty has foretold.

When the child grows up, the father gives him or her a name to make sure that they become a particular kind of person, a particular kind of girl or boy, and to define what kind of work they will do. He will give him a name which is of a special kind that we in Ambae call *Garae* or *Gmweta* or *Tambe* or *Waileleo* and that are meaningful. We don't have anything that is special to us and that makes them special, but according to tradition, fathers must put coconut cream on a child to find out what kind of boy or girl the child will become. When the child grows up, they will do whatever their mother or father has said they would do.

They also perform a ceremony in order to strengthen the child. When the father makes this ceremony he must give things to the child's aunties in order to ensure that they back him up and strengthen the words that the child should learn at home. When the child is a baby, he doesn't yet know anything, and so the mother begins to sing, to teach *kastom* songs to him to make sure that he can move his hands, move his legs and head, and to make sure that when he grows up he becomes a healthy child. He sings a song to ensure that he does what the father and mother do. And when he wants to say these kinds of things, he utters short words like his father in language, and in this way he starts to teach the child language. How to address one's father, which we call *tata*, the child begins to learn his first word and it is to say 'father'. When he reaches the stage in which he can talk, the child's father and mother will teach them *kastom* stories. And when they teach these stories the child begins to learn about their family. They show that this is your sister, this is your mother, and they start to teach other words, such as how to address one's brother or uncle, in language. And at this time when he is learning to talk the child's mother and father will make sand drawings, writing in the ground, in order to teach the child. (For example) when I come home I see that you are not there, but you are somewhere in my village, and there is a sign for this that has been taught in childhood that can be written on the ground to show that this is so. During this education, the father teaches sand drawings starting with small things and then progressing in order to more complicated things. When he begins to reach a stage in which he must command respect, the children's father must tell them the things they cannot do. In the past there was not a lot of this kind of talk, but they communicated these things by way of leaf signs or other natural signs rather than through speech. So the child learns that when he walks along a road this sign means 'taboo', you don't do this. This is communicated by way of leaves only that are put on the ground, and when we pass, we don't ask, we just see the meaning of the leaf and know what it communicates. When we grow big, our fathers teach us everything that we need to know to protect ourselves, or to make our way, and our mothers to make food.

I have tried to put these things down on paper for everyone to read, and also see pictures. At the same time as they see what he talks about in our language, like I teach in school the ABC in our own alphabet, and we do it in our own language. And in this way we teach all the children in school on Wednesdays and Fridays, and I also teach these things to children at home.

Thank you very much. I have had a researcher who has come to stay with me, her name is Catriona [Malau] and she is from Australia. She has come to stay with me and provided much help in language. When she stays with me she writes our language, and tells me how to make small booklets. These are the people of the Summer Institute of Linguistics (SIL), who trained me at the University of the South Pacific (USP), how to make small booklets. In my time there have been workshops and conferences that have improved my work, and made it possible for me to do things I wasn't previously able to do, for example now I can do them to help my children in the home. Thank you.

15. Risej long Kakae blong Disasta long Tanna

Numalin Mahana

Mi nem blong mi Numalin Mahana, mi kamaot long aelan blong Tanna long Waet Sands. Mi bin wok olsem filwoka blong Vanuatu Kaljorol Senta fo naen yias nao. So taem we mifala i kam stap givimaot ol ripot blong mifala long ol risejas we mifala i stap mekem, mifala i faenemaot se topik we mifala i stap kavremap hemi plante mo i go konektem wetem ol narafala laef long aelan. So from we mi mi kamaot long wan eria we ol taem nomo i gat disasta mo disasta ia i gat volcano, hariken mo drae sisen i stap afektem mifala be evri taem we ol disastas ia oli kasem mifala, mifala i stap askem kakae aot saed. So go go taem we risej wok blong mifala i stap go on ale mi mi faenemaot se no long ol bubu bifo olgeta oli gat ol stret fasin blong lukaotem ol famili blong ol taem we i gat disasta oli neva askem help. Mo ol help we i stap kam aot saed oli kostem vatu samtaem ol man oli stap givim help oli glad blong givim. Samtaem we oli sot long vatu bae mifala ino tekem eni samting so mi sidaon mi tingting se wanem nao wok blong mi olsem filwoka blong save mekem blong helpem komiuniti blong mi. Okei mi singaotem ol mama blong kam blong mi tokabaotem tingting from olgeta oli nomo save ol fasin blong ol bubu blong bifo we oli stap priperem kakae blong during long disasta mekem se mi mi go aot saed mi toktok long ol famili aot saed and oli agri long tingting ale mi mi askem long olgeta long ples ia blong givhan long mi. Blong smol smol samting olsem wanem we mi bin stap askem long olgeta ol bus naef blong save givim long ol mama mo ol naef blong kijen, baket blong kasem wota. Taem we mi tekem samting ia i go long fil mi faenem se oli intres mo mifala i gohed long ol tingting. During long 2003 mi bin holem sikis smol smol woksop blong ol disasta kakae mo long during long woksop ia mi disaed se bambae oli no yusum ol dishes mo naef mo kokonat kreta iven faea so evri samting mifala i mekem long kastom fasin nomo iven dresing ap olgeta oli bin dresap nomo long kastom, faea oli yusum wud nomo long traditional wei blong yumi blong bifo mo mi faenemaot se oli intres blong mekem. Bat long narasaed olsem yumi ol risejas yumi save wok blong yumi long fils samtaems hemi no isi mi mi karem fulap toktok. Ol toktok oli go agens ol fasin ia be mi mi jes ignorem nomo mo mi kontiniu blong wok wetem ol mama we oli gat intres.

Taem we mifala i mekem ol woksop ia mifala i givim long ol yangfala blong oli testem. Olgeta we oli plei futbol oli talem long mifala se taem mifala i kakae ol kakae ia mifala i go long fil mifala ino taet mifala i save plei long taem. Mo wei we mi mi traem blong mekem se taem oli get yus blong bringim bak ol kastom fasin blong kakae ale bae mifala i grupim se kakae ia blong mama we i gat bel, kakae blong mama we i givim birth mo kakae ia i blong wan pikinini we i smol kam kasem hemi kam bigwan mo kakae blong ol boe we oli go long sakomsaes mo ol narafala erias long yumi long aelan. Mi mi traem blong putum ol kakae ia long grup sofa nao ia fulap mama oli stap intres mo mifala i stap gohed iet, mifala i stap gohed iet mo ating afta woksop bae mi go bak mi mi kontiniu nomo long wok we i stap. So ating hemia nomo smol ripot we mi mi save givimaot long saed blong disasta kakae. Taem we afta long hariken mi faenem se speseli ol banana oli wes kwiktaem se fes samting mi save se i gat gudfala fasin we yumi save kipim ol banana ia i stap fo anata sikis o wan yia. So fes samting ia nao mi mekem, i gat ol spesel banana blong hem nomo we mifala i kretem wasem long solwota putum long basket ale hangem. Be i gat ol narafala aelan o iven Tanna yumi save berem mo putum antap long ol foktri be hemia we mi mi mekem mifala i hangem. Ale mi faenemaot se oli mekem komen long hemia se hemia we mi mi mekem ino smel be stael laplap ia hemi smel tumas be hemia we mifala i mekem hemi oraet be from ating mifala I, mi mi mekem se mifala i jenisim lif evri tu wiks.

Narafala fasin blong wan kakae bakegen we konkon yam we fulap long yumi i lego i stap wes nomo long ol aelan blong yumi be from mi save se i mas gat wan gudfala wei blong hem so mi go tru long risej karem save long ol samfala mama ale mifala i wokem, mekem se yam ia ino konkon nating taem mifala i wokem folem fasin blong bifo. I gat narafala hemi wan rus blong wan rop we mifala long saot evri aelan long saot, long Aneityum tu oli yusum we oli stap tekem mi kil kilim afta kukum. Hemia tu mi faenem se hemi gud from ol kakae ia speseli konkon yam ia mo rop ia oltaem oli stap andanit long kraon. I gat taem we trifala disasta i save kam in wan yia blong mekem se oli waepem gud ol kakae blong mifala. Be mi faenem se ol kaen kakae ia hemi stap andanit long kraon so hemi sef i stap so mi faenem wei blong mifala i lukaot gud long hem mo tijim ol mama. Sori mi no save tokabaot ol narafala aelan be mi mi tokabaot long aelan blong mi, yes Tanna nomo we tingting blong mi se mifala i mas grupum ol kakae akoding long helt blong man. Mi gat kakae blong sikman, kakae blong ol yangfala boe mo gel olsem. So hem blong mi nao ia we VKS hemi stap inkarejem mifala blong mekem moa awenes and blong mi se mi mas traem faenemaot ol grup blong ol kakae ia. Ating hemia nomo. Tangkiu.

Researching Disaster Food on Tanna

Numalin Mahana

My name is Numalin Mahana and I am from Whitesands in Tanna. I have worked as a fieldworker for the Vanuatu Kaljoral Senta (VKS) for nine years. When we make our reports to all the other researchers we find that each topic connects with all other aspects of life in the island. I am from an area which has lots of disasters—volcanoes, cyclones and drought—which affect us and so we have to find food from other places. So, as our research proceeded I found out that the old people had their own ways of looking after their families during disasters and they never asked for help. And if you got help from outside it cost *vatu*, sometimes it came as charity. Sometimes if they had no money we couldn't get any food. So I thought, what is my role as a fieldworker in helping my own community? I asked all the women to come and talk and, since they also didn't know about the old people's way of preparing food for disaster times, I asked if we could get some help from outsiders and they agreed that I could. We asked for small things like bush knives, kitchen knives to give women to work in their kitchens, buckets to carry water. When I took this out to the field they were all interested and we could go ahead with the project. In 2003 I ran six small workshops about disaster food and we found that they knew how to do without dishes and knives and coconut graters and even fire, so all of this could be done in a *kastom* way, even clothes, they wore *kastom* clothes and we found that people today were still interested in making clothes in this way. On the other hand, we know that our work as field researchers is not always easy. Some people criticise us, but I just ignore them and continue to work with the women who are interested.

When we ran these workshops we gave food to the youngsters to taste. Footballers said that when they ate this food they don't get tired on the field and can play a long time. And the way I tried was, as they got used to reintroducing *kastom* food, then we would group the food. Some is for pregnant women, some for the time of giving birth, and food for small babies until they grow, and food for boys who are being circumcised and all other categories that we have on the island. So we are trying to put all these foods into groups and a lot of women are interested. After this workshop I'll go back and continue with this work. That's all I wanted to say about disaster food. After a cyclone I found that bananas went bad very quickly so I found there was a good way of preserving bananas so they lasted another six months or one year. So the first thing, there are special bananas we grated them and washed them in salt water and put them into a basket to hang. On other islands, or even on Tanna, you can bury them, or even put them in a tree fork, but what we did was to hang them. So I found that they made the comment that the way I did it didn't smell, but the *laplap* style smelled too much, because we changed the leaves every two weeks.

Another way of preparing food was the cheeky yam that most of us don't eat, but I thought there must be some way to eat it, so I did my research and got the information from some women and we tried it and found that the yam wasn't bitter, when we followed the *kastom* way of preparing it. There's another one, a vine root that is on all the southern islands, on Aneityum too they use it. You beat it and then cook it. I found that these were particularly good because the yam and the root are underground. When three disasters come in one year they can wipe out all the food. But I found that these foods that are under the ground are safe so we can look for them and teach all the women about them. Sorry I can't talk about other islands but I am talking about Tanna and I think we need to group the food according to people's health. I have food for sick people, food for young boys and girls and so on. So that's what VKS is encouraging us to do and to raise awareness and I think I need to find out more about different food groups. I think that's all. Thank you.

16. Olpoi Village Pottery Making Today

Yoko Nojima

Lapita marks the beginning of pottery traditions in Vanuatu history.[1] At the opposite end of this chronological sequence are the two pottery traditions known on the western coast of Santo: namely, Wusi in the southwest and Olpoi in the northwest (Figure 16.1).[2] The well-known Wusi pottery certainly highlights the contemporary Santo pottery culture. In contrast, pottery production stopped almost half a century ago in the northwest, even though people still retain the knowledge of pottery manufacturing. This paper focuses on this latter case, the current situation of the pottery-making tradition among the people of Olpoi Village, based on my field experience in Northwest Santo in 2000–2001.

I first visited the village of Olpoi briefly in 1998, and returned for a year in 2000–2001 to conduct a dissertation research. Although pottery making was not the primary focus of my research, the place of pottery in the cooking system was one of my research questions. My visit was timely because Olpoi villagers had produced about a dozen pots just prior to my arrival in August 2000. They once again made some pots in 2001, and I was able to observe and record the process. This paper thus aims to update the research of Olpoi pottery technology to the beginning of the twenty-first century. By doing so, the place of pottery among the people of Olpoi today, and the impact of interaction with researchers in conceptualising their own understanding of the pottery are reconsidered.

Pespia, Olpoi Village and pottery in Northwest Santo

The place where pottery was once in production in Northwest Santo was reported as Pespia (Speiser 1996 [1923]). Today, Pespia is known as the name of a river running south of the Olpoi Village, and Pespia as a place name refers to a number of old settlements that were located upstream of this river. Pespia River remains the major source of their livelihood, supplying extensive riverine

1   My deepest gratitude goes to the people of Olpoi Village who accommodated me during my research. In particular I am grateful to chief Tavue and olfala Pala for all the support they provided. Alti Ezekiel and Helen Mark, fieldworkers of the Vanuatu Kaljoral Senta (VKS) in Northwest Santo also assisted me during my research. I would also like to thank J.-C. Galipaud for introducing me to the region in 1997, and Elizabeth Pascal for sharing the interest through personal communications regarding Olpoi pottery and Northwest Santo.
2   An area from Wusi to the north is generally known as 'West Coast Santo', while further north from Penaoru to Hokua in the western side of Cape Cumberland, is usually called 'Northwest Santo'.

food resources and water for irrigated taro gardens and other daily purposes. Pespia Village might have been once located approximately eight kilometres up into the mountain (Mackenzie 1995), but current villagers do not know the exact location of this old village. Instead, they generally explain that there were many small family hamlets along the river, and that people used to relocate their settlements from time to time. There are no villages or settlements along the Pespia; however, the area is owned by the people of Olpoi Village, who are the descendents of Pespia potters.

Figure 16.1. Map of Espiritu Santo

Olpoi is a Christian village formed after the establishment of the Presbyterian Mission in Nokuku in 1890. Olpoi was likely founded in the early 1920s as a new Christian settlement of about 40 people (Miller 1978: 324). This small settlement was gradually joined by the people who used to live upstream of Pespia River, and eventually became one of the major villages in the northwest. During World War Two, however, villagers returned to the interior to avoid the war. As a result, many of the elderly in the village were born, not in Olpoi, but in the inland territories. They are the people who possess the knowledge of pottery making and retain memories of using pots through their parents. Pottery was frequently used by people until relatively recently. Typically, elderly individuals are familiar with the taste of food cooked in clay pots, and often say, 'This is what my mother used for preparing food for me.'

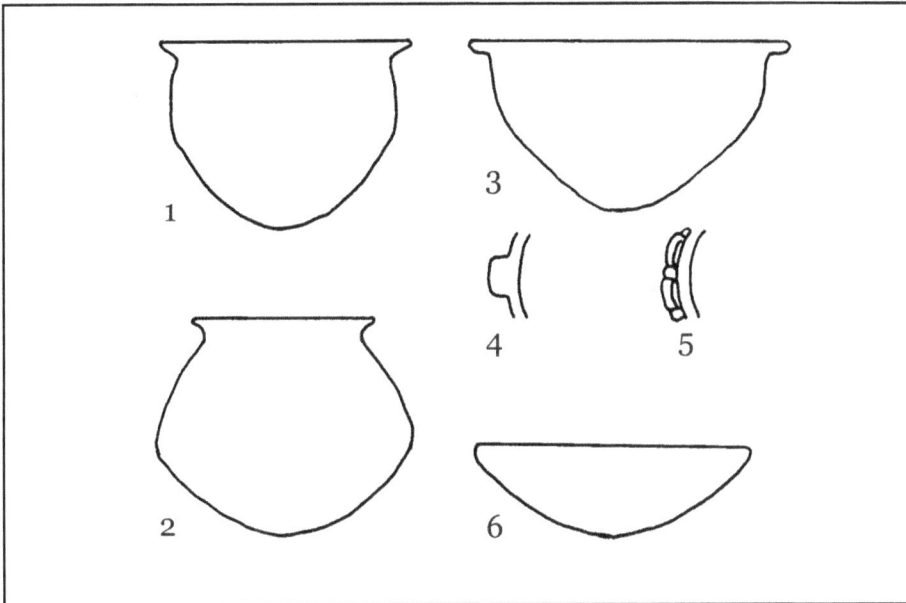

Figure 16.2. Schematic drawing of Olpoi-style pottery

(Yoko Nojima, c. 2000)

An old story in Olpoi recounts that pottery was brought about by a legendary man named Taval. According to the story, Taval went to his yam garden and found that a bamboo pole for supporting yam vines was swinging in the strong wind. The bamboo was tilted in all directions and created a round hole in the ground. Taval picked up this hole with curiosity, which became the shape of pottery. Variants of this story can be heard in the entire region of Northwest Santo including the Big Bay side. Interestingly, Taval is also the name of a source where people of Olpoi collect clay required for manufacturing pottery, although clay sources seem to be known in multiple locations in Northwest Santo. At

Pesina on the Big Bay, for instance, there once was a known clay deposit. This source, however, is said to have been spoiled by a man contaminating the clay with sea water, and thus the pottery technology has been lost there.

Pottery in Northwest Santo is called *welep*, meaning 'a saucepan of ground'. There are four major forms in Olpoi-style pottery (Figure 16.2): 1. a pot with neck and an outcurving rim (*wepran*); 2. a pot similar to 1., but with a narrow neck relative to the large diameter of the body (*weaotot*); 3. a tall, bowl-like pot with a straight rim (*weanlan, wepatpat*, or *wepatmot* depending on the decorative motifs on the rim); and 4. a shallow dish or bowl (*ov*). Among them, the first three are used for boiling, and are associated with the preparation of crops, cabbage and meat respectively, although the same pots are often used for any kind of food (Nojima 2010). Based on my observation, a particular fish called *maj* (a kind of freshwater goby) was the food most commonly cooked when pottery was used for cooking. This fish is frequently eaten in the western coast of Santo, usually boiled. When cooking this fish in pottery, sea water is used and boiled until all the water is evaporated (Figure 16.3). This cooking method, called *waktos* (*wak*=dry; *tos*=sea water), works better with a clay pot than with common metal pots, probably due to the different evaporation rate of water content. The preference towards the taste and texture of food cooked in pottery is recognised by the people. The major reason people do not use pottery for this cooking, they say, is a shorter cooking time and the easy handling of metal pots. Some informants in Northwest Santo mentioned that pottery was needed for cooking small portions of food, notably in relation to the grade system in which high-ranked individuals possessed their own fireplace to be separated from the others of lower status. This does make some sense because some pots found in old settlement sites in the bush are relatively small (with a maximum diameter of 15 centimetres or less), and some pottery employing the decorative motif of a boar's tusk is described as 'a pot for the chief' (Figure 16.4).

Pottery has been in intermittent production for at least half a century. Villagers remember that some pots were produced sometime in early 1980s,[3] although this seems to have been a one-time event. The major explanations provided by the Olpoi people for not making pottery today are twofold. First, the people's shift from the interior to the coastal settlement distanced them from their clay sources so that it is now much harder to obtain materials for making pots. Second, it is often expressed that the current village environment is extremely dry, which is not good for making pottery. It seems most likely that the needs for clay pots have diminished to a great extent as the lifestyle of the people has been transformed as a result of Christianisation and increased Western influences. However, the availability, durability and expediency of metal pots rarely came up from the villagers as a reason for not making pottery; instead, they are the reason for not using pottery.

---

3 People remember there was a flood that year, most likely caused by a cyclone.

Figure 16.3. Maj Cooking

(Yoko Nojima, photographer, 2000)

Figure 16.4. Olpoi Pottery

(Yoko Nojima, photographer, c. 1998)

Pottery making in 2001

Ethnographic accounts in the early twentieth century attest that pottery was made only by females (Harrison 1936; Mackenzie 1995). Some elders in Northwest Santo also explained that pottery used to be made by females, while males helped them in the first step of clay preparation. Today in Olpoi, pottery is made by both men and women, although the majority of potters seems to be male. There is also an old man in a small settlement of Ravlepa to the south of Nokuku, who occasionally makes pots, because he used to observe his mother making Olpoi style pots.

The pottery making events in the years 2000 and 2001 were both organised by the Presbyterian Youth Group of the Olpoi Village, more or less as a project to learn their *kastom* of pottery making. Making pottery in 2001 was also a promise villagers made to me when I arrived in Olpoi in August 2000. However, when the season for pottery making came closer, the village youth became somewhat reluctant, saying that there was no time to go to the mountain to dig out clay and that they were too busy doing other work such as preparing copra. In the end, pottery making was carried out on a somewhat smaller scale than the previous year (pots were made by seven individuals, one piece each). Three of them were village elders who already had some experience making pots, and they helped others to learn how to make pots.

The basic process of pottery making remains the same as that recorded by F. Speiser, M.E. Shutler (1971), and more recently by Jean-Christophe Galipaud (1996). The following description summarises the pottery making carried out in 2001.

Preparing clay and bamboo platform

The clay is spread on a large flat board made of *nakatambol* wood (*Dracontomelon vitiense*).[4] Before pounding a lump of clay, gravels contaminating the clay must be removed. Some water is added while pounding to attain ideal plasticity (Figure 16.5).

Shaping pottery

A bamboo cylinder is planted upright in front of the potter who is seated on the ground, on which clay, made into coils, is placed to form the body of the pots. Bamboo cylinders are occasionally rotated, serving as turntables for pottery making. After placing several layers of clay coils, it is smoothed and adjoined with wet fingers. Then the coiling process is repeated until the bottom half of the body of the pot is finely shaped (Figure 16.6). Then a flat disk of clay about

---

4   In Speiser's account (1996), however, the use of a stone table is noted.

the size of a palm is placed inside to create the bottom of the pot. The upper body of the pot is then shaped in the same manner of coiling. When making a *weanlan*, one or two sets of handles (*anlan*=ear) are attached. Handles are created by applying 3–4 short clay strings of about the length of a finger. This style is considered easier to form because of its simple vessel shape and open profile, and is often chosen by young people in their pottery-making practice.

Figure 16.5. Preparing clay

(Yoko Nojima, photographer, 2001)

Figure 16.6. Coiling the clay

(Yoko Nojima, photographer, 2001)

Decoration

It seems that the systematic decorative patterns or motifs are no longer in practice and that much knowledge regarding the decoration of pottery has vanished. While Shutler (1971) notes that Olpoi potters at the time of her visit possessed precise names for each decorative motif, I was unable to hear any explicit explanations. As a knowledge base for the decoration of pottery, the application of clay ropes and the use of fingernails, coconut midribs or citrus thorns for creating incisions are commonly shared (Figure 16.7). These are identical to the set of techniques recorded by Speiser. A motif employing a series of semi-circle clay ropes around the rim, known as *patpat* or 'a boar's tusk', is an exceptional case of well-known pottery design.[5] When decorative patterns are applied to the surface, the pottery is finally removed from the bamboo base, and its exterior bottom surface is smoothed with fingers.

Figure 16.7. Decorating the pot

(Yoko Nojima, photographer, 2001)

Applying red slip

Red clay (*ta'me*) is applied to the entire surface of the pot after a week of production, and pots are subsequently dried in a cool place for about a month. This process took longer than the case recorded by H. Mackenzie in

---

5   This pattern is also commonly applied for their large wooden plates for making *nalot*, an important dish in northern Vanuatu cuisine.

which red paint is applied after two days and pots are dried for only five days (Mackenzie 1995: 69). Red clay is mixed with water inside a bamboo container, and softened fibre from a coconut husk made into an application brush is used for painting pots. When pots are dried and ready to be fired, extra red clay is scraped off and the scabrous surface of the pot is smoothed with large, disk-shaped seeds of snakerope (*Entada phaseoloides*) (Figure 16.8). A sharp bamboo edge recorded by Mackenzie (1995) was not used in my observation.

Figure 16.8. Smoothing the surface of the pot

(Yoko Nojima, photographer, 2001)

Figure 16.9. Placing firewood against the pots on the hearth platform

(Yoko Nojima, photographer, 2001)

Figure 16.10. Fired pots are left outside until next morning

(Yoko Nojima, photographer, 2001)

Firing pots

Firing was done at midnight (some villagers mentioned that it should be before dawn). Some stones are lined on the ground to create a hearth platform to place pots ready for firing. This hearth is first pre-heated by making a fire on top. The pot surface is rubbed with specific *kastom* leaves before firing. This magic ensures a successful firing without any cracks. Pots are then placed upside down on top of the pre-heated platform, and firewood is set against pots to cover them from the surroundings. Firewood for this purpose is supposed to be *navenu* (*Macaranga*), although people used *burao* (*Hibiscus tiliaceus*) at the time of my observation. Only two to three pieces of pottery were fired at once, but a larger platform could accommodate more pots. Firing takes only about 25 minutes. Although Shutler (1971: 82) writes that 'the pots are fired in a slow smouldering fire and left in the ashes until completely cold,' I observed firing done with a strong, flaming fire. Fired pots are immediately removed from the fireplace with wooden tongs. Fired pots are believed to be as strong as iron, so they could be picked around without any particular attention. These pots are then left outside until the next morning, with some charcoal pieces placed inside.

There are some taboos and magic (or what villagers also call *kastom*) associated with pottery making. It is said to be taboo for a potter to eat salt when he/she is making a pot (Shutler 1971). This is generally taken literally and even consuming food containing salt is avoided. 'To eat salt' in fact is a connotation of sexual intercourse, and this is what has to be avoided before making pottery. The red colour symbolises Olpoi pottery as a product of strong *kastom* blessed by their ancestors. The red colour is a metaphor for the blood of ancestors. When villagers dig red clay, the names of the clan members who were deceased or killed are called, so that the blood of the dead will redden the soil. Digging sticks must be cut from a tree named *a'a* (*Myristica fatua*), whose sap is also red. When pots are fired, they have to be left outside so that spirits of the dead will come around to decorate them with their blood.

Olpoi pottery in transition

Archaeological evidence attests that pottery was once used almost everywhere in Vanuatu until about 2000BP in the south, 1200BP in the centre, and in Northern Vanuatu the pottery tradition lasted much longer and persisted in some regions to the ethnohistoric period (Bedford 2006, Bedford and Spriggs 2008). In the past 200 years, however, Santo was the only place in which pottery was produced and documented in ethnographic records. Geographical marginality and relative isolation of the west coast of Santo would have contributed greatly to the survival of pottery technology, without being heavily entangled in the wave of post-contact cultural transformations. Accordingly, this process made pottery an item more closely and distinctively associated with the people in this region.

The production and use of pottery among the people of Santo has been recorded in major ethnohistoric and ethnographic accounts. The earliest remarks on Santo pottery come from the accounts related to the voyage of Pedro Fernandes de Quirós in 1606. Regarding the people of Big Bay, Quirós' journal says, 'the natives make from a black clay some very well-worked pots, large and small, as well as pots and pans and porringers in the shape of small boats' (Markham 1904: 269). Fray Martin de Munilla also writes, 'In this land was found something that has not been seen in any of the islands already discovered—namely many pots and pans of very good baked clay, and many wooden dishes and spoons' (Kelly 1966: 215). These records suggest the uniqueness and richness of pottery culture throughout the island of Santo. In the early seventeenth century, pottery could have also been in use on the other islands in northern Vanuatu (Bedford and Spriggs 2008: 110–12).

During the late nineteenth and early twentieth centuries, missionaries and ethnographers left some records on Pespia and its pottery (Mackenzie 1995; Rannie 1912). F.A. Campbell, a Presbyterian missionary who visited the area in the late nineteenth century, noted that pottery was made only in Santo (Campbell 1873). Steel (1880: 332) also left a brief remark on Santo pottery, saying 'they make a kind of unglazed pottery, which they use for culinary purposes; but they all say that their fathers made a far superior kind.' Acknowledging the existence of pottery in the region, it is noteworthy that a certain degree of technological limitation has already been mentioned.

Speiser was the first ethnographer to have left an in-depth documentation of pottery making in Pespia and Wusi. He records that pottery was made only in these two villages at the time of his visit, indicating the pottery production was no longer ubiquitous in the western coast of Santo. He also writes, 'the quality of the pots has sadly deteriorated. The examples of the older production which are still to be seen are markedly superior to modern wares in general shape, in the thinness of their walls, and in the delicacy of the ornamentation' (1996: 231–2). About 25 years later, T.H. Harrison (1936) notes that a female he saw at Pespia was the last potter. These statements point out that there was considerable transformation in pottery production during the late nineteenth and early twentieth centuries, probably in association with increased western influence upon their lifestyle. The spread of western cooking ware might have reduced the demand for hand-made pottery, which would have also lessened its value in exchange.[6] Epidemics induced through Western contact causing population decrease might also have had considerable impact in transmitting the knowledge of pottery technology.[7]

---

6   The network of exchange connecting the islands of Vanuatu itself would have undergone considerable change concurrent with the sociopolitical transformation triggered by Christianisation and Western colonisation.

7   For instance, there was an outbreak of influenza in 1926 (Miller 1978).

It was also in the early twentieth century that Santo pottery became the focus of ethnographical and anthropological research as a part of Melanesian pottery traditions (MacLachlan 1939; Schurig 1930). Since the 1950s, as archaeological investigations in the Pacific progressed with the discovery of Lapita and other traditions such as incised and applied relief potteries (Gifford and Shutler 1956) and the long-term history of pottery traditions in Melanesia became evident, ethnographic Santo pottery became the subject of researches, particularly by archaeologists. Shutler, who visited Santo in 1967, recorded pottery making in Wusi and Olpoi (Shutler 1968; 1971). While Wusi pottery technology was also recorded by Guiart (1956) in the 1950s, Shutler's brief article (1971) is the only source from which we can learn about the state of Olpoi pottery making during this time. She notes for Olpoi pottery that 'an admiring audience surrounds the potter and especially good pots are treasured as pieces of art,' whereas Wusi pots were made in haste for sale (Shutler 1971: 82). This statement would indicate that pottery making was no longer a common practice at Olpoi, while at Wusi pots seem to have been produced in quantity. The time of Shutler's visit probably marks the demise of pottery production at Olpoi, at least on an annual basis.

More recently, in the 1990s, Galipaud in association with Vanuatu Cultural and Historic Site Survey (VCHSS) did extensive surveys on surface pottery collections in the west coast, and recorded pottery making by an old man in Ravlepa (Galipaud 1996). This Ravlepa potter occasionally makes pottery as his mother who was from Olpoi used to do it. The same could be said for an old man in Olpoi who is also well-known as a potter. He principally learned how to make pottery by watching his mother making pots, rather than being trained to be a potter. Pottery making for them is a means of remembering their *kastom*. Some other Olpoi villagers also try making pottery from time to time most likely for similar reasons: because pottery is their *kastom* and an object reflecting their memories of the past.

Pottery, Olpoi people today, and us

Two ethnographically-known pottery-making villages have followed contrasting paths in the last century. The Wusi pottery tradition, despite the danger of its demise when devastating epidemics in the early twentieth century killed almost the entire Wusi population (Baker 1929), has been inherited and revived by the inland population who migrated to the coast and founded a new Wusi village (Galipaud 1996).[8] Pottery is produced annually by Wusi women and sold to tourists in Luganville and Port-Vila, rather than being used for cooking by the

---

8   The contemporary Wusi language is thus different from the original one. In 2000, there was only one person who spoke the original Wusi language.

local people. In contrast, Olpoi pottery gradually shifted to decline as its practical value in food preparation and exchange became diminished. Nevertheless, up to the present day, throughout the entire west coast, Olpoi pots are regarded as excellent cooking vessels.

The quality of pottery manufactured today is not as refined as pieces from older times. This would point to the current state of pottery technology among the Olpoi people, in which considerable knowledge has been lost. Considering that the diminishing quality of pottery was recognised almost a century ago, it is notable that the knowledge somehow endured this period of critical transformation and survived up to this century. The reason behind this would be the people's attachment to their own *kastom*, culture and history, all of which are symbolically materialised in pottery. At the same time, the westerners' admiration of their pottery and occasional visits of researchers who were interested in their pottery would have influenced the local people's perception of pottery as an item representing their history.

It is noteworthy that pottery was made in 2000 and 2001. In 2000, Olpoi people did it principally on their own initiative, although brief visits of researchers such as Galipaud and myself in the late 1990s might have indirectly encouraged their decision making. Nonetheless, it seems that people are facing difficulties in deciding how they should handle the situation. A person in the village noted that pottery making is a very important *kastom* for them, but he doesn't know how keeping this tradition would benefit their lives. Due to the geographical isolation, people often face considerable economic difficulties. The income of the people comes almost entirely from copra and cacao plantations; the produce from both can be sold only when a cargo ship passes through the west coast of Santo, a few times a year. For the Olpoi people, improving their economic situation is the most critical issue. Such economic hardship in turn is limiting their appreciation of traditional knowledge and time spent for making pottery. After 2001, pottery making in Olpoi did not continue into the following years to fully revive the practice. However, there was an unsuccessful attempt in 2007, suggesting that at least some people still possess a will to make pottery. Also, there has been some news from Ravlepa where families of the deceased old man who used to make pots have started learning and producing pottery in the past few years (Pascal, personal communication).[9]

Archaeologists tend to view the contemporary pottery technology overlaid on a chronological timeline relating to the prehistoric pottery sequence, and as a clue to understanding the history of the Pacific people, rather than evaluating it within a contemporary sociocultural context. Similarly, local people themselves seem to regard pots as objects that embody their history. As long as it is regarded

---

9   The updated information regarding pottery making in Olpoi and Northwest Santo is credited to correspondence with a researcher, Elizabeth Pascal, who has been visiting this area since 2004.

as something of the past and distanced from their contemporary lives, it will be difficult to keep pottery alive. What is critical is to establish a solid foundation where pottery could be embedded in the lives of people in Northwest Santo. Finding a commercial route would be a way to do this—like the Wusi people are doing. It would also be possible for pottery to be developed again for culinary purposes. In any case, pottery making could be effectively used as a means of learning about *kastom*, as some Olpoi youth tried about a decade ago. Whether this art of pottery making will be carried through to the next generation depends on the people's decision and efforts today. Encouragement and support from researchers and the Vanuatu Cultural Centre are certainly beneficial in this critical process, as evidenced by the success of revitalising the *kastom* mat production on Ambae through the Women's Culture Project and the active involvement of researcher L. Bolton (Bolton 1994, 2003).

References

Baker, John R., 1929. *Man and Animals in the New Hebrides*. London: Routledge Press.

Bedford, Stuart, 2006. *Pieces of the Vanuatu Puzzle: Archaeology of the North, South and Centre*. Terra Australis 23. Canberra: Pandanus Books, Research School of Pacific and Asian Studies, Australian National University.

Bedford, Stuart and Matthew Spriggs, 2008. Northern Vanuatu as a Pacific crossroads: the archaeology of discovery, interaction, and the emergence of the 'ethnographic present'. *Asian Perspectives* 47: 95–120.

Bolton, Lissant, 1994. *Bifo yumi ting se samting nating*: the Women's Culture Project at the Vanuatu Cultural Centre. In *Culture, Kastom, Tradition: Developing Cultural Policy in Melanesia*, ed. L. Lindstrom and G.W. White, 147–60. Suva: Institute of Pacific Studies, The University of the South Pacific.

Bolton, Lissant, 2003. *Unfolding the Moon: Enacting Women's Kastom in Vanuatu*. Honolulu: University of Hawai'i Press.

Campbell, F.A., 1873. *A Year in the New Hebrides, Loyalty Islands, and New Caledonia*. Geelong: G. Mercer.

Galipaud, Jean-Christophe, 1996. Le rouge et le noir: la poterie Mangaasi et le peuplement des îles de Melanésie. In *Mémoire de Pierre, Mémoire d'Homme: tradition et archéologie en Océanie*, ed. M.J.M. Julien, M. et C. Orliac, *et al*, 115–30. Paris: Publications de la Sorbonne.

Gifford, Edward W. and Richard Shutler, 1956. *Archaeological Excavations in New Caledonia*. Anthropological Records 18. Berkeley and Los Angeles: University of California.

Guiart, Jean, 1956. *Grands et Petits Hommes de la Montagne, Espiritu Santo (Nouvelles Hébrides)*. Nouméa: Institut français d'Océanie.

Harrison, T.H., 1936. Living in Espiritu Santo. *Geographical Journal* 88: 243–61.

Kelly, Celsus, 1966. *La Austrialia del Espíritu Santo: The journal of Fray Martin de Munilla, O.F.M., and other documents relating to The voyage of Pedro Fernández de Quirós to the South Sea (1605–1606) and the Franciscan Missionary Plan (1617–1627)*. Cambridge: The Hakluyt Society.

Mackenzie, Helen, 1995. *Mackenzie, Man of Mission: A Biography of James Noble Mackenzie*. Melbourne: Hyland House.

MacLachlan, R.R.C., 1939. Native pottery of the New Hebrides. *Journal of the Polynesian Society* 48: 32–55.

Markham, Clements (trans and ed.), 1904. *The Voyages of Pedro Fernandez de Quiros, 1595-1606* vol. 1. Nendeln/Liechtenstein. London: Hakluyt Society.

Miller, J. Graham, 1978. *Live: A History of Church Planting in the New Hebrides to 1880*. Sydney: Committees on Christian Education and Overseas Missions, General Assembly of the Presbyterian Church of Australia.

Nojima, Yoko, 2010. Pottery as cooking vessels: the persistence of pottery technology in the western coast of Espiritu Santo, Vanuatu. *People and Culture in Oceania* 26: 57–79.

Rannie, Douglas, 1912. *My Adventures among South Sea Cannibals: An Account of the Experiences and Adventures of a Government Official among the Natives of Oceania*. London: Seeley, Service & Co. Limited.

Schurig, M., 1930. *Die Südseetöpferei*. Leipzig: Druckerei der Werkgemeinschaft.

Shutler, M.E., 1968. Pottery making at Wusi, New Hebrides. *South Pacific Bulletin* 18(4): 15–18.

Shutler, M.E., 1971. Pottery making in Espiritu Santo. *Asian Perspectives* 14: 81–3.

Speiser, Felix, 1996. *Ethnology of Vanuatu: An Early Twentieth Century Study*, trans. D.Q. Stephenson. Honolulu: University of Hawai'i Press (originally published 1923).

Steel, Robert, 1880. *The New Hebrides and Christian Missions, with a Sketch of the Labour Traffic and Notes of a Cruise through the Group in the Mission Vessel*. London: J. Nisbet and Co.

17. The Kastom System of Dispute Resolution in Vanuatu

Miranda Forsyth

This paper is a short report of the progress of my doctoral research into the indigenous, non-state system of dispute management in Vanuatu, which is called the *kastom* system for the purposes of the study. This paper will discuss the research questions the study is based on, the operation of the *kastom* system generally, two of the leading principles of the *kastom* system, the challenges facing the *kastom* system today, the relationship of the *kastom* system with the state system and finally the problems with that relationship.[1]

Research questions

The central issue with which the study is concerned is determining what the relationship between the *kastom* system and the state system is, and how it can be improved. In addressing this issue there are a number of sub-questions which must be asked: How is the *kastom* system currently operating in Vanuatu? What is perceived by the stakeholders as being the current relationship between the *kastom* system and the State justice system? What do the stakeholders consider to be the current problems with the relationship between these two systems and what reasons do they suggest are the cause of these problems? Do the stakeholders think the two systems should remain working in their current relationship or might another form of relationship better meet the needs of the people of Vanuatu? What model or models of a relationship between the two systems would allow the two systems to better meet the needs identified by the stakeholders?

Research methodology

The methodology which was used to conduct the study utilised a variety of approaches, many of which involved collaboration with the Vanuatu Kaljoral Senta (VKS). The principal methodology was in-depth interviews with key actors in both systems, and these were conducted throughout Vanuatu. In addition,

---

1   Subsequent to this paper being presented, the doctoral research has been completed and published as a book (Forsyth 2009).

to overcome the problem of my inability to attend actual *kastomkot* meetings, the VKS fieldworkers assisted me in filling out '*KastomKot* Observation Forms' to provide information about the actual cases which were dealt with in their communities. Over the course of two years, twenty of these completed forms were returned to me and were very useful in giving examples of matters decided and the types of procedures which were followed. The VKS's Young People's Project (YPP) was another focus of collaboration which involved a list of my questions being attached to a general questionnaire the YPP was administering throughout Vanuatu. Two additional methods of finding out information came from my experience of working in the Vanuatu Public Prosecutor's Office for a year and also through the holding of the Vanuatu Judiciary Conference 2006 which had as its focus the relationship between the two systems, and which brought together chiefs, police, lawyers and the judiciary to discuss a number of the issues involved with their co-existence (Forsyth 2006).

The operation of the *kastom* system

The kastom system in one form or another exists in every village and town in Vanuatu. It is indisputably the place where the vast majority of disputes in every rural and urban community in the country are dealt with. The central idea of the kastom system is that the chief or chiefs of a community are responsible for managing disputes and they do so through holding a public meeting with the parties involved at which the dispute is discussed, responsibility allocated and amends made through the payment of a custom fine by one or both of the parties. This fine is generally in the form of pigs, mats, kava, food and increasingly cash. Around this base there is a large diversity in the means of resolving disputes throughout the archipelago. For example, one respondent describes the process in Ambae:

> Once the parties have put their cases and [their points of] view the meeting breaks off after having elected some judges. These judges are not formally nominated; it is just known which people have the most knowledge and wisdom and have been fair in the past. These people then go away and discuss between themselves what to do and then return and announce how the reconciliation is to be reached. The parties are then called to comment on the decision and if there is disagreement then the meeting will not end until agreement is reached. The contribution of both parties is significant in coming to a reconciliation.

In contrast, in North Pentecost the process was said to be as follows:

> When there is a meeting everyone gathers in the nakamal and the chairperson of the village council tells the chiefs that they will be

responsible for making a decision. The chairperson directs the meeting. He is chosen by the village but is not necessarily a chief. Everybody talks, to give evidence and so on. At the end of the talking everyone goes outside and leaves the chiefs to discuss the issue and come to a decision. Then they come back inside and the chiefs say what their decision is. Then everyone goes back to their houses to look for pigs and red mats…. There is never any negotiation about the fine.

The matters that the kastom system in each area deals with depends on a number of factors, including the beliefs of the chiefs as to what cases they can manage to deal with, community support, and the accessibility of the state system. Thus in some places it only deals with minor disputes, whereas in other places it deals with everything, including murder.

Guiding principles of the *kastom* system

Restorative principles

The basic principles of the kastom system as enunciated by the chiefs and as practiced in the vast majority of cases are restorative, in that the focus is on restoring relationships that have been broken by the dispute. Two of the main stated aims of any kastom meeting are: 'blong mekem [tufala pati] shake han mo kam gudfala fren bakegen' [to make the two parties shake hands and become good friends again] and to allow the defendant to 'mekem gud fes' (literally 'clean [the person's] face', meaning to get respect in the community again). The purpose of this second aim is so that the defendant can once again become a functioning member of the community and any avoidance that may have been practised before the meeting can cease, which is important in small and inter-dependent communities.

The *kastom* process generally takes a holistic approach to the disputes, taking into account a wide variety of matters including the underlying causes of the conflict. It is for this reason that the payment of goods and cash are often in both directions, rather than having a single winner and a single loser as in the state system. For example, a chief gave an example of the holistic approach taken in kastom:

> In kastom if John comes and looks at Brown and Brown swears at him, John fights him. In court if a man says that he fought the man then he is punished but the one who swore does not get any punishment. So John goes and fights him again. The way that the ni-Vanuatu look at it is to ask who started the dispute and to punish that person as well.

This approach also means that sometimes even people other than the parties are fined. This is illustrated by a case about 'jealousy' which occurred in Ambae. A man suspected that his wife, a nurse, was having an affair with Z, one of her co-workers. Initially a village court heard the case and it was settled, but then Y started to talk to the jealous husband, stirring him up and suggesting that his wife and Z had been lying. The case then was taken up again at the area level where the chiefs 'found' that although the wife had not had an affair with Z she had provoked the jealousy because she had once telephoned him when she was away and had told him she was calling from a different place than the place she actually was. The end result was that the wife was ordered to pay a fine, but the heaviest fine was imposed on Y who had to pay a fine to the chief, to Z and to the husband for the trouble he had caused.

Importantly, at times the restorative principles are not always followed and the *kastom* system is used as a means of punitive control. An example of this is given by a respondent who stated:

> I will tell you about a case of a relative of mine. She had 'flatem' [finished] all the men around her and made lots of women very angry with her. The chiefs tried everything they could to stop her—they cut off her hair, and they all whipped her. Then finally they sent her back to the island. She stayed there for ten years and she saw how hard life was there, not like getting paid money for sex, and now she has come back to Vila ten years later a changed woman. Now she stands next to the chiefs to assault the women who have children with no fathers!

Peace and harmony in the community

Another central principle of the kastom system is that of restoring peace and harmony to the community. At times this principle conflicts with the restorative notions of the kastom system; for example victims who may not really be happy with the decision are forced to accept it and 'shake hands' for the good of the community. This principle may also conflict with notions of individual rights as the peace of the community is prioritised over individual justice.

Challenges for the *kastom* system today

There are significant challenges facing the operation of the kastom system today. The major problem with the kastom system today from the point of view of the chiefs is that many chiefs find it difficult to effectively wield authority, as people refuse to listen to their orders, to come to meetings and to pay the fines levied upon them. The reasons for this are partly created by the chiefs themselves (disputes over chiefly title, biased decision-making and chiefs acting contrary to their own kastom laws lessen peoples respect for them); partly a result of the increasing westernisation of society (increasing emphasis on individual rights and a materialistic approach to life lessens the force of community ties and respect); and partly a result of the existence of the state system (community members challenge the chiefs on the basis that they have no authority under the Constitution, the police prevent them from using force to enforce their orders and people take disputes to the state system if they are not satisfied with the chiefs' decision thus undermining their authority).

The main problems identified by non-chiefs with the system are: in many places the *kastom* system discriminates against women and youth, both procedurally by denying them a voice and also substantively, for example by fining a woman more than a man in a case of adultery; the widespread perception of bias among the chiefs, and even more problematically, the fact that there is no real way of dealing with biased, unfair, lazy or incompetent chiefs. As a result, many communities face the problem of believing in the kastom system and its advantages in principle, but not being able to access them because of their particular chief.

One positive finding is that despite these problems, the kastom system today is generally well-supported by the whole population, including women and youth, for its many benefits, including its essentially restorative nature, its accessibility; its familiarity; its ability to bring about peace and the fact that it is 'their' system.

The relationship with the state system

The kastom system itself is not legally recognised by the state, although the Constitution does recognise substantive customary law as a source of law. Elements of the kastom system are also recognised in a few minor ways by the state system, such as in provisions in the Criminal Procedure Code which allow the court to take customary settlements into account while sentencing. Essentially, however, at present the two systems operate very much in parallel rather than together, and their points of intersection are fluid and subject to negotiation by the individuals involved.

Each of the different state agencies (police, courts, prosecutors etc.) has an informal and dynamic relationship with the state system, which varies from place to place and from time to time. For example, in some areas the police require people to put the disputes before the chiefs before they lodge a complaint, whereas in others there is no such requirement.

The approach of the state towards the chiefly system has essentially been to rely upon it to maintain law and order where the state resources cannot reach, or are not accepted, but to deny any requests from the chiefs for state power to assist them in carrying out their duties, claiming that the source of the chiefs' power should be kastom and respect rather than state power. It is argued that this approach fails to take into account the fact that it is largely the presence of the state system itself which undermines the chiefly system, and that the kastom system cannot rely on the strength of respect alone to keep functioning in the changing circumstances of Vanuatu today.

The problems of the relationship between the state system and the kastom system

Whilst there are many benefits to having a degree of flexibility in the relationship, especially in light of the enormous variation in circumstances throughout the country, the unregulated nature of the relationship also generates many problems.

A fairly typical scenario demonstrates some of the major problems in the relationship:

> Jane is raped by her step-brother John. The chiefs of Jane's community call a meeting and John is fined. Two months pass and John has not paid his fine. Jane asks the chiefs what to do and the chiefs say they have no power to force John to pay. Jane goes to the police and makes a complaint. The police investigate but find it difficult as much evidence has been lost and the witnesses have become compromised. A file is prepared and it goes to court. John then comes to the chiefs and says he is willing to pay his fine if the case is withdrawn and so Jane is pressured by her family to withdraw the case. Jane goes to withdraw the case and the police and prosecution get angry with her and accuse her of wasting their time. John does not pay the fine. The police will not accept another complaint from Jane.[2]

The problems shown in this case study are just a few examples of the problems which exist. Although the nature of the problems varies throughout Vanuatu, the following are the most common. The uncertainty about where the dispute should be dealt with puts complainants in a vulnerable situation (this is shown by the example of Jane above). There is considerable dispute and confusion about which system should hear which types of cases (even in areas where there is an informal policy that the chiefs decide 'minor' cases and the state decides

---

2   This is not an actual case study, but is a simplified imagined one based on a number of actual cases.

'serious' cases there are arguments because of different views of what constitutes each type of case). There is an unresolved problem of which system should deal with a case first (this is problematic when a case goes to both systems and for example the chiefs want to hold a reconciliation ceremony before the defendant makes a plea). The problem of 'double jeopardy' (often defendants feel they have been 'doubly punished' if they are sentenced in the court as well as in kastom). The operation of the state system creates feelings of disempowerment on the part of chiefs and also frustration as they are told to be responsible for their communities but hindered by the state system in carrying out their duties in the following ways:

- sometimes courts make orders that interfere with chiefs' ability to do their work (for example, bail conditions, protection orders);
- sometimes the state prosecutes chiefs for making various orders (for example, the case of Public Prosecutor v Kota);
- sometimes courts make different orders to those the chiefs have made, which again undermines the chiefs' authority and respect in the eyes of the community;
- the ability to 'appeal' to the state system undermines the enforcement power of the chiefs; People challenge the chiefs on the basis that what they do is not in the Constitution;
- the existence of the kastom system also hinders the operation of the state system; cases are often withdrawn from the system after they have been 'dealt with' in kastom, creating feelings of frustration for prosecutors and police who have worked on the cases;
- people see the state system as 'foreign' in comparison: this is demonstrated by the courts are often being called 'kot blong waetman';
- people can de-legitimise decisions made by the state by saying the kastom system would decide differently

Conclusion

This short paper has shown many of the challenges and possibilities of the plural legal order in Vanuatu. The work that lies ahead is to identify some changes which can be made to both the state and the *kastom* systems to allow them to work better together, in a way which supports, rather than undermines, each other.

References

Forsyth, Miranda, 2006. *Report On The Vanuatu Judiciary Conference 2006: The Relationship Between The* Kastom *and State Justice Systems.* Online: http://www.vanuatu.usp.ac.fj/sol_adobe_documents/usp%20only/pacific%20 law/forsyth3.htm, accessed 11 May 2011.

Forsyth, Miranda, 2009. *A Bird that Flies with Two Wings:* Kastom *and State Justice Systems in Vanuatu.* Canberra: ANU ePress.

18. Heritej Saet blong Roi Mata

Douglas Kalotiti

Mi nem blong mi Douglas Kalotiti mi blong Efate long wan smol aelan nem blong hem Lelepa aelan. Mi mi wan filwoka blong Vanuatu Kaljoral Senta mi mi kam tekem ples blong wan olfala spika blong yumi we hemi Richard Leona hemi bin jeaman blong ol man filwoka ten afta we tem blong hem i finis. Mi bin stap wok long ples ia ating 9 yias nao. Bifo mi kam i gat ol bigfala grup blong Matthew Spriggs we oli kolem olgeta ol tim blong akioloji, ol man blong digim kraon oli bin kam oli bin kam tru long saed blong mifala ten oli kam stret long ples we mifala nao ol famlis we mifala i bin lukaotem ples ia. Hemi mekem se long taem ia nao long bigfala grup blong akioloji oli bin kam daon mo mi bin joenem olgeta an ten hemi mekem se mi bin joenem grup blong olgeta ating fo o faef yias trening long saed blong akioloji. Mo men tingting we hemi stap se hemi abaot wok ia long saed blong filwoka i mekem se mi kam joenem grup ia an bigfala tingting we grup oli bin kam blong mekem longwe hemi abaot wan saet longwe from hemi kam lelebet long Vanuatu, Pasifik mo long Europe. An long saet we mi mi ripresentem i kam hemi kam wan bigfala akioloji saet we sins long 1960 fes akiolojis we hemi kam in hemi José Garanger hemi bin statem akioloji, wok blong hem long ples we mi mi kam long hem. Topik we bae mi toktok long hem hemi long saed blong nominesen blong Wol Heritej we hemi long ples we mi mi kam long hem. Tingting blong nominesen ia hemi blong proteksen blong saet. Taem we ol risejas oli stap mekem fulap wok long saet ia fulap man oli bin karem aedia se wok bambae hemi olsem wanem? Oli ting se no ol man ia oli stap mekem wok blong olgeta nomo. Be afta we mi bin joenem olgeta mi bin faenemaot se wok ia hemi blong tokbaot ol histri blong yumi o hueva we hemi fes kam long ples, so i mekem se fulap man oli bin intres long wok an i mekem se miusium hemi gat fulap taem, janis blong kasem ples ia blong mekem wok.

An men tingting we hemi bin stap blong akioloji i blong digim kraon an ples we oli bin digim oli bin stap dig long wan baondri we yumi evriwan yumi save wan bigfala jif we nem blong hem i popiula lelebet we nem blong hem hemi *jif Roi Mata* long ples we hemi stap liv long hem. Bat bifo tat ol famle an pipol we oli liv tat saet oli bin protektem tat saet sins 1680 we hemi bin liv. Mekem se ol risejas mo mifala i gat tingting blong nominetem saet ia i kam wan list, i kam long wan list blong Wol Heritej—hemi wan nem we hemi niu long Vanuatu an Wol Heritej nominesen mo wok blong hem hemi veri veri had wok mo hemi veri, wan sensitif wok. Bifo yu wantem atraktem ol land onas, atraktem hu nao hemi gat infomesen, atraktem hu pipol nao oli long ol saets we yu nominetem. So i mekem se mifala i mas tekem fulap woksops bifo mifala i go luk ol land onas, mifala i mas aedentifae ol isius we land onas bae oli resem an taem ol isius ia mifala i save se bae oli resem mifala i gat ol ansas blong mekem o talemaot. So i mekem se projek blong CRMD, *Chief Roi Mata's Domain* an nominesen we hemi stap hemi stat long 2005. Insaed long projek ia i gat plante defren pipol mo oganaesesens oli inkludum ol man ples blong tufala komiuniti blong Lelepa mo Mangaliliu, Vanuatu Kaljorol Senta ol dipatmen blong gavman – Forestri, Fiseri Dipatmen blong Invaeremen, Australian National University, Bisops, yuts an pastas. Namba tu stret ples we oli bin nominetem olsem *Chief Roi Mata's Domain* hemi wan eria we hemi stap long nort-west Efate hemi Shefa provins we hemi Vanuatu. Namba tri eria blong solwota we hemi inkludum pat blong aelan blong Efate tu, narafala aelan mo Hat Aelan hemi wan ples we hemi stap long saet an bambae yufala i lukim hemia nao hemi baondri blong Wol Heritej. Ples ia nao mifala i gat bigfala jalenj long hem, hao nao bae mifala i mas protektem saet ia from Efate hemi stap long wan ples blong divelopmen. Bat rili mifala ino save protektem from se long ligel raets blong hem mifala ino honem an olgeta oli no saenem wan kontrak o talem yes se saet ia mifala i wantem putum long nominesen blong Wol Heritej. Ol saets ia i gat trifala saets: fes wan we yumi luk i stap long Efate oli kolem 'Mangaasi' seken saet oli kolem 'Kev' we oli kolem 'Feles Kev' hemi wan bigfala kev. 'Mangaasi' hemi ples we hemi residens blong hem. Long 2005 ia mifala i kontaktem fulap kaljorol heritej seves mo man we mi wok plante wetem hem hemi Chris Ballard long ANU Australia. Hem nao hemi bin kontaktem ol sevei an mifala i sevei long olfala vilej, ol passej, ol majik ston, ol rif an mifala i bin rikodem mo makem stret lokesen long evri saet. Wan map long olgeta saet ia hemi stap tru nao long Vanuatu Kaljoral Senta hemi pat long wok ia. Map long saet we mi bin tokbaot yu save luk lokesen blong hem ol blak stons oli stap mo ol big bigfala tris i stap long hem. Travel tu olsem pasej we bifo jif i wantem aot i aot long ples ia nao. Long 1849 Paul Vigors hemi bin lukim Hat Aelan hemi droem, ten hemi putum nem blong hem se Hat Aelan. Tede evri man oli lukim taem oli ron long sip oli talem se hemi Hat Aelan be hemi man ia nao hemi wan olfala riseja we mi faenem nem ia long 1849. Sevei blong ol ston long Hat Aelan mifala i bin sevei long wan smol eria nomo be mifala i faenem se gref , ol lokesen blong ol haos blong hem hemi bitim hemi bigwan hemi gref blong Roi Mata bodi hemi stap andanit long wan gref ston. Long taem blong wan woksop blong wan Wol Heritej i gat wan bigfala grup blong UNESCO oli bin go daon blong lukim saet ia.

Gref eria tede i gat gref ston mo ston baondri blong ples we José Garanger hemi bin digim an plan blong eria blong ekskavesen namba blong pipol we oli stap andanit long kraon we Roi Mata hemi bitim fifti. Plante pipol oli laef yet long taem we ol man blong bifo oli bin berem olgeta. Sam pipol oli bin dring kava festaem, oli posibol se oli gat mo bodi i stap yet an gref oli bin ekskavetem se hemi gat foti man be gref hemi stap yet long saet ia oli no bin finisim from we i gat mo leg i stap yet long saet ia an hemi stap yet an ekskavesen hemi disaedem blong oli stopem.

Nominesen hemi stap hemi no rili wan isi wok from mifala i mas kontaktem ol yuts, ol jifs, mo espeseli long saed blong jos, oganaesesen ol mama blong hueva hemia i gat stori blong ol defren trifala saets ia. Proteksen blong pavasones hemi kam big wan long awenes mo long saed blong sotej blong kraon, populesen grot an mifala i mekem ol sensas se long tis yia o long next yia taem olsem ia nao bambae kraon i mas sot from naoia ino gat stop long populating i mekem se mifala i gat smol fitbak long saed blong awenes we hemi stap.

Fulap long ol pipol oli talem se olsem wanem hemi wan Wol Heritej, hemi wan bigfala invest kampani? An mifala i talem se no hemi no wan invest kampani. Oli jes wantem kam nomo blong protektem from long sins long ded blong jif, pipol oli bin muvaot asaed sins pipol ino gat wan man i liv long taem ia kasem tede an jes bikos mifala nomo i bin protektem long taem blong ded blong hem. Mifala evriwan i bin muvaot long saet evriwan i bin muvaot long smol aelan ia oli bin berem evriwan oli nomo lukim kev so i mekem se storian an valiu an proteksens an sam impoten samting we i stap hapen long hem i mekem se mifala i liv wetem, hemi evri dei laef blong mifala an yu ting se ino impoten bat nem blong jif we hemi stap mifala i ting se hemi wan bigfala jif we evriwan oli respektem saet ia from fulap risejas we oli kam blong mifala i givim infomesen i mekem se pipol nao sam oli luksave so i mekem se mifala i traem blong talem se no Wol Heritej hemi no wan invest kampani hemi wan nem blong wan grup of pipol aotsaed long yumi we yumi neva gat nem ia oli jes wantem kam nomo protektem sam saets we oli veri impoten blong yumi o Vanuatu o long fiuja.

So hemia nao i mekem se nominesen blong saet ia hemi go insaed so mifala i veri laki tat mifala i wok wetem mebi faef onas nomo blong ajivim se saets we mifala wantem putum i go long list. Hemi stap long wan bigfala proteksens blong evriwan an long saed blong Efate mo Vanuatu hemi ol bratas blong jif Murmur an mifala i veri laki tat olgeta oli andastanem gud wanem nao mifala i tokbaot an mekem se olgeta tu oli rili help blong pasem tat mesej an proteksens blong saets longwe.

The Roi Mata Heritage Site

Douglas Kalotiti

I am Douglas Kalotiti from Efate, from a small island called Lelepa Island. I am a fieldworker with the Vanuatu Cultural Centre (VCC) and have taken the place of Richard Leona as chairman of the male fieldworkers after his term expired. I have been doing this work for nine years now. Before that I was part of the team that Matthew Spriggs organised—the people who dig up the ground, all the archaeologists who came to the place that we have been looking after. I joined their group and did four or five years of training in archaeology. The main thing they were interested in was the big site that was famous in Vanuatu and the Pacific and Europe. This site which I represented has been known since the 1960s, since the first archaeologist to work on it, José Garanger. The topic of my talk today is the nomination for World Heritage for the place I come from. The idea behind this nomination is the protection of the site. When the researchers were doing lots of work here, people from the village were saying, what kind of work are they doing? They thought the research was just for the researchers. But when I joined the group I saw that the research was about our history, the history of whoever came here first, and so lots of people were interested and the museum made more time to do this work.

The main motivation was to dig at the boundary of the now famous residence of Chief Roi Mata, at the place where he used to live. But before that everyone who lived near the site had been protecting it since he was alive in the sixteenth century. This is why the researchers and all of us wanted to nominate this site on the World Heritage list—something that was new for Vanuatu—and the nomination was very very hard work. You have to interest the land owners, interest those who have information, interest anyone who is on the sites that you are nominating. This meant that we had to run many workshops before we met with landowners to identify the issues which the landowners would raise and so we could prepare answers. So the Chief Roi Mata's Domain (CRMD) project for nomination began in 2004. Within the project there were many different people and organisations, including people from Lelepa and Mangaliliu, from the Vanuatu Kaljoral Senta (VKS) and all government departments—Forestry, Fisheries, the Department of the Environment, the Australian National University (ANU), Bishops, youth and pastors. The second place nominated for Chief Roi Mata's Domain was along the north-west of Efate in Shefa Province. The third area in the sea included part of Efate, another island and Hat Island, the place where the site is, and that is the boundary of the World Heritage area. So the big challenge now is: how to protect the site when Efate is going through so much development? Really, we can't protect Hat Island because we don't have any legal rights there, and the owner has never signed a contract or agreed to have the site nominated to the World Heritage list. There are three sites, the first, Mangaasi, is on Efate, the second is Feles Cave (on Lelepa). Mangaasi was Roi Mata's residence. In 2005 we carried out a number of heritage surveys with Chris Ballard, someone I have worked with before, from the ANU in Australia. He led these surveys and we looked at old villages, passages, magic stones, reefs and we recorded and marked the location of each site. A map of all the sites is available from the VKS. On that map you can find the location of all the black stones, all the big trees. You can see the passage that the chief used to use to travel along. In 1849, Paul Vigors saw Hat Island and he drew it and first named it. Today everyone who passes on a ship calls it Hat Island, but he was the first one to name it in 1849. In our survey of the stones in a small area on Hat Island we found the grave, the location of the houses, but Roi Mata's grave was found in one of the largest house yards or enclosures, his body was under a grave stone. During a workshop about the World Heritage listing a big group from UNESCO went down to look at the site.

The grave area today has a stone and the stone boundary of the place where José Garanger excavated, and the plan of the excavation shows there are over fifty people there. Many people were still alive when they were buried. Some drank kava before they were buried, and it is possible there are more bodies in the grave, there are 40 people, but they haven't finished digging and there are more legs coming out of the side of the excavation but they decided to stop.

The nomination isn't really easy because we have to contact the youth, the chiefs, and especially the church, the women's organisations and whoever has a story related to these three sites. Protection of buffer zones has become important because of the shortage of land and population growth and we made a census to say that this year or next year there will be a shortage of land because the population keeps growing so that we had feedback about the awareness project.

Lots of people ask what is World Heritage, is it a big investment company? And we say, no, it is not an investment company. They just want to come and protect it, because, since the death of the chief, people moved away and no-one lives there until today, because we protected it after his death. We all moved away from the site, from the small island where they buried everyone, and no-one went to look at the cave which means that we lived with the important value of the story. It may seem unimportant to others, but the name of that chief is important and is respected, and the fact that so many researchers come and ask us about the chief means that people today recognise him and this helps us to explain that World Heritage is not an investment company. It is a group of outside people who want to protect some sites which are important to us in Vanuatu and to the future.

So that means that the nomination of this site has gone ahead and we are lucky that we could work with maybe five owners to make sure the sites went onto the list. This protects everyone on Efate and Vanuatu, all of Chief Murmur's brothers and we are lucky that they all understand what we have been talking about and that they have helped to pass that message about protecting sites over there.

Postscript: Chief Roi Mata's Domain was the first site in Vanuatu to be granted World Heritage status in July 2008.

❦ Reflections ❦

19. Olfala Histri Wea i Stap Andanit long Graon. Archaeological Training Workshops in Vanuatu: A Profile, the Benefits, Spin-offs and Extraordinary Discoveries

Stuart Bedford, Matthew Spriggs, Ralph Regenvanu and
Salkon Yona

Archaeological research was included in the Vanuatu governmental moratorium on humanities-based research in Vanuatu from 1984 to 1994 (Bolton 1999: 1) and consequently it languished very much in a pioneering phase, reliant on interpretations from the results of a handful of influential projects that had been carried out through the 1960s and 70s. Right up to the mid-1990s fundamental questions relating to the initial colonisation and settlement of the archipelago and the succeeding cultural transformations which took place were still largely unanswered. Much of the country remained an archaeological *terra incognita* (Bedford *et al*. 1998; Bedford 2006a). However, the establishment of the Vanuatu Cultural and Historic Sites Survey (VCHSS) in 1990, a separate but associated entity to the Vanuatu Cultural Centre (VCC) and funded primarily by the European Union, was a major positive boost to archaeology. It started with a team of professional archaeologists, David Roe and Jean-Christophe Galipaud, and a less experienced but energetic group of ni-Vanuatu, some of whom would later go on to play influential roles in the long-term future of the VCC. The VCHSS initially comprised the manager Martha Yamsiu (later Kaltal) and field officers, Peter Kolmas, Ralph Regenvanu, Nicolas Vanusoksok, François Wadra and Fidel Yoringmal.

Its aims were to build and maintain a database of sites of cultural, archaeological and historic significance; to conduct surveys to identify and document these sites; train ni-Vanuatu staff in techniques of survey, research planning and execution; consider and establish procedures for determining, assessing and responding to threats to sites; encourage and develop the study of archaeology and history of Vanuatu and promote an awareness of its importance as part of the country's cultural heritage (Regenvanu *et al*. 1992; Roe and Galipaud 1994). The VCHSS organised and undertook site surveys in conjunction with the locally-based VCC *filwokas* and local communities. Focus was generally on the recording of historical and cultural/*kastom* sites, particularly in areas where development was being planned. Surveys were carried out on many islands in the archipelago. While archaeological research projects involving targeted excavations were not a component of the work of the VCHSS, its distinctly ni-Vanuatu approach, style and perspective that developed over a number of years (Regenvanu *et al.* 1992; Roe and Galipaud 1994; Roe *et al.* 1994), laid the foundations for collaborative archaeological research and training that was further developed following the lifting of the moratorium in 1994.

The VCHSS was incorporated administratively into the VCC in 1995 (Tryon 1999: 12–13), by which time staff included the late Jean-Paul Batick, Regina Batick and the late Willy Damelip. They were joined some time later by Marcellin Abong and Richard Shing, both of whom had completed some University training in archaeology. With the establishment of the VCC Research Policy and issuing of research permits in 1994 (Regenvanu 1999), research orientated archaeological projects were initiated. The first of these was the ANU-Vanuatu National Museum Archaeology Project which was started in 1994 on the island of Erromango by Matthew Spriggs, added Malakula Island and Bedford in 1995 and has continued in various guises until today (Bedford *et al.* 1998; Bedford and Spriggs 2008). A training component was first introduced in 1996 (Bedford *et al.* 1999; Spriggs 1996) based at the Mangaasi/Arapus site on the west coast of Efate.

Mangaasi/Arapus archaeological training workshops 1996–2003

The site of Mangaasi, on the west coast of Efate, was made famous throughout the archaeological world by the pioneering work of José Garanger who excavated a single area of 118 square metres there in 1967, uncovering both the remains of Chief Roi Mata's village near the surface of the site and evidence of much earlier occupation with thousands of pottery sherds at deeper levels (Garanger 1972). The site was dated at the time to 2700 BP (BP = 'Before Present', with 'Present' taken conventionally as 1950) and the distinctive pottery style found there and in other areas of Efate and the Shepherd Islands was named 'Mangaasi' in honour of the site. No further archaeological work took place at the site for another 30 years. Meanwhile a large number of other archaeological research projects had been carried out in different countries around the Pacific, and a huge amount of new information collected which was beginning to cast doubt on some of the conclusions of Garanger and other earlier researchers in Vanuatu. Pleistocene occupation had been identified in Island New Guinea and the Northern Solomons which opened up the same possibility for Vanuatu. Questions were also beginning to be asked about how the Mangaasi ceramic tradition fitted into the general picture. Claims that it was unrelated to Lapita and represented a separate cultural group contemporary with Lapita, were being seen as increasingly problematic (Spriggs 1984, 1997; Ward 1990).

In 1996 with these research questions in mind the Mangaasi site was added to the sites to be investigated under the umbrella of the ANU-Vanuatu National Museum Archaeology Project. It was decided that a significant training component should be added (Bedford *et al*. 1999). The necessary additional funding that facilitated the training component came from grants to the National Museum of Vanuatu, coordinated by Yosihiko Sinoto of the Bishop Museum in Honolulu, as part of the pilot archaeological training program of the Sasakawa Pacific Island Nations Fund (SPINF) for 1996–8 and from the Japanese Government via a grant to the Pacific Islands Development Program at the East-West Center in Honolulu in 1999. In 1996 the South Pacific Cultures Fund of the Australian Federal Government also made a significant contribution. For Project reports during this period, see Regenvanu and Spriggs (1996), Spriggs (1996) and Spriggs and Bedford (1999).

The site was ideally located in terms of logistics not far from the VCC in Port Vila. More importantly there was widespread support from the local community, some of the more senior members of which had worked with Garanger decades before. In 1996 the emphasis was on the training of VCC and VCHSS staff and members of the local community, but as both funding and the numbers of experienced VCHSS staff increased over the next three years the workshops could accommodate larger numbers. These comprised primarily VCC *filwokas* from both Efate and other islands who, except for a very few, had no experience of archaeology. A range of skills were imparted to the participants, depending in part on their literacy and other educational skills and in part upon their previous archaeological experience. VCHSS staff took on increasing responsibility for training as their experience developed. From 1999, excavations at different parts of the site were directed by Richard Shing and Marcellin Abong, while site survey and mapping were overseen by Willy Damelip. The program was conducted largely through informal practical training sessions, with participants being introduced to all aspects of archaeological excavation and survey throughout the five-week workshops. The skills and understanding developed through the program included the following: the purpose and value of archaeological research; basic principles of archaeological excavation and recording techniques; basic principles of stratigraphy and the recognition of different layers; techniques of wet and dry sieving of excavated sediments; artefact recognition and sorting of screened sediments into artefact classes; artefact handling and specialised collection techniques for such things as *in situ* charcoal; how archaeologists construct a site picture from the remains found, and why they use particular excavation strategies; basic concepts related to archaeological constructions of Pacific colonisation and settlement.

The training workshops proved to be very successful in terms of their primary objectives, and the research clarified the place of Mangaasi pottery in the local cultural sequence (Bedford 2000, 2006a). In addition, when in 1999 excavations were extended to Arapus, across the Mangaasi Creek which marked the southwest boundary of the site, they uncovered both earlier and much more extensive deposits than those identified at Mangaasi. These have ultimately been revealed to represent one of the best-preserved archaeological sites of its type in the Pacific (Bedford and Spriggs 2000; Spriggs and Bedford 2001). The famed Mangaasi site could now be seen as simply the periphery of a much larger site which had the potential to extend much further along the coast towards Mangaliliu Village. Funding was sought for a further three years from the Pacific Biological Foundation, and subsequently attracted further contributions from the New Zealand High Commission in Port Vila. Thus, with a break only in 2000, the training workshop on Efate continued from 2001 to 2003 (for project reports see Spriggs 2002, 2003, 2004a). For the first time there was participation by the women *filwokas* as well as the men. Excavations and training were focused at the Arapus site but small teams extended the sphere of the workshop to Mangaliliu further southwest, where Richard Shing supervised investigations, and to the neighbouring small islands of Lelepa and Nguna (Bedford 2004; Valentin, Shing and Spriggs 2005). Direct VCC *filwoka* and local community involvement in the excavations again proved to be the most effective method of raising awareness and the understanding of archaeological sites and what they represented as the project's area of operation was extended.

Figure 19.1. Excavation, sieving and sorting, Arapus site, West Efate 2001. Minister of Education Joe Natuman (centre) visits the site

(Stuart Bedford, photographer)

Figure 19.2. Excavators Joel Iau (filwoka south Tanna) and Douglas Kalotiti (*filwoka* west Efate) recording excavated depth, Arapus site, West Efate 2001

(Stuart Bedford, photographer)

Malakula archaeological training workshops 2001–2004

In 2001 a further archaeological training workshop was started on the island of Malakula. It was the Vanuatu component of a project funded by the Sasakawa Pacific Islands Nations Fund (SPINF) entitled *Distance Education in the South-West Pacific: Cultural Heritage Training 2001–2003*. The program was jointly run by Glenn Summerhayes and Matthew Leavesley (Papua New Guinea component), Bedford (Vanuatu), the VCC and the Papua New Guinea Museum (Bedford and Leavesley 2004; Leavesley *et al.* 2005). The broad objectives of the Vanuatu component of the program were to train ni-Vanuatu in the following areas of cultural heritage management:

- identifying and recording cultural sites of significance;
- cultural and archaeological survey techniques;
- archaeological excavation methods;
- raising community awareness through liaison, education and dissemination of information.

The Malakula archaeological training workshops were a natural development from those that had been carried out on Efate. They were specifically located on one of the northern islands of Vanuatu as they are more under-resourced in terms of trained personnel and previous educational programmes. The increasing threat from proposed mining activities and other development projects on these islands made the need for training and survey particularly urgent as little of the cultural heritage of these islands has been recorded. The training workshops were also designed to further develop and enhance: 1. the established structure of site survey and 2. the recording processes that were employed by the VCHSS. VCC *filwokas* from islands who had not previously participated in earlier training on Efate were particularly encouraged to join the new programme. The small islands of northeast Malakula and the Maskelyne Islands of the southeast were selected for the workshops (Bedford and Regenvanu 2002, 2003).

Heightening of community awareness was a major objective of the Malakula workshops and it was felt that this could be most effectively achieved by running the workshops in a number of different areas. This posed a number of logistical challenges, with a core group of around 15 people being together for five weeks and shifting between different islands and communities where archaeology was virtually unknown. Crucial to the success of the workshops was Numa Fred Longga, curator of the Malakula Cultural Centre (MCC) who had participated in excavations at Mangaasi/Arapus in 1999 and the by-then fully experienced staff of the VCHSS. The workshop started on Uripiv Island, the home island of Numa Fred, where both his standing as curator of the MCC and his ability to explain in local language the objectives of the workshop proved a major benefit. VCC *filwokas* mostly from northern Vanuatu made up the majority of the trainees, including *filwokas* from other small islands of Malakula where the workshop was to be shifted to following Uripiv. Fidel Yoringmal, long-retired from the VCHSS, joined the workshop on his home island of Wala and was again able to explain in detail in local language the objectives of the workshop. A similar scenario eventuated on Vao Island with the participation of Vianney Atpatoun, ex-curator of both the VCC and MCC, who had some experience of archaeological investigations including touring Lapita sites in New Caledonia.

There were two main aspects to the training workshops on Malakula. One was focused on archaeological investigation and survey in an attempt to build up a picture of the long-term history of the islands. The other was surveying the islands for ceremonial structures and old villages which were then recorded in detail. Traditional stories relating to these structures or sites were also recorded. The archaeology of the small islands of Malakula had up until that time been barely touched, so it was with some relief that after only four days on Uripiv Island we were able to identify well-preserved deeply-stratified deposits including evidence of Lapita, the foundation culture for Vanuatu about 3000 years ago (Bedford 2003). This ensured the success of both the archaeological aspect of the training workshop but also greatly facilitated community interest and awareness. Ultimately, archaeological workshops were held on seven small islands of Malakula (Uripiv, Uri, Wala, Atchin, Vao [NE Malakula] and Uliveo and Sakao [Maskelynes]). Following the identification of particularly well-preserved Lapita deposits on Vao in 2003, funding was sought for further excavations. An additional, more research-orientated workshop was held on Vao in 2004 with the increasingly experienced Malakula *filwokas* making up the greater part of the excavation team (Bedford 2005).

Figure 19.3. Excavation, sieving and sorting, Vao Island 2003

(Stuart Bedford, photographer)

Benefits and spinoffs

Direct participation and collaboration of VCC and VCHSS staff, *filwokas* and local communities in actual excavations carried out during the training workshops were fundamental in facilitating a basic understanding of archaeology and its wider relevance and importance. The archaeology in those areas where the workshops were held was also particularly amenable for such awareness programs. The deeply-stratified well-preserved sites regularly revealed features through the different layers such as hearths, various items of material culture and midden debris, with which people were generally familiar. Certainly when some of these features or midden debris were being recovered from depths of more than two metres below the ground surface a sense of the development of stratified deposits over time or the idea that *graon i stap gro* could be more easily appreciated.

The workshops proved also to be fertile venues for exchange of information between trainers and trainees. Roles could often be reversed when particular artefact forms from more recent deposits were recognised by *filwokas* or local villagers. Environmental and cultural information in relation to faunal remains and particularly shellfish could also be readily accessed. When a 'shellfish workshop' was established on Uripiv in 2002 to identify the large numbers of shellfish being recovered from the site there, it provided an ideal platform for discussions ranging from size variation and variety of species over time, through the identification of species no longer found in the area, to the traditional usage of various species. Extinct species have also been identified in the course of the excavations, such as the extinct land crocodile found at Arapus (Mead *et al.* 2002), as well as several extinct or locally extirpated bird species. These discoveries have helped raised environmental issues and awareness in communities.

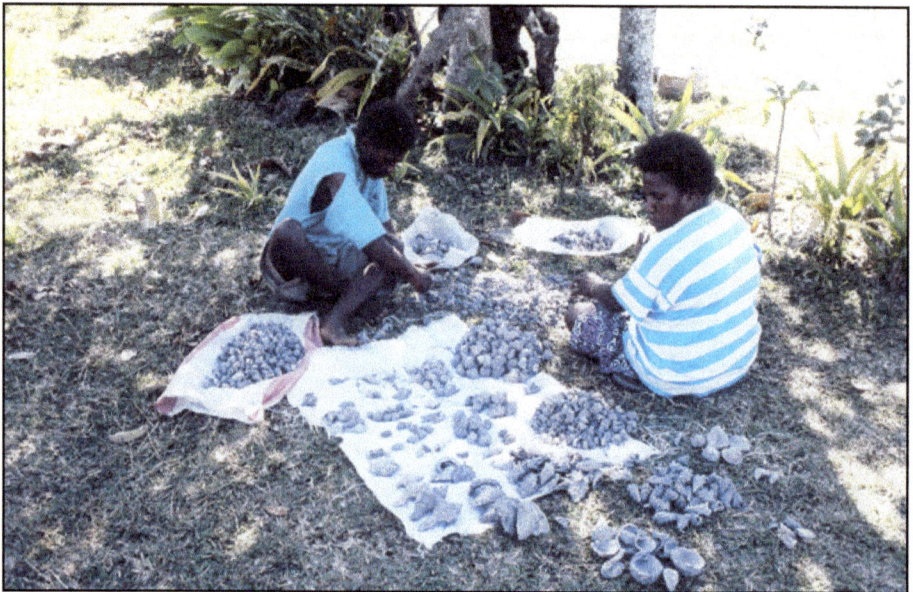

Figure 19.4. Shell analysis workshop, Uripiv Island, Malakula 2002

(Stuart Bedford, photographer)

Communities benefitted greatly from the workshops being held in their immediate area, not least financially. Accommodation in the villages was paid for, local labour was hired to participate, most food was sourced locally and its preparation involved the paid participation of local women's organisations. For small communities with limited opportunities to participate in the monetary economy, the projects' financial inputs were significant. The participation over many years of most of the men and a smaller number of the women VCC *filwokas* greatly facilitated the much wider dissemination of archaeological information and awareness. *Filwokas* play a crucial liaison role between foreign researchers and local communities, and in this regard are able to explain what archaeological work entails and its aims and values. After participating in the workshops, all trainees became fully conversant with the processes involved in archaeological work and were able to explain them to their home communities, who sometimes confuse archaeology with mineral exploration activities. *Filwokas* also provide an archipelago-wide network of VCC representatives who, having now participated in the archaeology training workshops, have been able to relay information to the VCHSS on the appearance of archaeological remains uncovered during local village activities or larger development projects.

Following now some eleven workshops, various staff of the VCHSS have accumulated substantial experience and understanding of archaeological method and theory and would be capable of running such workshops independently. The research aspect of the workshops has also aided the work of the VCHSS in other ways. A detailed cultural sequence for Central Vanuatu has now been established beginning with Lapita to Erueti to Mangaasi and beyond (Bedford 2006a). The outline of a similar cultural sequence is also available for Malakula (Bedford 2001). This now means that sites found during surveys can be dated and their historical significance assessed without incurring significant extra costs such as radiocarbon dating.

Local and wider community awareness was further raised through regular oral presentations to local communities, landowners, the Friends of the Vanuatu National Museum group and school and university students who toured the sites in large numbers. Educational groups ranged from pre-schoolers to students from teacher training institutions and the University of the South Pacific, Emalus Campus in Port Vila. Other visitors included Government MPs, Provincial government officials, and representatives from Diplomatic missions. Visits from schools provided a rare opportunity for the students to see first hand, and in some cases participate in, the excavations. An added bonus of the school visits is the fact that most high schools in Vanuatu comprise students from all over the country, which further contributes in the dissemination of interest and information to a wider audience. Martha Yamsiu-Kaltal and Richard Shing particularly have taken the principal lead in community and visiting group presentations. The response from all educational institutions was extremely positive, but teachers and students alike lamented the fact that they did not have ready access to information on the archaeological history of Vanuatu or the Pacific generally.

Figure 19.5. Richard Shing leads a public presentation on Vao Island 2003

(Stuart Bedford, photographer)

In a major effort to address this very issue the VCC initiated the National History Curriculum Project in 2003 that produced the three-volume publication *Histri Blong Yumi Long Vanuatu* (Lightner and Naupa 2005), aimed at ultimately providing a basis for a core curriculum high school subject on the history of Vanuatu. A French translation of the first two of these volumes appeared in 2010. Archaeological information, much of which was generated during the training workshops, makes up a substantial component of Volume One. At a less academic and less ambitious level, but one that serves well the needs of grassroots ni-Vanuatu in terms of providing basic archaeological information, was the production of a cartoon format booklet *Wokbaot Bakagen wetem Olgeta Blong VCHSS. Saet Sevei mo Akaeoloji* (Kaltal, Nojima and Bedford 2004). Developed during the Malakula workshops it is essentially an update, with the addition of archaeology, of the original VCHSS cartoon publication which introduced and highlighted the role of the VCHSS site surveys in the early 1990s (Regenvanu *et al.* 1992). In line with obligations outlined under the VCC research policy, annual reports on the workshops and their results were produced in both Bislama and English for distribution to local communities and deposition in the Vanuatu National Library.

The increasing accessibility and use of the World Wide Web has also been taken advantage of with many of the reports and latest results able to be viewed on the VCC web site (www.vanuatuculture.org). During the Mangaasi workshop in 1998 a pioneering web-based interactive learning site was established where field data and photographs from the excavations were posted on a daily basis, inviting feedback and discussion from a world-wide audience. This was the first time anywhere in the world that a 'live' archaeological excavation was presented on a day-by-day basis on a dedicated web site (Spriggs 1999, 2000). The innovative project design led to Spriggs being awarded a prize-grant to undertake the web project from the Kon-Tiki Museum – Telenor 'No Barriers' Fund of Norway. Additional equipment support came from the Apple University Development Fund in Australia, and a satellite phone base was temporarily established at Mangaliliu Village during the course of the project to put material up on the web. For a brief moment at least, Vanuatu led the world in this sort of web-based learning.

A series of academic papers have also been generated from the archaeological results of the workshops (Bedford 2000, 2003, 2006a, 2006b; Bedford and Spriggs 2002; Bedford *et al*. 1998; Horrocks and Bedford 2005; Spriggs and Bedford 2001) which in the case of the Mangaasi/Arapus excavations have made a valuable contribution to the nomination of the Chief Roi Mata's Domain as a UNESCO World Heritage Site (Spriggs 2006). Another spin-off was that the same excavations were used as the basis of an artistic reconstruction of this colonising period which was ultimately used on the Vanuatu Lapita stamps issued by the Post Office in 2005 (Figure 19.6).

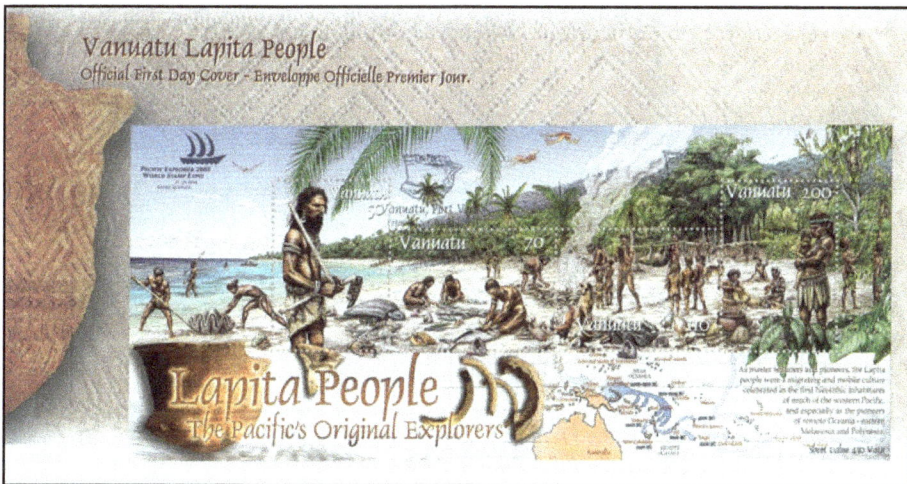

Figure 19.6. Vanuatu Lapita stamp issued in 2005

(copyright Vanuatu Post)

Radio interviews have been broadcast nationally on a regular basis discussing the aims and results of the workshops. As radio is the only form of communication to which the whole of the country has access, regular features on Radio Vanuatu were seen as essential. Much of their success can be attributed to Abong Thompson, former Vanuatu National Radio presenter now at the VCC, who recorded the interviews and compiled the shows that were most often broadcast on Saturday nights on the VCC *Kastom mo Kalja* half hour. Feature articles have appeared on a regular basis in Vanuatu newspapers and coverage has also been extended to TV Vanuatu. The Vanuatu National Film and Sound Unit of the VCC has filmed many of the excavations over the years and produced a number of films. They include *Footprint blong Bubu* (Pathways of the Ancestors) and *Yumi tokbaot Roy Mata* (Stories about Roy Mata), the second of which was developed directly out of the excavations at Mangaasi/Arapus and was the first-ever documentary made explicitly for the new TV Vanuatu channel. Both of these films were shown to local community and school groups on Malakula during the workshops there as their content had a direct relation to the archaeological methods used and the materials that were being uncovered on those islands.

Extraordinary discoveries

Prior to attendance at the various archaeological training workshops most VCC *filwokas* had little idea that the sherds of pottery they regularly came across in their gardens had anything to do with the cultural heritage. In a number of cases they were seen as having biblical connections (Bedford 2006a). This was certainly Salkon Yona's experience prior to his attendance at the Mangaasi/Arapus workshop of 2003.

> *Bifo mifala long Epi oli bin lukim plante pis sospen graon long ol garen blong mifala. Mi bin askem ol olfala papa mo mama blong mifala wanem samting ia? I gat tufala storian blong hem. Wan i talem se olgeta oli ol pispis blong ten komanmen wea Moses i bin sakem mo i brokbrok i go olbaot. Wan narafala storian i talem se olgeta oli ol pis blong wan bigfala wotatank blong god spirit long Emae wea afta wan bigfala ren i bin filimap tumas i folfoldaon mo i go olbaot* (Yona 2006).[1]

It was a revelation to hear that through archaeological research it had been established that, as on Efate and clearly in evidence in the midden deposits he was excavating, communities on all islands of Vanuatu had once produced pottery, dating as far back as 3000 years. Yona's enthusiasm for the workshop was regularly shared with fellow Epi islanders resident in Vila.

---

1   On Epi we find a lot of pieces of pottery in our gardens. I have asked the older people in the community what they were. There are two stories associated with it. One is that they are pieces of the Ten Commandments which having been discarded by Moses broke into thousands of pieces and were spread around. Another is that they were once part of a large water-tank owned by the spirits of Emae which burst into many pieces following heavy rain.

Mi bin storian long woksop plante wetem ol fren blong mi wea oli stap long Vila. Wan blong olgeta [Charlie Nati] i bin talem se hem tu i bin lukim fulap samting olsem sospen graon long Teouma wea hemi draevem buldos blong makem ples blong fidim naora. Mi bin askem hem blong karem wan pis i kam olsem mi save lukluk gud long hem. Taem mi lukim bigfala pis sospen wea man ia i bin karem i kam mi tingse hemi mas Lapita from i gat wan difren disaen olgeta. Mi bin karem pis ia long Kaljoral Senta blong soem long olgeta (Yona 2006).[2]

Yona's identification of the sherd ultimately led to the discovery of one of the more important archaeological sites yet found in the Pacific, the Lapita cemetery of Teouma (Bedford *et al.* 2004, 2006).

The Australian National University-Vanuatu National Museum led excavations took place initially at Teouma over three seasons (2004–2006) (Shing *et al.* 2005, 2007a) with support from (among others) the National Geographic Society (Spriggs 2007) and the Pacific Biological Foundation (Spriggs 2004b). Subsequently, between 2008 and 2010, further excavations have been carried out with funding from the Australian Research Council (Bedford et al. 2010). The excavations have generated unprecedented interest both locally and worldwide. The spectacular remains uncovered at the site and its accessibility facilitated a major public awareness campaign. School visits and guided tours for the general public and government and diplomatic officials were particularly promoted and even included a visit by the President and the First Lady and party in 2005. Display boards were set up at the excavations, and a pamphlet (Shing and Bedford 2005 [updated in 2007 (Shing *et al.* 2007b)]) and poster about archaeology and the excavation were provided on site and have subsequently been distributed to schools and communities throughout the country. The pamphlet and poster were funded by the Snowy Mountains Electricity Commission (SMEC) Foundation. Excavation participation by school students was encouraged and facilitated through the screening of deposits to retrieve artefacts in an area of the site that had been disturbed by quarrying. In 2004 alone, more than 1000 schoolchildren visited the site. The excavations received regular high profile coverage in Vanuatu and international newspapers, radio and television, as well as several overseas documentary filmmakers, and were the focus of the *Friends of the Vanuatu National Museum* calendar for 2006.

Although the Teouma excavations were conceived within a 'rescue' framework, to establish how much damage had been done by quarrying activities and how

---

2   I talked on a regular basis with friends in Vila about the workshop. One of them [Charlie Nati] said that he had seen pieces of pottery at Teouma where he was driving a bulldozer on the prawn farm construction site. I asked him to pick up a piece next time so that I could have a good look at it. When I saw the sherd that he had brought from the site I thought that it looked like Lapita as it had a very distinctive design. I took it to the Cultural Centre to show it to people there.

much of the site remained intact, it did provide some further opportunities for training. In 2005 community representatives from Eton village in South Efate participated in the excavation. In 2006 the funding from the National Geographic Society facilitated the participation of five students—Solomon Islanders and ni-Vanuatu—from the University of the South Pacific main campus in Suva, Fiji and a further USP participant from Vila (Spriggs 2007). There were also opportunities in all years at Teouma for volunteer participation by Vanuatu-based and international participants from Australia, France, New Caledonia and New Zealand, as well as the professional collaboration of French, New Caledonian and New Zealand researchers.

A major Lapita exhibition was opened at the National Museum in 2006 following the return of four reconstructed Lapita pots from the Australian Museum in Sydney that had been recovered at Teouma in 2004 and 2005. The homecoming of these pots was an event to celebrate, particularly so for VCC curator Takaronga Kuautonga who had spent two months in Sydney collaborating in their reconstruction, funded by ICOM (International Council of Museums) Australia. With a further two complete vessels having been recovered from the site in 2006, Vanuatu can now boast of having 70 per cent of the world's collection of whole early Lapita vessels. The pots were transported to the Musée de Quai Branly in Paris for exhibition for two months from November 2010, along with other complete pots from New Caledonia. This Lapita exhibition represents the first ever exhibition dedicated to Pacific archaeological material to be held outside the Pacific and Australasian region. A 350-page bi-lingual catalogue was published in Paris for the exhibition (Sand and Bedford (eds) 2010), and at the same time, a tri-lingual companion booklet was produced by the Vanuatu Cultural Centre (Bedford, Sand and Shing 2010).

The second tranche of excavations, starting in 2008, led to an application for AUSAID funding to further develop School participation. Funding was obtained, and a very successful program of school visits and participation in excavation of the site took place in 2008 and 2009, with tours in English and French led by Richard Shing and by Jean René of the Alliance Française in Port Vila. Feedback reports were given to individual schools discussing the objects that their students had found during their work at the site. New booklets and posters in English, French and Bislama were produced and distributed to the students and teachers as part of this program. Although funding had run out by 2010, a less-ambitious program of school participation continued during that year.

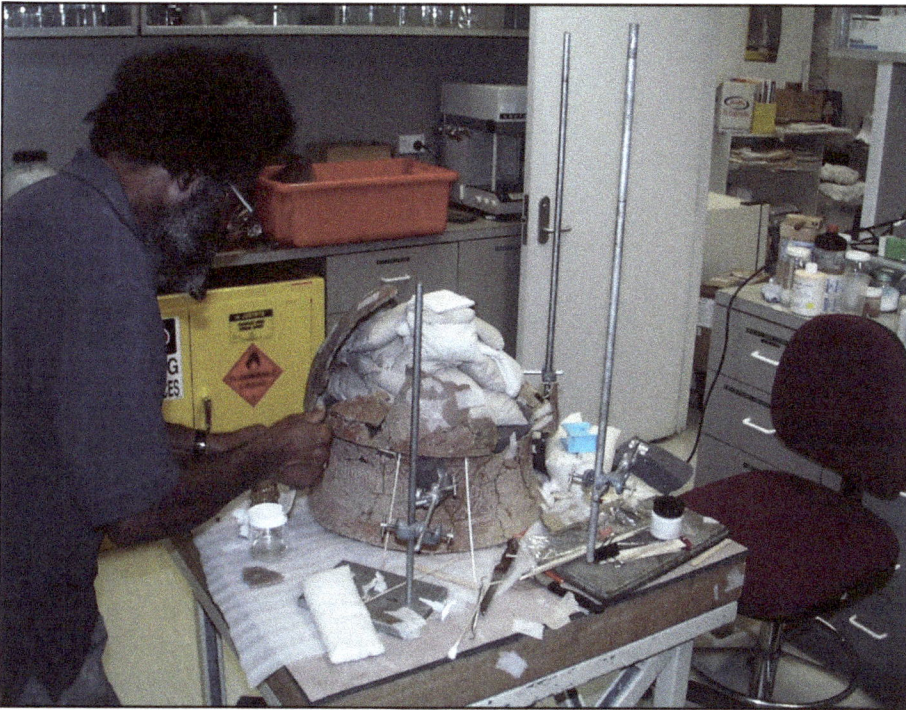

Figure 19.7. Takaronga Kuautonga at the Australian Museum restoring the Lapita pots

(courtesy of the Australian Museum)

There have also been additional reports more recently from *filwokas* of archaeological deposits turning up in different parts of Vanuatu. *Filwoka* Paul Vuhu, who attended the 1999 workshop on Efate, reported large sherds of pottery being eroded by the sea on the east coast of Ambae. A subsequent visit to the island confirmed a series of cultural deposits buried by volcanic ash. Excavations took place in 2007, and a report on them is in preparation. They revealed evidence of catastrophic volcanism that had buried sites over a wide area about 900 years ago; there are implications here for current volcanic hazards research. On Erromango ex-VCC *filwoka* Sempet Naritantop reported deeply buried cultural deposits with pottery at two sites adjacent to the Williams River in Dillons Bay, making a special trip to Port Vila to brief VCC staff in 2007. These are very significant discoveries; pottery is extremely difficult to find on Erromango as people gave up using it there around 2000 years ago (Bedford 2006a). An ANU team working with the Dillon's Bay community and Erromango *filwoka* Jerry Taki, conducted excavations at these sites in the second half of 2010, again providing an opportunity for community awareness activities. A major site probably going back about 2700 years appears to extend under much of the village at Dillon's Bay.

Conclusion

The archaeological training workshops have been collaborative projects that evolved and improved through experience, have achieved their objectives and, through a momentum of their own, have realised much more. The outcomes are witnessed by the broadened skills-base and understanding of VCC, VCHSS staff and *filwokas* and by the greatly-increased information about Vanuatu's rich cultural heritage which has been disseminated through TV, radio, newspapers, web sites, educational manuals, pamphlets, comic books and exhibits in the National Museum. A wide range of the ni-Vanuatu public has been exposed to archaeology and cultural heritage issues through these media.

The deeply-stratified and well-preserved archaeological deposits at the sites chosen for the workshops have highlighted the fact that Vanuatu has some of the best preserved archaeological sites in the Pacific. There is now worldwide recognition of the significance of the archaeological heritage found in Vanuatu, confirmed in 2009 by the success of the nomination of the Chief Roi Mata's Domain in northwest Efate to the World Heritage List. This formed, along with the Kuk Swamp Early Agricultural Site in Papua New Guinea, the first successful World Heritage cultural nomination by independent Pacific Island countries. The major Lapita exhibition in Paris in 2010–11 is further evidence of such international recognition.

What has been absolutely crucial to the success of the workshops and excavations has been the opportunity to tap into the resources of a well-respected and well-run national cultural institution such as the VCC. Without its collaboration the workshops would not have taken place. The VCC *filwoka* system, which operates across the islands, facilitated the wide dissemination of information. Vanuatu can now arguably claim to have one of the best educated populations at a grassroots level in relation to archaeology anywhere in the Pacific. With the inclusion of information about the archaeology of Vanuatu in the High School history curriculum its acceptance and importance can only be further enhanced.

An obvious and immediate major benefit, certainly in archaeological terms and highlighted by Yona's discovery, is the reporting archipelago-wide of archaeological deposits or materials being uncovered by knowledgeable and informed ni-Vanuatu. A more long-term benefit is archaeology's contribution to a developing sense of identity for the population of what is still comparatively the young nation of Vanuatu. The notion of a *taem blong daknes* (time of darkness) referring to Vanuatu before the arrival of Christianity was hammered into the national psyche by missionaries during the nineteenth and twentieth centuries. It is one that still pervades much Vanuatu thinking today (Regenvanu 2005:39). Archaeological evidence is being used to present a more balanced perspective on the nation's past. To find out that your ancestors were the first explorers and colonisers of all the islands of Eastern Melanesia and Western Polynesia more than 1000 years before the birth of Christ, and participated in the greatest maritime colonisation episode in world history, can have a salutary effect in helping to achieve a more balanced historical perspective.

In 1996 the then Minister of Culture Joe Natuman in his opening address to the Lapita Archaeology Conference held in Port Vila stated that 'We in Vanuatu will need to do more work in establishing firmly our early history because it is important for our identity as a people, as a country, and as a nation in the region and the world at large' (in Galipaud and Lilley 1999: 15). While the Minister's sentiments will always hold true as far as the need for more work to be done is concerned, revealing the early history of Vanuatu through projects such as the archaeological training workshops has without question made substantial advances over the years since the lifting of the research moratorium. Equally important has been the dissemination of information gleaned from those workshops and other research projects through such networks as the VCC *filwoka* system. Together they have substantially raised the profile of the nation's approximately 125-generation history in ni-Vanuatu consciousness.

Acknowledgments

As noted in the text, funding for the workshops at Mangaasi/Arapus came from the Australian Federal Government's South Pacific Cultures Fund (1996), the Sasakawa Foundation (1996–1998) and the Japanese Government through the Pacific Islands Development Program in Honolulu (1999), the Pacific Biological Foundation (2001–2003) and the New Zealand High Commission (2002–2003). For the workshops on Malakula funding came from the Sasakawa Pacific Island Nations Fund (2001–2003) and the National Geographic Society (2004). Funding for the Teouma 2004–2006 project as a whole was provided by the Pacific Biological Foundation, the National Geographic Society, the Australian Research Council, the Snowy Mountains Electricity Commission Foundation, ICOM Australia and Mr Brian Powell. The 2008–10 Teouma excavations were funded by the Australian Research Council, with the Schools program funded by AUSAID during the same period. In addition, critical financial and logistical support has been provided throughout the period 1994 to the present by the Department of Archaeology and Natural History and School of Archaeology and Anthropology at the Australian National University.

The smooth running of the workshops would not have been possible without the full support and participation of staff at the Vanuatu Cultural Centre, and particularly so the staff of the VCHSS and VCC accountant Jennifer Toa. The *filwokas* from the various islands were enthusiastic and attentive for the full period of the workshops and often provided training to the trainers. The VCC *filwoka* for West Efate Douglas Kalotiti was crucial to the success of all the work at the Mangaasi and Arapus sites, as was Numa Fred Longga, Curator of the Malakula Cultural Centre for the workshops on Malakula. *Filwoka* for South Efate Silas Alben has fulfilled a similarly critical role at the Teouma site during 2004–10. Although they are too many to list here individually, a special thank you goes to all Chiefs, landowners and local members of the fieldwork crews for their co-operation, assistance and friendship—literally hundreds of people have been involved in one way or another. Many thanks are also due to the local communities who supported the workshops with their hospitality and assistance.

References

Bedford, Stuart, 2000. Results from excavations at the Mangaasi type site: a re-assessment of the ceramic sequence and its implications for Melanesian prehistory. *Bulletin of the Indo-Pacific Prehistory Association* 19: 159–66.

Bedford, Stuart, 2001. Ceramics from Malekula, northern Vanuatu: the two ends of a potential 3000-year sequence. In *The Archaeology of Lapita Dispersal in Oceania: Papers from the Fourth Lapita Conference, June 2000, Canberra, Australia*, ed. G.R. Clark, A.J. Anderson and T. Vunidilo, 105–14. Canberra: Pandanus Books. Terra Australis, 17.

Bedford, Stuart, 2003. The timing and nature of Lapita colonisation in Vanuatu: the haze begins to clear. In *Pacific Archaeology: Assessments and Prospects*, ed. C. Sand, 15: 147–58. Nouméa: Les Cahiers de l'archéologie en Nouvelle-Calédonie.

Bedford, Stuart, 2004. Ripot i go long ol man Nguna long saed blong stadi blong Stuart Bedford mo Taman Willie long Arkeoloji blong Nguna, Julae 14 Kasem 18 2003. Report to Vanuatu Cultural Centre and Nguna community. Typescript, on file Vanuatu National Library.

Bedford, Stuart, 2005. The timing and nature of human colonisation of Vanuatu. Report to National Geographic Committee for Research and Exploration (Grant 7738-04). Typescript, on file Vanuatu National Library.

Bedford, Stuart, 2006a. *Pieces of the Vanuatu Puzzle: Archaeology of the North, South and Centre*. Canberra: Pandanus Press, Australian National University. Terra Australis 23.

Bedford, Stuart, 2006b. The Pacific's earliest painted pottery: an added layer of intrigue to the Lapita debate and beyond. *Antiquity* 80: 544–57.

Bedford, Stuart and Matthew Leavesley, 2004. Distance education in the South-West Pacific: culture heritage training 2001–2003. Report presented to the Sasakawa Pacific Island Nations Fund, Tokyo. Typescript, on file Vanuatu National Library.

Bedford, Stuart and Ralph Regenvanu, 2002. Summary report to the Vanuatu Government on distance education in the South-West Pacific: cultural heritage training 2001–2003. Workshop and Training Program on Uripiv and Wala Islands, Malakula 2001. Typescript, on file Vanuatu National Library.

Bedford, Stuart and Ralph Regenvanu, 2003. Summary report to the Vanuatu Government on distance education in the South-West Pacific: cultural heritage training 2001–2003. Workshop and Training Program on Uripiv, Uri, Atchin and Vao Islands, Malakula 2002. Typescript, on file Vanuatu National Library.

Bedford, Stuart, Christophe Sand and R. Shing, 2010. Lapita Peoples/Peuples/Pipol. In *Oceanic Ancestors/Ancêtres océaniens/Bubu blong ol man long Pasifik*. Port Vila: Vanuatu Cultural Centre.

Bedford, Stuart and Matthew Spriggs, 2000. Crossing the Pwanmwou: preliminary report on recent excavations adjacent to and south west of Mangaasi, Efate, Vanuatu. *Archaeology in Oceania* 35: 120–6.

Bedford, Stuart and Matthew Spriggs, 2002. Of shell, stone and bone. a review of non-ceramic artefacts recovered from the first 1000 years of Vanuatu's archaeological record. In *Fifty Years in the Field. Essays in Honour and Celebration of Richard Shutler Jr's Archaeological Career*, ed. Stuart Bedford, Christophe Sand and D. Burley, 135–52. Auckland: New Zealand Archaeological Association Monograph 25.

Bedford, Stuart and Matthew Spriggs, 2008. Northern Vanuatu as a Pacific crossroads: the archaeology of discovery, interaction and the emergence of the 'ethnographic present'. *Asian Perspectives* 47(1): 95–120.

Bedford, Stuart, Matthew Spriggs, Hallie Buckley, Frédérique Valentin, Ralph Regenvanu and M. Abong, 2010. Un cimetière de premier peuplement: le site de Teouma, sud d'Efate, Vanuatu/A cemetery of first settlement: Teouma, South Efate, Vanuatu. In *Lapita: Ancêtres océaniens/Oceanic Ancestors*, ed. Christophe Sand, and Stuart Bedford, pp. 140–61. Paris: Musée du quai Branly/Somogy.

Bedford, Stuart, Matthew Spriggs and Ralph Regenvanu, 1999. The Australian National University-Vanuatu Cultural Centre Archaeology Project 1994–7: aims and results. *Oceania* 70(1): 16–24.

Bedford, Stuart, Matthew Spriggs and Ralph Regenvanu, 2006. The Teouma Lapita site and the early human settlement of the Pacific Islands. *Antiquity* 80: 812–28.

Bedford, Stuart, Matthew Spriggs, Meredith Wilson and Ralph Regenvanu, 1998. The Australian National University-National Museum of Vanuatu Archaeological Project 1994–7: a preliminary report on the establishment of cultural sequences and rock art research. *Asian Perspectives* 37(2): 165–93.

Bedford, Stuart, Andrew Hoffman, Martha Kaltal, Ralph Regenvanu and Richard Shing, 2004. Dentate-stamped Lapita reappears on Efate, Central Vanuatu: a four decade-long drought is broken. *Archaeology in New Zealand* 47:39–49.

Bolton, Lissant 1999, Introduction. *Oceania* 70: 1–8.

Galipaud, Jean-Christophe and Ian Lilley (eds), 1999. *The Western Pacific from 5000 to 2000 BP. Colonisation and Transformations*. Paris: IRD Éditions.

Horrocks, Mark and Stuart Bedford, 2005. Microfossil analysis of Lapita deposits in Vanuatu reveals introduced Araceae (aroids). *Archaeology in Oceania* 40: 67–74.

Kaltal, Martha, Yoko Nojima and Stuart Bedford, 2004. *Wokbaot Bakagen wetem Olgeta Blong VCHSS. Saet Sevei mo Akaeoloji*. Port Vila: VCHSS, Vanuatu Cultural Centre.

Leavesley, Matthew, Bernard Minol, H. Kop, Vincent Kewibu, 2005. Cross-cultural concepts of archaeology. Kastom, community, education and cultural heritage management in Papua New Guinea. *Public Archaeology* 4: 3–13.

Lightner, Sara and Anna Naupa, 2005. *Histri Blong Yumi Long Vanuatu*. 3 volumes plus teacher's guide. Port Vila: Vanuatu Cultural Centre.

Mead, Jim I., David W. Steadman, Stuart H. Bedford, Christopher J. Bell and Matthew Spriggs, 2002. New extinct mekosuchine crocodile from Vanuatu, South Pacific. *Copeia* 3: 632–41.

Regenvanu, Ralph, 1999. Afterword: Vanuatu perspectives on research. *Oceania* 70: 98–101.

Regenvanu, Ralph, 2005. The changing face of custom. *People and Culture in Oceania* 20: 37–50.

Regenvanu, Ralph, Peter Kolmas, Martha Yamsiu, David Roe and Jean-Christophe Galipaud, 1992. *Wokabaot Blong Olgeta Blong VCHSS*. Port Vila: The Vanuatu Cultural and Historic Sites Survey.

Regenvanu, Ralph and Matthew Spriggs, 1996. Ripot i go long ol man Mangaliliu mo Lelepa long saed blong stadi blong Kaljoral Senta long Arkiologi blong Mangaasi, Okis kasem Septemba 1996. Typescript, on file Vanuatu National Library.

Roe, David, Ralph Regenvanu, Francois Wadra and Nick Araho, 1994. Working with cultural landscapes in Melanesia: some problems and approaches in the formulation of cultural policies. In *Culture-Kastom-Tradition. Developing Cultural Policy in Melanesia*, ed. L. Lindstrom and G. White, 115–30. Suva: Institute of Pacific Studies, USP.

Roe, David and Jean-Christophe Galipaud, 1994. *The Vanuatu Cultural and Historic Sites Survey: Project Description, Evaluation and Recommendations. Final Report*. Port Vila: The Vanuatu Cultural and Historic Sites Survey.

Sand, Christophe and Stuart Bedford (eds), 2010. *Lapita: Ancêtres océaniens/ Oceanic Ancestors*. Paris: Musée du quai Branly/Somogy.

Shing, Richard and Stuart Bedford, 2005. *Wanem ia arkioloji*. Port Vila: The Vanuatu Cultural Centre.

Shing, Richard, Stuart Bedford, Matthew Spriggs and Ralph Regenvanu, 2005. Ripot long saed blong stadi long arkioloji long Teouma 2004. Typescript, on file Vanuatu National Library.

Shing, Richard, Stuart Bedford, Matthew Spriggs and Ralph Regenvanu, 2007a. Ripot long saed blong stadi long arkioloji long Teouma 2004, 2005, 2006. Typescript, on file Vanuatu National Library.

Shing, Richard, Stuart Bedford, Matthew Spriggs and Ralph Regenvanu, 2007b. *Wanem ia arkioloji*. Port Vila: The Vanuatu Cultural Centre.

Spriggs, Matthew, 1984. The Lapita Cultural Complex: origins, distribution, contemporaries and successors, Journal of Pacific History 19(4), pp. 202-223.

Spriggs, Matthew, 1996. Report to the Vanuatu Government on archaeological research and training program at Mangaasi on the island of Efate, August to September 1996. Typescript, on file Vanuatu National Library.

Spriggs, Matthew, 1997. The Island Melanesians, Oxford, Blackwell.

Spriggs, Matthew, 1999. Remote delivery of archaeological discovery results to a classroom context. In *Archaeology, Communication and Language. No Barriers Seminar Papers*, ed. Paul Wallin, vol. 1, 1998: 5–7. Oslo: Kon Tiki Museum.

Spriggs, Matthew, 2000. The Pacific archaeology teaching project: an experiment in remote delivery of archaeological results to a classroom context. In *Essays in Honour of Arne Skjolsvold. Occasional Papers of the Kon-Tiki Museum*, ed. P. Wallin and H. Martinsson-Wallin, volume 5, 122–31. Oslo: Kon-Tiki Museum.

Spriggs, Matthew, 2002. Report to the Australia and Pacific Science Foundation on the project 'Investigation of the initial human colonisation of Vanuatu and its later transformations' for 2001. Typescript, on file Vanuatu National Library.

Spriggs, Matthew, 2003. Report to the Pacific Biological Foundation on the project 'Investigation of the initial human colonisation of Vanuatu and its later transformations' for 2002. Typescript, on file Vanuatu National Library.

Spriggs, Matthew, 2004a. Investigation of the initial human colonisation of Vanuatu and its later transformations. Report to the Pacific Biological Foundation for 2003 and Final Report. Typescript, on file Vanuatu National Library.

Spriggs, Matthew, 2004b. Archaeological investigation of the Lapita site of Teouma: The critical missing piece in the study of Central Vanuatu environmental and cultural history. Final Report to the Pacific Biological Foundation. Typescript, on file Vanuatu National Library.

Spriggs, Matthew, 2006. World Heritage values for the Roy Mata-Mangaasi Complex, Northwest Efate, Vanuatu. Report as part of the nomination papers for the proposed World Heritage area, submitted to UNESCO. Typescript, on file Vanuatu National Library.

Spriggs, Matthew, 2007. Research report on NGS grant number 8038—06: Solving the riddle of Pacific Settlement: the archaeology of an Early Lapita cemetery and village site at Teouma, Vanuatu. Typescript, on file Vanuatu National Library.

Spriggs, Matthew and Stuart Bedford, 1999. Summary report to the Vanuatu Government on archaeological research and training program at Mangaasi, West Efate 1997–1999. Typescript, on file Vanuatu National Library.

Spriggs, Matthew and Stuart Bedford, 2001. Arapus: a Lapita site at Mangaasi in central Vanuatu? In *The Archaeology of Lapita Dispersal in Oceania: Papers from the Fourth Lapita Conference, June 2000, Canberra, Australia*, ed. G.R. Clark, A.J. Anderson and T. Vunidilo, 93–104. Canberra: Pandanus Books. Terra Australis 17.

Tryon, Darrell, 1999. Ni-Vanuatu research and researchers. *Oceania* 70: 9–15.

Valentin, Frédérique, Richard Shing and Matthew Spriggs, 2005. Des Restes Humains Datés du début de la période de Mangaasi (2400–1800 BP) Découverts à Mangaliliu (Efate, Vanuatu). *Comptes Rendus Palévol* 4: 420–27.

Ward, G., 1990. The Mangaasi pottery and the Mangaasi site. In *Saying So Doesn't Make It So*, ed. D. Sutton, 153–67. New Zealand Archaeological Association Monograph 17.

Yona, Salkon, 2006. Excerpts from joint presentation with Stuart Bedford at 26 Years Collaboration Conference (Recorded 8/11/06 [Copy held by National Film, Photo and Sound Archives, Vanuatu Cultural Centre]).

20. Smol Toktok long Risej blong Kastom

Martha Alick

Tangkiu, mi nem blong mi Martha Alick mi mi kam long Epi long Laman aelan. Mi bin stap long wok ia olsem wan woman filwoka ia hemi eit yias blong mi nao. Mi mi gat wan woman filwoka long narasaed long wes we hemi stap staon longwe mo mi gat wan man filwoka tu i stap long Epi we hemi save stap blong wok wetem mi long risej blong mifala. Bae mi talem olsem ia se taem mi kam insaed olsem wan woman filwoka blong mi karemaot wok ia, mi faenem lelebet i had ia from mi mi ting se kastom hemi blong ol olfala man nomo blong oli karemaot be taem we mi kam tru long plante tu, tri yias we mi stap aot wetem ol topiks blong evri yia mi faenem hemi intres long mi. Mi faenem se hemi helpem mi tu blong mi save tijim ol pikinini blong mi mo hemi helpem mi tu blong mi save tijim ol narafala man long ol kastom blong mifala we hemi bin lus bifo finis blong mifala i save faenemaot bakegen blong bringim ap i kam antap blong mifala i save lanem. Mi faenem se komiuniti blong wok olsem mi save we mi kari aot wok ia mi dil plante wetem ol komiuniti mo mi involv plante long ol aktiviti blong ol jifs mo ol woman olsem mi mi pat long plante, mi bin komitim mi long plante wok blong ol komiuniti mekem se mi faenem wok ia i isi nomo. Be olsem bae mi talem se mi mi glad from mi gat janis blong sam samting we i bin lus bifo we ol abu blong mifala i ded finis ale i gat risej long hem blong faenemaot olsem bae mi mi save bae mi mi faenem long mi se mi bin save plante samting long kastom bitim ol olfala man we ating oli ting se kastom hemi taem we yumi stap long deilaet hemi lus i lus nao. Oli ting se taem yumi kam ol kristen man hemi nomo taem blong yumi go bak long ol kastom fasin blong yumi bifo. Fo eksampol, topik blong mifala long tis yia hemi kastom dresing. Mi mi faenem i had lelebet ia blong traem faenemaot se bifo we ol waet man oli no kam long yumi long New-Hebrides yumi stap werem wanem o yumi stap yusum wanem. Hemi wan intresting topik we mifala i traem blong mekem risej long hem be mifala ino faenem evri ditel blong hem mo ol kastom histri blong kastom stori ia i kam wea hemi stap yet blong mifala i save go kontiniu blong mekem risej long hem.

Ating hemia nomo hemi smol toktok mifala i glad blong stap long ol pleses blong mifala sapos yufala ol riseja yufala i glad blong kam joenem mifala long ples blong mifala blong mekem risej blong yufala, mifala i welkam blong mitim yufala mo lukaotem yufala. Tangkiu tumas.

Some Brief Words on Researching Kastom

Martha Alick

Thank you. My name is Martha Alick and I come from Laman Island, Epi. I have been working as a woman fieldworker for eight years now. There is another woman fieldworker working on the west and a male fieldworker on Epi who is able to work with me on our research. I will put it like this: when I started working as a woman fieldworker I found that it was a little hard because I thought that *kastom* was only for old men to perform, but over the years, and as we have gone through different topics, I have found that my work is very interesting to me. I have also found it helpful in teaching my children, and also in teaching other people about our *kastom* that has been lost for a long time, and that we can learn about it and promote it. I find that I work a lot with the community, and I'm very involved and committed to the activities of Chiefs and women. In this I find that my work becomes easy. I am glad to have a chance to revive some things of the ancestors that were lost, and that through research I have come to know many more things than the old men, many of whom think that once we are in the daylight (as converted Christians) *kastom* is lost forever. They think that when you become Christian it is not possible to go back to the *kastom* ways of the past. For example, our topic this year is *kastom* clothing. I have found it a little difficult to try to find out what clothes we wore before whites came to the New Hebrides. This is an interesting topic for us to attempt research on, and we have not uncovered every detail, and the *kastom* histories and *kastom* stories are still there for us to research.

I think that this is all that we have to say. We enjoy staying at our home islands and places, and if you researchers would like to come and join us there to undertake research projects, we will welcome you and look after you.

21. Learning How to Relate: Notes of a Female Anthropologist on Working with a Male Fieldworker in Vanuatu

Sabine Hess

In 1999 I visited Vanua Lava for three weeks to find a fieldsite for my doctoral research. Eli Field had been recommended to me as an experienced fieldworker from the Vanuatu Cultural Centre (VCC). During this first trip I was adopted by Eli Field as a daughter and my new family, his wife Joana and their five sons and two daughters, looked after me. Eli helped improve my Bislama by speaking what seemed to me in hindsight almost non-stop and high speed. My mother, Joana, took me to the creek to wash, showed me how to grate coconuts and how to sit properly. It was a crash course in village life in Vanuatu. I was also introduced to other villagers and the chiefs; and I managed to record a few stories.

In October 2001, almost two years later I returned, this time to stay for one year to undertake doctoral research in anthropology for which I had secured funding from the Australian National University (ANU). Again, Eli Field and Joana welcomed me as their daughter. During the following year I learnt what exactly this entailed: how I was supposed to behave and also what I could get away with due to my being a different kind of daughter, for example living in a house by myself.

From anthropological literature like Charles Briggs' (1986) book *Learning How to Ask* (1986) we learn crucial lessons on how important it is to pay attention to meta-communicative aspects of the culture we study: how people talk to each other in different situations and social settings, what questions one may ask of whom, and which topics are left out. Coe's (2001) article 'Learning how to find out', a kind of follow-up to Briggs, makes us aware of different kinds of knowledge. Inspired by Bloch (1993), she distinguishes three kinds of knowledge: practical knowledge (everyday tasks, cooking, washing), specialised knowledge (carpentry, weaving), and knowledge focused on history (family and chiefly genealogies, the history of a town) (Coe 2001: 403). Furthermore, what people consider important knowledge may differ from what the anthropologist considers important knowledge.

Like Coe, I had read Briggs before going to the field, and I was indeed paying attention to people's meta-communication. How people interact with each other is dependant on three structuring social categories: kinship, gender and generation. While I recognised these, I also have to admit to trying to partially circumvent what I learnt. I wanted to ask questions despite these restrictions. This of course proved unsuccessful but made for a good lesson. I learnt that the basis for learning how to ask, or meta-communication, is learning how to relate.

In what follows I will trace my own (at times steep) learning curve through discussion of some anecdotes from my fieldwork. I can only speculate on how Eli Field experienced these incidents and what he may have learned from them. I hope that he will have the chance to present his views on the progress of our cooperation and relationship. If he does so I think the reader or listener will gain more than the sum of the two parts.

Father and fieldworker; daughter and guest

Not long after my arrival a death occurred in the neighbouring village, Vatrata. Arrangements were made for everyone to go, except my mother Joana, who was to stay behind to look after me. When I realised what was happening in the general rush for departure I caught Eli and said that I wanted to come too, that in fact I needed to go because this was part of my work. At first he seemed sceptical whether I could walk the distance through the bush, crossing three creeks on the way, as quickly as required but eventually he agreed that I could come. I, on the other hand, was surprised that he had seemingly tried to exclude me from ritual activity which—surely as an experienced fieldworker he should know—would be important for me to record.

So what happened? The only explanation I had was that he thought of me as a daughter and guest and therefore was more concerned with my wellbeing than with my task as a researcher. Up to my arrival his role as a fieldworker had been very much defined by the relationship between him and the VCC in Port Vila, and not so much by the relationship between him and another researcher living in his own village.

As already mentioned, being adopted into a kin network meant that people knew how to relate to me. I, in turn, had to learn how to relate to them. Interaction in cross-sex relationships are imbued with restrictions of all kinds. This is particularly true for a father-daughter relationship, which is marked by mutual respect and partial avoidance, for example we may not look at each other for prolonged periods of time. Doing interview-based research this aspect was difficult to remember as the Western style of communication is keeping eye contact to signal attentive listening and interest.

In addition to this problem I was also faced with restriction on the topics I could discuss with Eli. Topics related to women and sexuality were taboo. Any suggestion to temporarily 'forget' our father-daughter relationship for an hour or so and work as fieldworker and anthropologist were unacceptable, unthinkable. A division of work and private life, from kinship as the way of relating, was impossible. Initially, this caused quite some frustration on my side. On a number of occasions I mentioned that if there ever was another anthropologist coming he or she should be adopted as Eli's sister's child because this is the least restrictive relationship in terms of flow of knowledge. Eli seemed hesitant and commented with a 'yes, maybe' rather than 'yes, what a good idea'. Maybe such a relationship would pose a whole new set of problems.

Key informant and gatekeeper

The special situation and good fortune of the existence of the Vanuatu fieldworker system practically delivers us a key informant at our doorstep, or rather us to theirs. And, indeed, fieldworkers are very valuable to us and often our work would not flourish or be possible without them. However, there are also some challenges. Talking to other researchers working in Vanuatu we frequently arrived at the topic of the fieldworker as key informant and the power he or she has. Because of their specific knowledge, their practice at articulating it, and their initial exclusive access to the freshly arrived researcher, they are simultaneously key informant and gatekeeper. Fieldworkers can be gatekeepers in two related ways. They control the flow of resources and of knowledge. I have heard stories where the fieldworker tries to keep the researcher and the resources that come with him or her to the benefit of his family only. This is understandable from a local perspective. But as a fieldworker—and maybe this has been covered in the fieldworker-workshops already—assistance to researchers means also assistance in access to other people, even people that the fieldworker may not agree with. If this means that the researcher gives some rice to someone else for a change, then so be it!

A fieldworker is more than an ordinary member of society. He or she is (or should be?) also a mediator enabling access to knowledge. Researchers usually come to find out information about a specific topic. They would like to talk to various people, not just one or two. While the fieldworker may be an expert, other people in the community may also have valuable knowledge to contribute. The great strength of the fieldworker is that he or she knows whom to ask for specific knowledge. This is usually straight forward if the person in question is a relative of the fieldworker. But if the fieldworker has no obvious family ties to this other person, or there are personal tensions between them, it is, in my understanding, the task of the fieldworker to find a way to make this contact possible, even though his or her own proper way of behaving would be avoidance.

In this last section which was addressed as much to fieldworkers as other audiences, my own bias towards putting research first, before kinship and rules of sociality became apparent. If I was doing research in a place that had no fieldworker system this expectation may never have occurred. To me, fieldworkers are cultural brokers who more or less understand the principles (or ideology?) of research as a worthy end in itself and can mediate or switch between the two cultures and their expectations. My assumption might be wrong, or may be asking too much. Is it really possible for a fieldworker to push his or her relationships into the background for someone else's research with a slim chance of usefulness to locals? Maybe every person can answer this for him or herself. I wonder what the official VCC's advice would be?

At this point I would like to tell an anecdote of my research as a gentle reminder to other researchers to respect restricted knowledge: Together with my colleague Sophie Caillon we had elicited a restricted story about the creation of taro gardens from two of our uncles. No need to say Eli Field, was furious. To us the story was significant as it allowed us to create a theoretical link between taro and people in a new way. But other than that, we could see nothing in the story that was particularly worthy of secrecy, although it was highly amusing. I tried to explain the importance of the story to our work to Eli, but he threatened to withdraw from the research altogether if I continue to seek this kind of knowledge. I was furious too and for about three weeks we hardly talked to each other. These weeks he also used to prepare every person in the village about what kind of information they were not allowed to pass on. I had to give in so that I could continue my research.

Initially it felt like defeat, but I came to understand his point of view. To me this story was 'just another story', one of many I recorded. To Eli Field and to many others, if women know the story in detail the existence of the irrigated taro gardens would be threatened by drought. So my knowledge of the story was a potential threat to people's survival on the island. Who am I to say whether this is 'real'? No research is that important! And I did get my PhD without this story after all. So, here is a plea to all researchers: don't lose perspective in the name of science and respect the limits of people you work with.

Father and daughter

What would you do if an anthropologist turned up at your doorstep? One must not forget that I had more time and resources to prepare for this encounter than Eli Field. What had he known about anthropology or the strange questions these people ask about the most obvious things? I assume that his learning curve was at least as steep as mine and that he has some pretty good anecdotes and insightful observations about our time together to tell, too. May be he can give some hints to fieldworkers on 'what to expect' and some advice to researchers on the dos and don'ts of fieldwork.

Over the year that I lived on Vanua Lava I think we learned to live and work together and respect each other as father and daughter *and* as fieldworker and anthropologist. Because I learnt how to relate I learnt how to ask. And I noticed changes in Eli Field's relating and responding too. While I learnt how to ask properly, Eli learnt that my questions where different from the ones he was used to from his normal interlocutors. Initially I asked about incidents I observed to learn about the principles of behaviour. For example I would ask: Why did you give so-and-so some money? Coming from some other person in the community this question could be understood as a kind of social control, a criticism, or a demand, to name a few possibilities. The answer for this person would have been, a *justification* and not so much an *explanation*. In the beginning I had trouble understanding Eli's response because they were often more justification than explanation. After some time of getting used to what must have seemed the most obvious questions his answers became less defensive and more explanatory, not so much concerned with personal detail (burdened with a reluctance to reveal) but more abstract, trying to convey the principle. Eli learnt very quickly to respond to my expectation of this kind of answer. This transition, I think, was not easy. As I became more familiar with the principles, however, I wished more for the 'normal' kind of answer. Once I learnt to use questions as the locals did, my expectations of an answer became mixed. Sometimes I wanted an explanation, sometimes just an 'authentic' kind of answer. And in Eli's particular case I sometimes wanted to see how the justification was framed as an explanation. Eli in turn became competent at distinguishing what I was after and giving answers that he thought appropriate. We had, after all found a kind of middle ground where I could ask questions that were within the limitations of a father-daughter relationship, and he could answer in a way that would not be understood as gossip. With this mutual understanding of appropriateness, sensitive topics, such as land rights, could be discussed using particular people's situation as a 'case study' rather than as a claim to land or a doubt of their rightful ownership.

To conclude I have to say that despite the restrictions and challenges that such a relationship poses I am glad to be in a father-daughter relationship with Eli Field because of the respect and protection it affords. I think his suggestion of female researchers working with female fieldworkers, and male researchers working with male fieldworkers where possible is a good idea in some cases. Another consideration might be how the relationship and the work would be affected if the researcher would be adopted into the same generation as the fieldworker, for example as a sister or brother, something fieldworkers expecting a researcher may want to think about.

I doubt whether there really would have been a shortcut for acquiring this kind of embodied knowledge of how to relate beforehand. Relating to people is dependant on many things—words like sympathy, sense of humour, understanding, and sincerity spring to mind, not really something one can practice before one actually gets there. As advice for researchers I would say: try to work with people you like, and think of making mistakes as part of your method.

I would like to, again, thank Eli Field for his support and conclude with his summarising comment about our (working) relationship on my day of my departure: we had a good hard time.

Postscript

At the conference this paper was presented for me by my former supervisor Margaret Jolly, which I was delighted to hear. Weeks before I had first asked the linguist Catriona Malau if she would read a paper for me at the conference. Catriona and I had been working together on Vanua Lava, so she seemed an obvious choice. But since then she had become my 'sister-in-law' because she had actually married Eli Field's son Armstrong Malau. When we met in Amsterdam three weeks before the conference she read the paper and realised that it would be impossible for her to read it at the conference since she cannot say Eli's name. She stressed that for her the in-law-relationship is a very real one, not a fictitious one like 'adopted' researchers might have. As a daughter-in-law she could clearly not read a paper on a daughter-father relationship. I guess this anecdote of my omission and her position, again, emphasises how important it is to consider relating in the right way first (even at an international conference)—before doing anything else.

Unfortunately Eli Field did not arrive in Port Vila in time for the conference, so his side of the story is still missing.

References

Bloch, Maurice, 1993. The uses of schooling and literacy in a Zafimaniry village. In *Cross-cultural Approaches to Literacy*, ed. Brian Street, 87–109. Cambridge: Cambridge University Press.

Briggs, Charles L., 1986. *Learning How to Ask: A Sociolinguistic Appraisal of the Role of the Interview in Social Science Research*. Cambridge: Cambridge University Press.

Coe, Cati, 2001. Learning how to find out: theories of knowledge and learning in field research. *Field Methods* 13, 392–411.

22. Wok Olsem wan Filwoka

Elsy Tilon

Tangkiu tumas mi gat bigfala hona mo rispek blong stanap long fes blong yufala blong talemaot smol tingting blong mi olsem mi kam mi olsem wan woman filwoka. Mi nem blong mi Elsy Tilon mi kam long wes blong Ambrym. Mi angkel blong mi ia hemi stap long fored ia, from mama blong mi i kam long not blong Ambrym. Mi wok mi kam olsem woman filwoka hemi eit yias nao, be mi gat wan man filwoka festaem hemi Ramel be ko-operesen blong hem wetem mi hemi nogud tumas. Be taem hemi finis Philip hemi kam in ko-operesen blong mitufala hemi gud. Mitufala wok tugeta wan we hemi tingbaot blong hem i mekem i kam talem long mi. Sins we mi no kam mi no atendem woksop blong 2004, 2005 be taem man filwoka i kam long woksop i go bak hemi talemaot wanem we olgeta oli mekem ale mitufala i wok tugeta. Blong talem nomo se festaem blong mi mi kam long woksop hemi 1997. Topik blong mifala hemi rang blong ol woman be festaem we mi kam, mi mekem risej blong rang blong ol woman ia ale mi go bak mi stap, mi disaed blong tekem wan rang blong mi. Nao afta 2000 an 1997 mi mekem olsem mi kilim pig nao blong mi kam tekem narafala step blong mi mo mi stap olsem ol wok, mi bin wok kolosap long olgeta an we mi bin aot olgeta oli harem. Mo sins tu yias mi no atendem woksop mi olsem mi stap mekem wok blong big man olsem mi mekem wok blong jos mi nomo. Go kolosap long jif mi mi bin atendem ol jif mitings. Long tis yia mi tekem narafala step bakegen mi kam elda blong Presbyterian jos, be wok blong mi i stap, mi lukluk wok blong mi olsem kastom wetem jos mi mekem tufala wok ia i balans nomo. Mo taem mi mi tok mekem awenes mo toktok, ol woman ol man ol jif oli harem mi oli lisin long mi ating hemia nomo smol toktok blong mi tangkiu.

Working as a Fieldworker

Elsy Tilon

Thank you very much. It is with great honour and respect that I stand before you to tell you a little about me, and how I came to be a woman *filwoka*. My name is Elsy Tilon, and I come from the west of Ambrym. The man sitting at the front here is my uncle, because my mother comes from the north of Ambrym. I worked as a fieldworker when he was just eight years old. Back then there was a male fieldworker by the name of Ramel, but the cooperation between him and me wasn't very good. But when he finished Philip came in, and the cooperation between us is good. We two work together as one, and when he thinks about something regarding his work he comes and tells me. I was not able to attend the workshops in 2004 and 2005, however after he had returned from the men's *filwoka* workshop, he told me of everything they had done—we work together. I should say that the first time I came to a workshop was in 1997. Our topic was 'women's rank'. Alright, after I went back to my island I decided to take my own rank. Next, after 2000, like 1997, I killed a pig to take another step. And this is how I work, I worked closely with them and when I went to the workshop they heard about it. And for the last two years I have not been able to attend workshops because I now work as a big man, that is, I make my own work now. I am close to being a chief, and I attend all the chief's meetings. This year I took another step by becoming an elder of the Presbyterian Church. And so I have work to do. As I see it, in my work in *kastom* and church, I make it so that these two areas of work are balanced. And when I make awareness speeches, women, men and chiefs hear me and listen to me. I think that this is all I have to say. Thank you.

23. Shifting Others: Kastom and Politics at the Vanuatu Cultural Centre

Benedicta Rousseau

Assessing the origins of the Bislama term, *kastom*, anthropologists have highlighted its essentially oppositional nature (Bolton 1999; Lindstrom 1982; Rousseau 2004). Emerging in the context of colonisation and missionisation, *kastom* provided a discursive marker of a lifestyle apart from that of *skul*—the way of the mission (Bolton 1999). Over the next century, it found itself enmeshed in a variety of 'evaluative dualisms' (Lindstrom 1982), as practices, material culture and demeanour became linked with the descriptor, *kastom*. Vanuatu's experience of modernity could be characterised as a series of 'otherings', with the category of *kastom* positioned in oppositional relationships that provide a definition of indigeneity (Taylor 2010). In some ways, though, *kastom* works to resist or obscure this action, carrying with it ideological connotations of stability, primordialism, constancy. This chapter seeks to expose the fluidity of *kastom*, charting the fluctuating relationship between the spheres of *kastom* and politics over the past 30 years, and the multiple 'others' created through that interaction.[1]

Those familiar with Melanesian anthropology over the last two decades will recognise the dualism of *kastom* and politics as one of the most over-discussed areas of recent investigation, as well as an ideological opposition that has been employed within Vanuatu. However, the purpose of this chapter is not to rehash arguments surrounding the 'invention of tradition' or the 'hijacking' of *kastom* by an educated elite (or those who have 'lost theirs'—see Philibert 1986). Instead, I aim to illustrate the way in which *kastom* relies on its dialectical partners for its definition, and how such partnerships shift. The ethnographic focus for this analysis is the work of the Vanuatu Cultural Centre (VCC) over the past thirty years. The VCC has been chosen for a number of reasons: it holds a unique place in the country as the longest-established state institution to work explicitly in the area of *kastom*; it has provided a public forum for representations of *kastom*, creating a repository that enables the type of historical investigation

---

1   This chapter is based on fieldwork carried out in Vanuatu in 2000–01 and 2005. Funding for fieldwork was provided by the Cambridge Commonwealth Trust, the William Wyse Fund, the Emslie Horniman Fund, the Smuts Memorial Fund, the Richards Fund and the British Academy (SG-40371). I am grateful to the Vanuatu Cultural Council for permission to carry out research. I would also like to thank the staff and fieldworkers of the Vanuatu Cultural Centre for their assistance, support and friendship throughout my time in Vanuatu.

necessary to illustrate changes in the relationship between *kastom* and politics; in addition, anthropological researchers must work through the VCC, so I have been involved in some of the projects discussed below, and affected by the shifting parameters of *kastom*.

A short history of the Vanuatu Cultural Centre

A cultural centre was first opened in Port Vila in 1956 by the Condominium administration. It was run by a Board made up of expatriate and indigenous members with facilities comprising a museum, archives and library. Its main aim was to provide for 'the exhibition of objects which illustrate the history, literature and natural resources of the New Hebrides' (Bolton 2003: 3). However, the displays veered away from many objects that would today be labelled *kastom*, incorporating into the exhibition policy concerns regarding 'heathen' practices that were prevalent amongst some colonial agents, but also expressed through the distinction between *kastom* and *skul* employed by many indigenous converts to Christianity.[2]

The arrival in the 1970s of researchers such as Jean-Michel Charpentier and Darrell Tryon, both linguists, Peter Crowe, an ethnomusicologist, and Kirk Huffman, an anthropologist, signalled a shift in the work of the VCC. The previous focus on museum displays lessened in favour of 'getting Melanesians interested' (Bolton 2003: 36). The presence of this new wave of overseas researchers helped push this work into the present, introducing the training of ni-Vanuatu researchers as a key area of VCC work. The reference point for the study of *kastom* became as much the contemporary practices taking place in island villages as the museum collection in Port Vila.

The Oral Traditions Project was the first project within the VCC to embody this new ethos, and is seen as the start of the fieldworkers' network. Under the tutelage of Peter Crowe, a group of male ni-Vanuatu were trained in the collection of *kastom* stories and knowledge, with an increasing emphasis on language preservation (through the influence of Darrell Tryon, still the facilitator of the annual men fieldworker's workshop). The effect of this programme of work was manifold: museum and research technologies were dispersed to a wider population than the (expatriate) staff of the VCC (eg: tape-recording, dictionary compilation, orthography etc.); museum work moved away from a simple focus on artefacts; the physical location of research shifted away from Port Vila; and *kastom* became connected to locality in a new way—the emblematic embodiment of the fieldworker.

---

2   For a more detailed account of the history and development of the VCC see Bolton 2003.

This change in orientation coincided with the growth of the independence movement through the 1970s, with the VCC's pro-independence agenda forging a link between political and cultural self-determination; *kastom* and politics. A key example of this was the National Arts Festival held in 1979 at which groups from around the archipelago were given the opportunity to present 'their *kastom*' to an indigenous audience. As a key organiser, the VCC took this opportunity to reinforce its message of 'unity in diversity': while *kastom* took many forms, its existence throughout the proto-state meant it could provide a means of showing how unified ni-Vanuatu were still different from each other, and how 'ownership' of *kastom* operated at a highly localised level.

Kastom, politics and anthropologists

It is around this time that anthropologists started to take an interest in the contemporary use of the term *kastom*, focussing particularly on the way it was being employed by the Vanua'aku Pati. While it had previously served as a means of differentiation from the alternative lifeway of *skul*, pro-independence politicians were now using *kastom* to valorise that which was indigenous, rather than non-Christian. Anthropological critiques of the use of *kastom* in the rhetoric and practice of the independence movement are numerous, positing an instrumentalist revision of the concept on the part of politicians. These assessments all share a suspicion of—and, in a few cases, an open dislike for—this 'new' type of *kastom*, and place it in opposition to what they see as having gone before. What unites these otherwise disparate accounts, too, is the construction of a dichotomous relationship between 'national' and 'local' in Vanuatu, frequently tying this to a supposedly temporal dimension of *kastom*, ideas of authenticity, and insinuations of 'incorrect' practice.

Tonkinson (1982), for example, discusses what he terms 'the problem of *kastom* in Vanuatu', pointing particularly to a divergence in interpretation amongst different sectors of the population: as ideology on the part of politicians; as pragmatic practice on the part of 'the populace' (Tonkinson 1982: 306). He recounts the uncertainty involved in the interpretation of the new 'valued' *kastom* on the part of the people of Southeast Ambrym as presented to them by representatives of the Vanua'aku Pati (in this case, a local Presbyterian pastor):

> People in some rural areas took the message quite literally. They worried about a return to grass skirts and penis-wrappers, spears and bows and arrows, and wondered whether they would have to destroy non-*kastom* things such as hunting rifles, aluminium dinghies, outboards and so on (Tonkinson 1982: 310).

For Tonkinson, the formulation of *kastom* in the lead-up to independence was so generalised as to become ideology. In fact, he argues that this was inevitable and necessary due to the 'loss of *kastom*' since European contact:

> *Kastom* has at no stage [in independence politics] been subject to clarification, codification, subdivision or any kind of close analysis or scrutiny. It is, however, hardly surprising that *kastom* has remained undifferentiated in political discourse, because its utility as a rallying point depends heavily on its confinement to an ideological level, indivisible and unexamined. The reasons for this are obvious, given the circumstances of cultural transformation in Vanuatu, where in many islands a great deal of *kastom* disappeared virtually without trace and where new patterns of mobility led to widespread diffusion of much of what remained (Tonkinson 1982: 310).

The argument that *kastom* has/had been 'lost' features again in the work of Philibert (1986). However, for him, it was only certain segments of the population who had lost their *kastom*—the same group who then attempted to use the concept in the interests of national unity. He argues that 'the proto-bureaucratic "class" is attempting to gain control over a symbolic code derived from traditional practices (*kastom*) so as to promote social cohesion and establish a civil polity' (1986: 1). His argument rests on the accentuation of a high level of class differentiation in Vanuatu at the time of independence—in particular, the construction of a homogenous 'elite', composed, it seems, of indigenous politicians. Their use of *kastom* in the promotion/creation of a national identity is called into question as much for who they are as for how they have defined it:

> It is tradition as defined by members of an acculturated political elite living in an urban environment, many of whom were, prior to independence, Presbyterian clergymen or civil servants in the colonial administration. In other words, this *kastom* policy is endorsed by those least able to define or codify such customs. In fact, one could go further and state that it is a political symbol that could only have been devised in an urban context, away from areas where 'traditional' culture has remained a lived practice (Philibert 1986: 3).

He equates the urban environment, overseas education and state political involvement with a lack of *kastom* (or 'dead custom, empty practice' (1986: 8))—'far from being a closely integrated, functionalist view of culture, the view of *kastom* to emerge from the political circles of the capital is one of a set of survivals. This is so because those who have to decide what *kastom* was/ is are precisely those who have lost theirs' (1986: 8). The 'incorrect' nature of the concept of *kastom* propagated in independence politics is addressed again by Larcom (1982; 1990). She recounts the lack of interest in the past that she encountered during her first fieldwork in the Mewun area of South West Bay, Malakula in the early 1970s. Bernard Deacon, a Cambridge anthropology student, had visited the area some 50 years earlier, and Larcom was keen to build on the ethnographic material provided in his posthumously published papers (Deacon 1934). When she enquired about slit-gong beats and rhythmns—a focus of Deacon's interest—'no-one…was able or willing to demonstrate them for me' (Larcom 1982: 331). Enquiries relating to other areas of supposed ethnographic interest were no more successful: 'Questions about their parentage or traditions were greeted with about as much interest as a question on the breakfast diet: they could, of course, have told me what they had just eaten for breakfast, but why would I possibly want to know about such things?' (Larcom 1982: 331–2).

On her return in 1981, Larcom found the situation on Malakula much altered, in line with changes in the national arena. Now the Mewun were 'acutely aware of *kastom* as a body of past traditions to be revitalised' (Larcom 1982: 332). She states that '*kastom* was now a critical national and local issue, something representing past authenticity in counterpoint to Western values' (Larcom 1982: 332). For Larcom, the expressions of *kastom* that she now found did not tally with previous Mewun usage: 'Specific information on the role of *kastom* in the Mewun past tends to support a view of historic social life as inventive. *Kastom* glossed today as revealed and revitalised authentic tradition has little to do with earlier use of *kastom* in Mewun' (Larcom 1982: 333). She emphasises the role of trade, exchange and purchase of *kastom* in the past—an 'inventive flow' that was also 'mirrored in the looseness of group boundaries' (Larcom 1982: 333). In Larcom's assessment the major change wrought by the model of *kastom* presented in independence politics was the imposition or adoption of fixity on the 'local' level. She presents this elsewhere as the establishment of a 'museological' version of culture:

> By endorsing a museum culture of its own, the nation implicitly challenges a most distinctive aspect of Vanuatu social life—its emphasis on relationships, creativity, and exchange. For many local groups, including the Mewun, the unabashed invention of artifacts as emblems and invitations for relationships may come as close as possible to an authentic ni-Vanuatu culture (Larcom 1990: 188).

In their assessments of *kastom* these anthropologists foreground an alignment of practice with 'the local' and ideology with 'the national', while an antagonistc division between *kastom* and politics provides the back-story. These accounts bear the imprint of theoretical preoccupations prevalent in anthropology in the early 1980s, particularly debates surrounding the place of history and tradition in post-colonial politics, exemplified most popularly in the 'invention of tradition' literature (e.g. Handler and Linnekin 1984; Hanson 1989; Hobsbawm and Ranger 1983). For this reason the examples cited above lean heavily towards assessments of authenticity, aiming to demonstrate the lived confusion of rapid political—and discursive—change. I would argue that, while the divisions pointed to by these authors typify the orientation of VCC activity through the 1980s and early 90s, the analysis given fails to pinpoint the reasons why *kastom* and politics were and had to be kept separate in its work.

On the one hand, the existence and expansion of the fieldworker network—ideally including one representative of each language area of the country—reinforced the local nature of *kastom*. At the same time, the VCC worked to extract its version of *kastom* from that which could be used for political purposes. The crucial component of this exercise though was not the maintanence of 'purity' or 'authenticity'; rather, it involved the redefinition of the relationship between *kastom* and land in the post-independence environment. Land alienation had provided one of the strongest propellants of pro-independence politics—for Nagriamel as much as the Vanua'aku Pati—resulting in the return of all land to customary ownership under the constitution of the Republic.[3] The effect of this was twofold, tying *kastom* to land but simultaneously introducing the possibility that *kastom* knowledge could be used to 'prove' customary ownership.[4] In encouraging the collection, preservation and resuscitation of *kastom* knowledge and practice, the VCC needed to establish itself as apart from this new, potentially divisive, discourse of *kastom*.

Assessing this change in the use of *kastom* in Vanuatu, Bolton states that the Cultural Centre has been consistently opposed to the involvement of fieldworkers in land disputes. While some men fieldworkers are community leaders who may be involved in the arbitration of such disputes, this should remain separate from their role as a fieldworker (2003: 75). Similarly, the use of *kastom* knowledge that has been collected in the name of the VCC in land disputes is seen to be against the mandate of the organisation (Bolton 2003: 74). In fact, Bolton delineates types of *kastom* into that which could be used for land disputes, and that which subscribes to the VCC ideal. She describes the Cultural Centre approach in this way:

> Land, subject to ownership...can be a source of dispute. While local knowledge and practice, invoked and disputed in conflicts over land, can be described as *kastom*, the *kastom* with which the Cultural Centre

---

3 Section 73 of the Constitution states: 'All land in the Republic of Vanuatu belongs to the indigenous custom owners and their descendants'.

4 Land disputes are ubiquitous throughout Vanuatu and have been the source of much legal consternation. At one point, 99 per cent of state court judgments relating to land were under appeal. In 2001, the Land Tribunal Act brought into existence a new legal forum for dealing with these disputes, aiming to use *kastom* processes of justice as well as *kastom* knowledge as evidence. So far though the Tribunals do not seem to be reducing the number of land disputes passing through the system, and in many areas they are not yet functioning. In addition, many minor court cases that come before island or magistrates courts involving trespass or criminal damage have their roots in land boundary disputes.

deals is explicitly characterised as uncontroversial. In the Cultural Centre context one fieldworker cannot dispute the knowledge and practice reported by another because each reports on his own place. *Kastom* is characterised by regional differences: different *kastom* derives from different places (Bolton 2003: 76).

The Young People's Project: changing conceptions of *kastom* and research

While the equation of localised place and *kastom* provided the orientation of VCC work, and became axiomatic in anthropological writing (eg: Jolly 1994; Bonnemaison 1994), through the 1980s and early 1990s, the VCC itself posed a challenge to this notion with the inception of its Young People's Project (YPP) in the mid-1990s. This project responded to two demographic characteristics of the country that had been so far ignored in most anthropological research and not constituted a place on the agenda of the VCC: urbanisation and the fact that close to 50 per cent of the population was under the age of 25 (National Statistics Office 2000). The Project set out to produce research about young people in Vila, conducted mainly by young ni-Vanuatu themselves using primarily quantitative research methods. Its first two products were a report, *Harem Voes blong Yangfala long Vila Taon* (VYPP 1999 translated into English as *Young People Speak*), and a film, *Kilim Taem*, to accompany the report.

The Director of the Cultural Centre, Ralph Regenvanu, explained the rationale behind the Project's initial research in his introduction to the report. In it he argued that the type of talk that goes on in Vanuatu about young people and their problems is ill-informed and unhelpful, as it is not based on any understanding of the opinions of young people themselves, or an accurate assessment of their situation. The research carried out by the Project could ensure more appropriate development planning, simply by asking young people about their lives:

> We can't discuss development if we don't know the fundamental needs and opinions of those at the grassroots level…. If we don't know the answers to those questions, then none of us—the government and the people—can find the most appropriate way to address issues facing young people in town today (VYPP 1999: 1, my translation).

This type of research, with its explicit involvement in the development agenda for Vanuatu, indicated a move away from the previous Cultural Centre definition of culture and *kastom*. This, too, was explained in the introduction:

Starting in the 1960s, the Cultural Centre has been recording our traditional culture to ensure that there is a record of it for future generations. Now, in the 1990s, we can see that there is a new culture emerging in Vanuatu—this culture is the young people's culture, many of who aren't living *kastom* but nor are they living a European life. This is a new culture for Vanuatu and it's the work of the Cultural Centre to study this new culture as well, to see how it joins up with *kastom* and how it is changing our *kastom*. It is also important to record this major change occurring at this point in the country's history so that we always have a record of it (VYPP 1999: 1–2, my translation).

The effect of the YPP on the work of the VCC was twofold, representing an expansion of the concept of *kastom* and the introduction of a new range of research methods. This approach was effective in terms of raising the VCC's international profile, in particular gaining praise and support from NGOs and donor agencies and inspiring such organisations to develop projects targeting young people. However, this new synthesis of *kastom* and formal research methodologies played out less comfortably in the context of the fieldworkers' programme. As mentioned above, one of the key components of YPP activities was to provide training in research methods and data analysis. Those who carried out the research were all young ni-Vanuatu who were not currently employed and had no previous experience of such work. Of those involved in that initial phase of research, some remained part of the project in the new category of YPP fieldworkers. As such, they participated in the annual men and women fieldworker workshops at the Cultural Centre. However, their manner of research and presentation, and, in particular, the way this was received by the older fieldworkers reveals much about the persistence of the connection between locality and *kastom* favoured by the anthropologists cited above and, up to that point, privileged by the VCC.

The annual workshops provide a focus for fieldworker activities through the year. Separated into two two-week blocks, one each for the men and women, the fieldworkers meet at the VCC in Port Vila to present reports on their work through the year and make presentations on a pre-announced topic. In 2000, the topic for the women fieldworkers' workshop was *Kastom kalenda blong garen* (the customary gardening calendar), with most presentations covering what gardening activities took place throughout the course of the year; types of crops that were specific to their area and how they had got there; *kastom* prohibitions relating to gardening practice; and songs and stories relating to all of these. That year, three YPP fieldworkers participated in the workshop, making their presentation as a group.

In locating their sources of information the young women made reference to *'komiuniti blong mi'* [my community] while also providing information about/

from other islands. The fieldworkers were from Tanna, Paama and Matasso, yet they reported details of *kastom* gardening practice from Ambrym, central and north Pentecost, and south east Malakula, having gained this material through research carried out in a number of areas of Port Vila. Their presentation was mainly met with 'corrections' from the other fieldworkers: the fieldworker from north Pentecost emphasised that you must work every day in the garden, not infrequently—'if you miss one day, you're hungry for one month'; an Ambrym fieldworker corrected their version of male/female co-operation in gardening— boys are just *folem rod*, rather than going to the gardens to help.[5]

In response to the latter the YPP fieldworkers stated that this was what they were told, but they were sorry for getting it wrong—an apology that was repeated again later in the session. Other corrections were put forward by the older fieldworkers and, in response to those, the facilitator suggested that practice might be different in town because people haven't been back to the islands for some time, yet this could also be of interest. This was met with general agreement. However, the overall attitude that the young peoples' presentation was in need of correction resulted in one of the YPP fieldworkers breaking down in tears, apologising for her lack of *kastom* knowledge, stating her desire to go back to her island to learn proper *kastom*, but explaining that this was hampered by her boyfriend's demands on her and a lack of money. This was met with sympathy from the older fieldworkers.

The tensions that emerged in the workshop's responses to the young people's presentations seem due to the fact that they were either reporting on places that they 'belonged' to but were not living in, or employing 'research methods' to collect information on places that they could not claim to belong to. They were not trying to speak about *kastom* in town; rather, they attempted to fit into the dominant paradigm of the fieldworker programme that locates *kastom* in the islands and obscures research methods. As Bolton (2003) argues, legitimation for knowledge in the context of the fieldworker workshops relies on connection to place—with this you are unassailable. Yet how that knowledge is obtained is not always made clear. The position of fieldworker brings with it certain opportunities and 'privileges'—a yearly visit to Port Vila, paid for by the Cultural Centre; access to—and some control over—visiting researchers; and a title that connects the fieldworker to a national institution. Most fieldworkers show a strong commitment to the mandate of the Cultural Centre—*blong leftemap kastom*—however, the urge for financial gain or the use of their title in local politics is not unknown. While the Cultural Centre sees fieldworkers as representatives of areas beyond just their own village (or family) there is no imperative placed upon them to indicate how representative the knowledge is

---

5 Literally, 'following the road'. In this instance it implies that the boys are just going to the garden for something to do, rather than work.

that they present at the workshops. Conflict may come from disputes between families or villages in an area, or sometimes between adherents of different religious denominations (sometimes with differing valuations of *kastom*).

For the most part, fieldworkers do not make explicit their sources of information. All fieldworkers tend to be of reasonably established status within their village: for men, *jifs* or of high rank, or connected to a family known to be knowledgeable in *kastom*; for women, married to such men, or respected as strong women in the village or church hierarchy. For this reason, they can speak without recourse to legitimating sources; their word is enough—they present themselves as natural informants. This is not the case for YPP fieldworkers: they are open to correction due to both their age, and their lack of personal authority. Their use of interviews to gain knowledge from women of islands other than their own, makes clear their inability to speak authoritatively. But, within the workshop model, no legitimating claim can arise from 'research'. The suspect nature of research has been noted by the Director of the Cultural Centre: a researcher is still perceived as someone who comes to Vanuatu, finds things out but neither brings back the knowledge, nor comes back themselves.[6] Also, when urging women fieldworkers to find out more information from *olfala* (elders) in their area, the facilitator of the fieldworkers' workshop suggested that they emphasise that 'this is not just research'; rather the women want the knowledge so as to be able to live it in their own lives.

Through the YPP, the VCC undertook an exercise in overt political engagement. However, it was not a direct engagement with state politics, choosing instead to bypass that problematic realm through alignment with external development agencies. While its aim of influencing that sector was successful, the YPP did not break down the definitional boundaries between *kastom* and politics within the VCC's work—the expansion of the concept of *kastom* was not accepted in the context of the fieldworkers' workshop; it was seen to contradict the equation of *kastom* and locality that allowed for the existence of a non-divisive, non-political form of *kastom*. And, it can be argued that the work of the YPP brought further controversy to the issue through its methodologies, aligning the carrying out of research with a lack of *kastom*. A more recent VCC initiative may, however, have found a way to move beyond these particular dualisms.

---

6 Paraphrased from Ralph Regenvanu's presentation to the 'Walking about: travel, trade, migration and movement' conference. ANU; Canberra, October 2000. Anthropologists are generally referred to in Bislama as *riseja*.

From politics to policy: the self-reliance and sustainability project

In March 2005, the VCC organised a meeting held on Uripiv, a small island off the coast of Malakula, to discuss ways of using the '*kastom* economy' to achieve what was termed 'national self-reliance'. This was followed up in July 2005 by a larger National Summit on Self-Reliance and Sustainability, held at the Chiefs' Nakamal in Port Vila. The impetus for these meetings came from the 'Traditional Money Banks in Vanuatu' project based at the VCC, but involving collaboration from the Malvatumauri National Council of Chiefs and the Vanuatu Credit Union. Sometimes referred to as the 'pig bank' project, it aims to document and encourage the use of indigenous forms of wealth such as tusked pigs, mats and shell money which play a central role in exchanges and various forms of payment through most parts of the archipelago.[7] Extrapolating from this project, the activities subsumed under the title of Self-Reliance and Sustainability constituted an entire new mandate for life in Vanuatu. The Uripiv recommendations, and those that came out of the National Summit, covered a variety of topics from reforming the school curriculum to placing a ban on the importation of rice to fundamentally changing the laws governing land tenure.

In a way, the banner of Self-Reliance and Sustainability subsumes multiple projects, with multiple target audiences. As with the YPP, the VCC is courting the NGO/aid donor sector. This is done with a glossy report, featuring a pig-tusk-as-art style photo on the cover, written in English predominantly by Kirk Huffman, and containing background information on the traditional economy of areas of Vanuatu such as southern Malakula and North Pentecost where these economic practices are seen as particularly strong. At the same time though, the Uripiv recommendations and, more recently, those of the National Summit have been distributed nationally—to provincial governments, community groups and councils of chiefs—written in Bislama and photocopied on plain A4 paper.[8]

Speaking about the project, the former Director of the Cultural Centre, Ralph Regenvanu, has referred to it as a 'Trojan horse'—a way of making what could be defined as *kastom* more palatable to the needs or desires of NGOs and government officials. It provides a broken-down version of what the VCC, Malvatumauri and other interested parties believe is *kastom*, but it is presented in such a way that *kastom* can appear as a bundle of practices or a resource available to the majority of the ni-Vanuatu population. The Self-Reliance and Sustainability project has required realignments in the relationships between various institutions within

---

7   This project is funded by UNESCO and the Japanese Funds-In-Trust for the Preservation and Promotion of the Intangible Cultural Heritage.
8   These ideas are updated and explored in more depth in Rousseau and Taylor (in press).

Vanuatu: government departments, politicians, bureaucrats, the VCC, the Malvatumauri. The Self-Reliance and Sustainability project has also required a broadening of the distribution and efficacy of *kastom*—it is portrayed as being evenly dispersed throughout society. And, simultaneously, it is demonstrated that *kastom* holds answers to all spheres of government activity: environment, economy, education, health, justice and governance. *Kastom* has become, again, a property of the nation, and, as such, the business of the government.

This is not to say that the Self-Reliance and Sustainability project is meeting with universal acceptance. Each bureaucrat that 'sees the light'—that is, reassesses their view of the possible futures of the country with reference to internal (indigenous) rather than external resources—is seen as a victory by many involved. And this points to the new lines of cleavage that I argue are emerging in Vanuatu: *kastom* was previously assessed on a national/local; ideology/practice continuum, and its legitimacy became anchored in place. Now, it is becoming tied to class issues: the markers of *kastom* put forward through the Self-Reliance and Sustainability project are economically based, rather than politically based. The ni-Vanuatu middle class may have taken the place of Christians, politicians, young people, researchers, and the urban population as the new 'others' in relation to *kastom*.

References

Bolton, Lissant, 1999. Radio and the redefinition of *kastom* in Vanuatu. *The Contemporary Pacific* 11(2): 335–60.

Bolton, Lissant, 2003. *Unfolding the Moon: Enacting Women's Kastom in Vanuatu*. Honolulu: University of Hawai'i Press.

Bonnemaison, Joël, 1994. *The Tree and the Canoe: History and Ethnogeography of Tanna*. Honolulu, University of Hawai'i Press.

Deacon, A. Bernard, 1934. *Malekula: A Vanishing People in the New Hebrides*. London: George Routledge and Sons.

Handler, Richard and Jocelyn Linnekin, 1984. Tradition, genuine or spurious. *Journal of American Folklore* 97: 273–90.

Hanson, Allan, 1989. The making of the Maori: culture invention and its logic. *American Anthropologist* 91: 890–902.

Hobsbawm, Eric and Terrence Ranger, 1983. *The Invention of Tradition*. Cambridge: Cambridge University Press.

Jolly, Margaret, 1994. *Women of the Place: Kastom, Colonialism and Gender in Vanuatu*. Reading and Chur: Harwood Academic Press.

Larcom, Joan, 1982. The invention of convention. *Mankind* 13(4): 330–7.

Larcom, Joan, 1990. Custom by decree: legitimation crisis in Vanuatu. In Cultural Identity and Ethnicity in the Pacific, ed. Jocelyn Linnekin and Lin Poyer, 175–190. Honolulu, University of Hawaii Press.

Lindstrom, Lamont, 1982. *Leftamap kastom*: the political history of tradition on Tanna, Vanuatu. *Mankind* 13(4): 316–29.

National Statistics Office, 2000. *The 1999 Vanuatu National Population and Housing Census: Main Report*. Port Vila, National Statistics Office.

Philibert, Jean-Marc, 1986. The politics of tradition: toward a generic culture in Vanuatu. *Mankind* 16(1): 1–12.

Rousseau, Benedicta and John Taylor (in press). Kastom ekonomi and the subject of self-reliance: differentiating development in Vanuatu. In, *Differentiating Development: Beyond an Anthropology of Critique*. Soumhya Venkatesan and Thomas Yarrow (eds). Berghahn Books: Oxford.

Rousseau, Benedicta, 2004. The achievement of simultaneity: *kastom* in contemporary Vanuatu. PhD thesis: Department of Social Anthropology, University of Cambridge.

Taylor, John, 2010. Janus and the siren's call: kava and the articulation of gender and modernity in Vanuatu. *Journal of the Royal Anthropological Institute* 16(2): 279–6.

Tonkinson, Robert, 1982. National identity and the problem of *kastom* in Vanuatu. *Reinventing Traditional Culture: The Politics of* Kastom *in Island Melanesia*, ed. R.M. Keesing and R. Tonkinson. *Mankind*, Special Issue 13(4): 306–15.

Vanuatu Yang Pipol's Projek. 1999. *Harem Voes Blong Yangfala Long Vila Taon*. Port Vila: Vanuatu Kaljoral Senta.

Epilogue: A Personal Perspective on Afta 26 Yia: Collaborative Research in Vanuatu since Independence[1]

Margaret Jolly

The Vanuatu Kaljoral Senta (VKS) was the venue this week for a unique conference. Conjointly organised by Director Ralph Regenvanu and a team of young Australian researchers, Jack Taylor, Nick Thieberger and Stephen Zagala, it was focused on the theme of collaboration in research, *wok tugeta*. But collaboration was not just the theme but the practice. The conference was well timed between the annual workshops of women and men fieldworkers of the VKS. Many fieldworkers and other ni-Vanuatu presented papers and participated in the conference. And although the conference was advertised to start in Bislama and then move into English and French, in the event most of the presentations and discussions were in Bislama. From the opening stirring speeches by Chief Paul Tahi, President of the Malvatumauri National Council and by Chief Murmur of Mangaliliu, reflecting on his conversion from Presbyterian elder to *kastom jif*, to the closing funny stories by Bob Tonkinson about his anthropological research in Mele-Maat and Ambrym during the colonial period, the three days offered a feast for all participants.

Several overseas researchers who started work before independence participated: Michael Allen (Ambae), Margaret Jolly (South Pentecost), Lamont Lindstrom (Tanna), Mary Patterson (North Ambrym), Margaret Rodman (Ambae), Bob Tonkinson (SE Ambrym and Mele-Maat), and Darrell Tryon (linguistics across Vanuatu). There were discussions of the weird protocols of the Condominium governments but also how approval by colonial authorities did not imply acceptance by people in local communities. Michael Allen told us stories of how the famous Church of Christ leader Abel Bani first rejected his request to study *kastom* in Nduindui, because he said they had left darkness behind in going *long skul*. Bob Tonkinson told us how Mele-Maat people were also reluctant about him, believing that his white skin may not survive the attacks of Anopheles mosquitoes but also that some suspected he might be a returning dead spirit.

Indigenous research started in the colonial period too, fostered by the development of the fieldworker system from 1980 by Kirk Huffman (a respected absent presence at the conference), together with Darrell Tryon, Advisor to the

---

1   This epilogue was published in the Vanuatu newspaper The Independent, on November 12, 2006, and has not been updated here for reasons of provenance.

men fieldworkers from then until now. Some of the earliest men fieldworkers, honoured in the closing ceremony, presented papers too: Richard Leona,[2] on the history of fieldworkers and their collaboration with outside researchers; Phillip Tepahae on his life's work on Aneityumese language and culture (including the Aneityum dictionary with John Lynch) and James Gwero, who worked both with his age-mate Michael Allen on Ambae in the 1960s and later with Lamont Lindstrom on the oral histories of World War Two from 1987 to 1989. Their conjoint research came out as *Big Wok*, an early model of collaborative research, with versions published both in Bislama and English.

We were also reminded of the long pause during the moratorium on most foreign research from 1984–1994, and how when it recommenced it did so with an exemplary set of research guidelines. These emphasise the importance of considering the aims of research in the context of the needs and priorities of communities and the importance of collaboration with ni-Vanuatu and with local fieldworkers where possible. These guidelines, introduced under the aegis of the then new Director Ralph Regenvanu, developed guiding ethical principles which have been used as a model both by UNESCO and the World Intellectual Property Organization (WIPO). Matthew Spriggs became the proud holder of VKS Research Permit Number One! We heard about how, from the late 1980s, the late Grace Mera Molisa insisted that since women were an integral and complementary part of Vanuatu's culture there should be a parallel stream of women fieldworkers. That started in 1994 and like the men's network has grown considerably with now close to 40 women fieldworkers from most parts of the archipelago.

Women fieldworkers were a notable presence as presenters and discussants at this conference. They had just finished another successful annual workshop with Jean Tarisesei, Co-ordinator and Lissant Bolton, Advisor, on the theme of *kastom* dress. Numalin Mahana gave a fascinating perspective from Tanna on indigenous disaster foods; Rosalyne Garae spoke with quiet eloquence about patterns of parenting and child nurture on Ambae; while Jean Tarisesei and some of the team of women fieldworkers gave interesting reflections on collaborations within Vanuatu. Margaret Rodman spoke to the collaborative project House Girls Remember, along with Numalin Mahana and Leisara Kalotiti. This research generated important insights about domestic workers from the colonial period to the present, not just about wages and eating and sleeping conditions but perceptions of their work and their relations with employers. The book from that workshop (*House-Girls Remember*, edited by Rodman, Kraemer, Bolton and Tarisesei, University of Hawai'i Press) was one of four launched during the conference.

---

2   Editors' note: regretfully not included in this volume due to a technical fault in recording conference.

Archaeology has been another area of exemplary collaboration between overseas and ni-Vanuatu researchers and between ni-Vanuatu. About a decade ago, VKS Director Ralph Regenvanu with Matthew Spriggs and Stuart Bedford of the Australian National University (ANU) initiated a new project of research focused not just on new excavations but also on educating ni-Vanuatu about '*olfala histri wea i stap andanit long graon*'. That research has proved hugely successful, generating exciting and well-publicised discoveries from the Roi Mata sites at Mangaliliu and the excavations at Teouma, and training many ni-Vanuatu men and women in the skills of archaeology while raising broader community awareness. As Stuart Bedford pointed out it was Salkon Yona, a ni-Vanuatu fieldworker from Epi who first identified the Lapita pot (dug up and kept by a bulldozer driver) which led to the extraordinary discoveries at Teouma. Because of the extensive coverage of volcanic ash, Lapita had been harder to find in Vanuatu than other Pacific sites, but since this work Vanuatu has become focal to the prehistory of Lapita. We celebrated such recent archaeological research with the launch of Stuart's book *Pieces of the Vanuatu Puzzle* (Pandanus, ANU, 2006). We also heard about the making of modern 'saucepans', the contemporary manufacture of pottery at Olpoi and Wusi villages from Yoko Nojima of the University of Hawai'i. The success of such public awareness and excitement about archaeology is perhaps partly behind the community support for the submission of the Roi Mata Heritage Site to UNESCO. Douglas Kalotiti (Co-ordinator of the Men Fieldworkers) explained the process of working through that submission (recently completed with the collaboration of Chris Ballard and Meredith Wilson of the ANU, who were unable to be present because their second baby is imminent). He explained how local custodians of the land were persuaded to move from and stop using the areas concerned because of the perceived significance of this site for future generations. Many participants joined in a visit to the Roi Mata domain in a tour after the conference.

Another area of research where we heard some stunning examples of recent collaborative research was in language, story-telling and music. Linguistic research has moved on from the days when, as instructed by Darrell Tryon, in my own recordings and learning of the Sa language of South Pentecost the main instruments were the reel-to-reel tape recorder, hours of painful transcriptions in International Phonetic Alphabet and translations with patient interlocutors. As Nick Thieberger demonstrated from his work on the language of South Efate (strangely neglected til now), new technologies include the video recording of conversations and stories, the use of new software, and the creation of multimedia dictionaries in which, for example, the detail of species of flora and fauna named in local languages can be accompanied with photographs. These new technologies evince a sense of vibrancy about language and culture and of collaborative conversation. Local interlocutors are no longer just the sources of words, stories, and voices in experiments in phonetic differentiation but like Phillip Tepahae, they may be co-authors of grammars and dictionaries. Together with linguists from the ANU and Sydney University, Nick has also been collaborating with the VKS in the digitisation and archiving of early audio recordings. We celebrated in launching Nick's recent book from his doctoral research, *A Grammar of South Efate,* which as he proclaimed to the non-linguists present, was not dry and technical but fascinating! Other interesting discussions of language and oral traditions came from Michel Wauthion and Patrick Rory on Vao language, Robert Early on the socio-linguistics of endangered languages and Janet Dixon and Takaronga Kuautonga on Futuna stories. Their book *Nokonofo Kitea: We Keep On Living This Way,* (Crawford/UH Press), also launched at the conference, presents Futuna stories not as frozen texts, but as living oral culture, articulating and reflecting on contemporary predicaments such as globalisation and climate change.

Another superb presentation came from Monika Stern, representing a French team from CNRS and Lacito, presently researching the music of Penama and Torba Provinces. We witnessed the differences of song poetry performed for a public dance performance, with the accompaniment of drum and resounding feet, and in the quieter context of solo and choral performance. The blue lines of computer sonic graphics graphically demonstrated the underlying structure of the music. The extraordinary beauty of the song poetry was then translated into French and the poignant melody line, translated into Western notation, was demonstrated by Monika on a violin.

It was especially gratifying to see so many younger researchers presenting at this conference, both from Vanuatu and overseas. I had a particular parochial pride in hearing papers by several younger researchers whom I have been fortunate to work with at the ANU. Stephen Zagala spoke on the relationality of sand-drawing and on how the UNESCO project which he authored declared sand-drawing a 'masterpiece of intangible heritage'. This entailed not just a collaboration between ni-Vanuatu and himself but catalysed new exchanges and collaborations between ni-Vanuatu, men and women. Jack Taylor spoke about his collaboration with Kolombas Todali, fieldworker in North Pentecost, and how he perceived that rites of accepting researchers as part of family, of advancing them in the stages of learning powerful knowledge, and celebrating with them the products of knowledge returned (theses, books, papers etc.) were all part of a process which gave rights to researchers through rites. It echoed a conversation I had had earlier in the week with Chief Telekon of Bunlap (now living in Erakor), when he affirmed that I was still family with people in Bunlap, and told me that my research and book had helped raise up *kastom* in South East Pentecost. I read a paper by Sabine Hess, now back in Heidelberg, whom I had supervised at the ANU, reflecting on some of the personal challenges while researching with fieldworker Eli Field on Vanua Lava. She explored the tensions between their relationship as father and daughter and as man fieldworker and woman anthropologist and agreed with Eli that her fieldwork had been a 'good hard time'. She reminded new researchers how important it was to respect local protocols about not breaching *tabu* places or *tabu* stories. This echoed local stories retold by Jack Taylor about Bernard Deacon's death on Malakula, not just the result of black water fever but because he visited a *tabu* place despite strong warnings.

As in Sabine Hess' talk, the collaborative system of research with fieldworkers was critically considered, in terms of the gendered dynamics of collaboration and in how it might re-emphasise a 'key informant' approach to anthropology rather than dynamic ethnography and participant observation. And, as Benedicta Rousseau pointed out in her paper, grounded in her work with the Young People's Project, it is important to be able to discuss *kastom* between islands (given patterns of exchange, mobility, urbanisation and inter-island marriage) and to discuss *kastom* at the shared national level and not just as the particular *kastom* of one place. It was heartening to see experienced researchers like Mary Patterson, renowned for her early work on kinship, place and sorcery on Ambrym working again in Vanuatu, between towns and villages, on national questions about 'managing modernity' with collaborators like Ileen Vira. Mary's past kinship connections are being remade in the present, as in her research collaboration with Koran Wilfred, grandson of her original host family.

Most younger researchers from overseas seem to have developed excellent collaborative relations either through the connections of the fieldworker system or more generally through VKS or through earlier work or volunteer experience in Vanuatu. Miranda Forsyth, who once worked as an Australian volunteer in the Public Prosecutor's Office is now completing an important study of the relation between state and customary systems of dispute resolution. Sara Lightner, who first came to Vanuatu as a Peace Corps Volunteer and is widely respected as the co-author of the wonderful *Histri Blong Yumi* (with Anna Naupa), is now doing pioneering research for her Masters at the University of Hawai'i on the indigenous Catholic sisters of Melsisi. Some research presented has a strong potential for a policy impact: Margaret Malloch and Morris Kaloran spoke to their conjoint work for AusAID on women and equity in Vanuatu: Catherine Sparks from Canada gave a scintillating presentation on whether ni-Vanuatu women's everyday commitment to food production and care of their children could be read as 'resistance' to the high church of neo-liberal economics; and Jacqueline Marshall spoke of her 'action research', on the possible introduction of backpacker tourism into the villages of Mele and Mele-Maat.

The centrality of the visual in recording, analysing and preserving contemporary Vanuatu culture was highlighted. Marc Tabani not only gave a passionate report on his continuing research on John Frum in Tanna, and his accumulating 'millenium archives', but also presented an excellent film. Jacob Kapere screened this and several other films during the lunch breaks and spoke to us about the crucial importance of the Film Unit of VKS not just as a '*kastom* bank' of visual records from the past but as a process of recording the living culture of Vanuatu, as in several films he has made or been associated with as advisor. As Lissant Bolton reminded us in a speech (and in an entertaining paper she gave about the dispute about the Unification Church in 2005), culture in Vanuatu is constantly being created and changing.

Several presentations stressed how crucial the VKS is as both a site and a source of research, in the resources of its museum, its library, film unit, and several associated projects and especially in the experience of its extraordinarily talented team of staff, fieldworkers and volunteers (including the dedicated Friends of the Museum). Martha Yamsiu spoke of the foundational work of the Vanuatu Cultural and Historic Sites Survey (VCHSS), and William Mohns explained how VKS was creating a digital archive of the collections. Susan Cochrane brought materials from a recent workshop involving South Sea Islanders in Brisbane and showed images of some of the *kastom* collection of objects associated with labourers on Queensland's sugar fields and their descendants, now held in the Queensland Museum. But, Peter Murgatroyd of the University of the South Pacific reminded us of how important it was to move knowledge beyond the walls of museums and libraries, beyond Vila to the outer islands and to the world, with the use of new digital technologies. Clearly digital libraries and websites such as he is building at USP are hopeful developments, as is increasing dissemination of research in Bislama, as well as English and French, and the use of open-access publications. But, as those with close experience of islands beyond Vila (and indeed in some villages and settlements just down the road) know accessibility is not just a matter of geography but of money and power. And so the earlier technologies of paper and videos may prove important for a while yet. In conclusion, I want to congratulate and thank the organisers, the presenters, the staff and the fieldworkers of VKS for a stunning event. It was a fitting tribute to Ralph Regenvanu who is due to retire at the end of December after having been an energetic and charismatic Director of VKS for about eleven years. The VKS has become a model institution in the Pacific region and internationally as a place dedicated to living culture and collaborative research. May it continue to thrive and let us hope this experience was not unique, in that something similar might be repeated before too long.

References

Bedford, Stuart 2006 *Pieces of the Vanuatu Puzzle: Archaeology of the North, South and Centre.* Canberra: Pandanus Press, Australian National University. Terra Australis 23.

Jolly, Margaret, 2006. *A Personal Perspective on After 26 Years: Collaborative Research in Vanuatu since Independence*, The Independent, 12 November 2006.

Keller, Janet Dixon 2007. Nokonofo Kitea: *We Keep on Living this Way: Myths and Music of Futuna Vanuatu.* Honolulu: University of Hawai'i Press.

Lightner, Sara and Anna Naupa 2005. *Histri Blong Yumi Long Vanuatu.* 3 volumes plus teacher's guide. Port Vila: Vanuatu Cultural Centre.

Rodman, Margaret, Daniela Kraemer, Lissant Bolton and Jean Tarisesei (eds), 2007. *House-Girls Remember: Domestic Workers in Vanuatu.* Honolulu: University of Hawai'i Press.

Thieberger, Nicholas. 2006. *A Grammar of South Efate: An Oceanic Language of Vanuatu Oceanic Linguistics Special Publication*, No. 33. Honolulu: University of Hawai'i Press.

www.ingramcontent.com/pod-product-compliance
Lightning Source LLC
Chambersburg PA
CBHW061244270326
41928CB00041B/3399